Fifty Letters of a Roman Stoic

Seneca
Fifty Letters
of a Roman Stoic

TRANSLATED WITH AN INTRODUCTION
AND COMMENTARY BY MARGARET
GRAVER AND A. A. LONG

The University of Chicago Press CHICAGO AND LONDON

The University of Chicago Press, Chicago 60637
The University of Chicago Press, Ltd., London
© 2021 by The University of Chicago
All rights reserved. No part of this book may be used or
reproduced in any manner whatsoever without written
permission, except in the case of brief quotations in
critical articles and reviews. For more information,
contact the University of Chicago Press, 1427 E. 60th St.,
Chicago, IL 60637.
Published 2021
Printed in the United States of America

30 29 28 27 26 25 24 23 22 21   1 2 3 4 5

ISBN-13: 978-0-226-78276-8 (cloth)
ISBN-13: 978-0-226-78293-5 (paper)
ISBN-13: 978-0-226-78309-3 (e-book)
DOI: https://doi.org/10.7208/chicago/9780226783093.001.0001

Library of Congress Cataloging-in-Publication Data
Names: Seneca, Lucius Annaeus, approximately 4 B.C.–
    65 A.D., author. | Graver, Margaret, translator, writer of
    supplementary textual content. | Long, A. A., translator,
    writer of supplementary textual content.
Title: Seneca : fifty letters of a Roman Stoic / Lucius
    Annaeus Seneca ; translated with an introduction and
    commentary by Margaret Graver and A. A. Long
Other titles: Epistulae morales ad Lucilium. Selections.
    English. 2021 | Fifty letters of a Roman Stoic
Description: Chicago ; London : The University of Chicago
    Press, 2021. | Includes bibliographical references and index.
Identifiers: LCCN 2021009510 | ISBN 9780226782768 (cloth) |
    ISBN 9780226782935 (paperback) | ISBN 9780226783093
    (ebook)
Subjects: LCSH: Ethics—Early works to 1800. | Stoics—Early
    works to 1800.
Classification: LCC PA6665.A1 2021 | DDC 876/.01—dc23
LC record available at https://lccn.loc.gov/2021009510

♾ This paper meets the requirements of ANSI/NISO
Z39.48-1992 (Permanence of Paper).

Contents

Preface

The surviving manuscripts of Seneca's *Letters on Ethics* contain no fewer than 124 letters, ranging in length from a single page to fifteen or more. Seneca writes about so many subjects and in so many different styles that any selection is bound to be partial, since every letter adds something fresh about the author's extraordinary mind and literary virtuosity. Nonetheless, in choosing fifty letters for this volume, we have tried to illustrate the range and variety of Seneca's subject matter, from the experiences of his daily life—the noisy neighbors, the footrace with a little child, the roar of a packed arena—to his intellectual interests in literature and philosophy. Our explanatory notes supply fuller information on people, places, and ideas mentioned in the text. These notes are adapted from the much longer commentary in our complete edition of the *Letters on Ethics* (Graver and Long 2015), with expansion at some points to serve the needs of readers who may be meeting Seneca for the first time. An asterisk in the main text (*) indicates an explanatory note at the back of the book.

Apart from one or two minor revisions, the translation given here is identical to the one in our earlier book. The Latin text followed is that of Reynolds (1965b). In those few places where we differ from Reynolds as to what Latin text best represents Seneca's intentions, the word or phrase that renders the different Latin wording is marked with a superscript circle (°), and our reading is given in the Textual Notes section. The translation itself aims primarily to convey Seneca's ideas exactly, while also conveying his ever-changing style and mood. Although word-for-word rendering is rarely possible (and would often be misleading), we do strive for consistency in translating key Latin words, taking pains especially with philosophical terms.

In preparing the explanatory notes, we have relied mainly on our own judgment, but we are often indebted to earlier commentators for assistance in locating the relevant ancient evidence. For historical and biographical matters, we have frequently consulted the comprehensive *Brill's New Pauly* (Cancik and Schneider 2002–10). Portions of the translation and notes have been improved as well by the acumen of undergraduate research assistants funded through the James O. Friedman Presidential Scholars Program at Dartmouth College: Brian Howe, John Kee, Michael Konieczny, Karen Laakko, Aaron Pellowski, Lea Schroeder, and Leslie Shribman.

The titles given to individual letters are supplied by us for ease of reference; they are not authorial.

Introduction

Margaret Graver and A. A. Long

The best way to learn about Seneca, as a person and as a philosopher, is to read his letters. Begun late in his life, the *Letters on Ethics* adhere to a format that he himself devised and that proved especially congenial to his talents.[1] These are serious writings, using the intimacy of the personal letter as a vehicle for a searching examination of values and life choices. In this, they resemble the letters of the philosopher Epicurus, which Seneca had studied extensively. Unlike Epicurus, though, Seneca addresses all his letters to one individual, his younger friend Gaius Lucilius Iunior. The collection does not include any letters written by the friend, and yet Lucilius is constantly made present to us through frequent references to his life experiences and his questions about philosophy. As readers, we come to feel that we know both men at a deep level. Still, these letters are not a private correspondence like Cicero's letters to his friend

---

1. The title *Letters on Ethics to Lucilius (Epistulae Morales ad Lucilium)* is attested already in the second century CE (Aulus Gellius 12.2) and is given in the oldest surviving manuscript copies, dating to the ninth century; see Reynolds 1965b. Whether or not Seneca himself referred to his work by that title, he makes clear that the project is defined by its epistolary format (21, 38, 40, 75) and by its prevailing interest in ethics: see for instance letters 38, 40, 75, 121.1.

Atticus. They are meant to be shared with a wider public, to bring comfort in difficult times, intellectual engagement, and sheer entertainment to those outside the author's own circle.

In this work we do not find much of the story of Seneca's life as reported later by the historians Tacitus and Dio Cassius: his tutoring the young Nero, his work as a speechwriter, and the charges of his political opponents. After all, he wrote the *Letters* in the two to three years before his death in 65 CE, after he had withdrawn entirely from the imperial court.[2] Nonetheless, there are elements of autobiography in the work. Seneca describes his early experience as a vegetarian, his travels in and around Pompeii, his daily routine. He mentions his wife Paulina, his brother Gallio, and his deceased father, whom we know as Seneca the Elder. At age sixty-five, he tells us what it is like to come near dying from shortness of breath. More than once he sketches an incident that makes him look ridiculous: his cluelessness on visiting an aging property of his own, his effort to cross the Bay of Naples in choppy seas, his sitting down in a schoolroom among teenagers. We do not get the big events of his life so much as the small but significant ones.

Reading more closely, we can collect some information about his personal situation. We see that he owns a great deal of property since he mentions visiting three of his own villas. While his personal habits are austere, he makes it clear that for someone like him, simple living is a matter of choice, not economic necessity. Similarly, it is by choice that he now has no

---

2. The period of composition must be after Seneca's retirement in 62 CE. Of events mentioned in the correspondence, only the fire at Lyon (91.1) is datable, to late summer of 64 CE.

influence on the affairs of state. Early in the correspondence, he establishes a parallel between the political career he has now abandoned and that of Lucilius, a man familiar with the imperial court who is still active as civil governor of Sicily. As Seneca urges his friend to withdraw from his public position and devote himself to a life of study, we catch the tensions that might attend such a decision. Those tensions were very real, for those who had entered public service were expected to stay on, not only by their peers but also by a powerful and unpredictable ruler. That same dynamic was to be explored later by Tacitus, who writes it as a dialogue between Seneca and the emperor Nero himself.[3]

Significantly, the letters make no direct mention of Nero or of his immediate family. On the face of it, Seneca's stance is apolitical. Sounding a theme that was already traditional in philosophy, he remarks on the gratitude that philosophers should feel toward those who provide the benefits of peace. His own retreat from politics is repeatedly explained as the consequence of ill health and a desire for study; it is not to be taken as criticism of the current regime. Yet the anxiety with which he speaks of the dangers of insubordination is highly revealing. Just as in another of his works he speaks of the "fires and torments" Lucilius had witnessed at the court of Gaius Caligula,[4] so here he speaks feelingly of imprisonment, torture, and execution as real possibilities for men like himself. His admiration for such historical figures as Publius Rutilius Rufus, Scipio Africanus, Quintus Aelius Tubero, and especially

---

3. Tacitus, *Annals* 14.53–56.
4. Seneca, *Natural Questions* 4a pref.

Cato the Younger suggests nostalgia for the old days of the Roman Republic, but he does not imply that those days could ever return.

More generally, Seneca uses his rhetorical skills and satirical wit to expose the decadence of the elite Roman society he knows so well. He is often critical of extravagant expenditures, on everything from glassware to bathing establishments, and he can be scathingly funny about the ridiculous habits of his contemporaries. The violence and cruelty of Roman reality are constantly brought to the fore, notably the gladiatorial contests, the harsh treatment of the enslaved and of prisoners, and the sexual exploitation of women and boys. Yet it is not the times alone that are at fault, for he also refers to one of Cicero's letters for an instance of shocking moral degeneracy in the time of Cato. The values and practices of contemporary Roman society are completely out of joint, but the vice that pervades Rome affects human societies in every era.

In all this, his point is about the corruption of existing human societies, not about human nature as such. However flawed our surrounding culture may be, our innate sociability is nonetheless a basic guide to action. As rational beings, we have a natural instinct to seek companionship and genuine friendship, and we can learn to recognize the responsibilities we have, not only toward our immediate communities but also toward the worldwide community. These are the Stoic values that Seneca finds quite absent from the dominant ideology of his time.

Ultimately it is this principle of the interconnectedness of all human beings that gives rise to the *Letters on Ethics* themselves. Seneca states the premise of his entire work near the beginning of letter 8, where he writes,

The work that I am doing is for posterity: it is they who can benefit from what I write. I am committing to the page some healthful admonitions, like the recipes for useful salves. I have found these effective on my own sores, which, even if not completely healed, have ceased to spread. The right path, which I myself discovered late in life when weary from wandering, I now point out to others.

He thus offers an answer to a question that had long been debated among philosophers, one that he himself had investigated in the brief essay *On Leisure.* If every one of us has a responsibility to serve the community throughout life, then how can anyone be justified in spending long periods in philosophical study and reflection? For Seneca, a scholarly retreat is itself a form of public service. Although philosophers may not be able to solve the immediate problems of their societies, their writings can still benefit others by teaching readers of every time and place how to live happy and productive lives.

To be sure, this stated purpose implies a rather limited range of objectives for philosophical writing. Not all philosophy offers social benefits of exactly that kind. But Seneca can find excuses to incorporate many different intellectual issues into his work, while still keeping his primary emphasis on the most basic themes of ethics: the importance of personal integrity, the foundations of friendship, the reasons not to fear pain and death, and the management of one's emotions.

Philosophy in Letters

The notion that material of high quality and lasting importance might be presented in the form of letters was one that could arise quite naturally in a Roman context. It was not only that Epicurus and other Greeks had sometimes written philosophical letters. Roman literary conventions allowed for works aimed at a wide readership to carry a formal dedication to some prominent individual whose name would appear in the first line or paragraph. Cicero's philosophical treatises had all begun in this way, as had Seneca's earlier essays on philosophical topics. Such dedications did not convey that the person named was actually in need of the information the work contained; rather, they offered a compliment to that person's literary taste and a promise to preserve his name for posterity. To some extent, this must also be the message conveyed to Lucilius in these letters. In letter 21, Seneca tells Lucilius,

> What Epicurus was able to promise his friend, I promise to you, Lucilius: I shall find favor with posterity, and I can bring others' names along with me, so that they will endure as well. (21.5)

Like the letters of Epicurus and even like Virgil's *Aeneid*, Seneca's letters will achieve a kind of immortality; in them, Seneca will live on after death, and Lucilius will live alongside him.

We may still ask whether the letters to Lucilius are real letters, in the sense that a real letter is one that is not only sent to the addressee but also composed with an exclusive eye to that person's specific needs, interests, and knowledge. To this question the answer is surely no. Aspects of Lucilius's life are indeed featured: Seneca makes a point of mentioning his hometown of Pompeii, his career in government, his travels, and his writings. But such observations do not restrict the work to Lucilius's sole perspective; on the contrary, they honor him by sharing information about him with a wide audience.

Nor do we find material in the work that is of merely topical significance. In contrast to the letters of Cicero, which constantly refer to circumstances, persons, and events that will be understood only by his friend Atticus, those of Seneca make a conspicuous effort to be intelligible to a broad readership. Particulars that might not be understood outside the author's immediate circle are either explained or reduced to the generic ("a friend of yours" in 3.1). Material directed ostensibly to Lucilius alone is thus overheard, as it were, by other readers, who will find in it their own forms of benefit or amusement. As the more general perspective is compatible with Seneca's retaining a genuine interest in the problems and motivations of the real Lucilius, it is often impossible to say whether Lucilius actually experienced the events described or whether these are only typical situations that any reader might be likely to confront.

A new literary endeavor demands some kind of introduction, but the notion of a correspondence with an intimate friend precludes the usual formal opening: such close friends as Seneca and Lucilius ought already to have been corresponding for some time. Seneca gets around this difficulty by means of a device like the *in medias res* openings of epic poems. The opening words of letter 1, "Do that," seem to refer to something Lucilius has said in a previous letter to Seneca, and yet the thing Lucilius is supposed to do is precisely to *begin* thinking about the matters Seneca is able to teach. In a powerful metaphor, this beginning is represented as an act of self-liberation. In Roman law, a slave was set free by the act of a vindicator (*vindex*), who formally claimed him or her into freedom; Lucilius, however, is told to "assert your own freedom" (*vindica te tibi*). He has been enslaved by various demands on his time;

now he must lay claim to himself, by drawing back from his previous occupations and devoting himself to a course of reading and study.

It matters also what sort of book one chooses to read. In the letter that immediately follows, Seneca instructs Lucilius not to go abroad, as it were, with his reading, but to settle down to one or two authors with whom he can become intimate, finding in their books a home and a source of sustenance. Further, he should extract from each day's reading some short maxim for subsequent reflection. To illustrate, Seneca provides a suitable example from his own reading, together with a brief reflection on it. As if to reinforce the recommendation, he then proceeds to supply a similar maxim at the close of every one of the next twenty-seven letters. The practice becomes a joke—it is Lucilius's "little gift" or "payment" or his "daily dole"—but it also serves to establish an important link between the reading of books and the business of living.

One distinct advantage of the epistolary format is its flexibility. Virtually anything in Roman life might be made relevant to ethics, and even themes that have already been introduced can be developed further or taken in another direction. There is no obvious reason why the sequence needs ever to end. To some extent, the format itself can also be altered without fundamentally changing the character of the correspondence. The initial practice of providing maxims for daily meditation is abandoned after letter 29, allowing for greater variety in the endings of letters. Longer and more demanding letters begin to appear, and some discussions develop more in the manner of a philosophical exercise, with problems clearly stated and arguments and counterarguments defending various positions. Seneca is careful, however, to maintain his practice of including some letters that are very short and some that treat the more colorful and amusing aspects of Roman life. He is intensely serious about philosophical matters, but the letters are never to become just another philosophical treatise.

A skilled rhetorician can find ways to include what he wants, even where the stated purpose of his work seems to exercise constraint. Despite the restrictive nature of the justification offered in letter 8, Seneca finds excuses to incorporate a wide variety of philosophical material, from tricks of logic to the philosophical analysis of being and causation. One of his favorite devices is to make a show of pulling himself back from some fascinating topic that has no immediate ethical payoff. In letter 58, for instance, he interrupts himself in the midst of explaining some points in metaphysics with an elaborate apology, as if he thinks such topics do not properly belong in his letters. Another verbal dodge is the ventriloquized question, in which the topic to be treated is presented as a response to some inquiry by Lucilius. Letter 113 begins by complaining that Lucilius is overly curious: the topic he has asked about is one of those that "are only right for people who go in for Greek shoes and cloaks." Yet Seneca will treat it nonetheless, and as the letter proceeds, it becomes obvious that the choice of subject matter is his own. These and similar devices allow Seneca to take credit for the specialized knowledge of philosophy he really possesses while still preserving the epistolary framework he has established.

Seneca's Philosophical Stance

At first the philosophical material contained in the letters is of the most general kind, exhorting readers to begin a course of study rather than providing them with technical details, and steering clear of any single doctrinal perspective. Indeed, it is not until the ninth letter that Seneca gives clear indication of his own commitment to Stoicism. When he does so, however, he speaks firmly and with some philosophical elaboration. The topic he addresses is one that will frequently occupy his attention: the kind of concern one should ideally feel for one's friends or for any of one's nearest personal connections. Right away, he seeks to differentiate the Stoic view from that of the old Cynic philosophers, for whom the word "impassivity" (*apatheia*) meant that one should actually be insensitive to the death of one's friends. This is not what Stoics have in mind. For them, even the best and most mature person will feel the loss, but wisdom means that they can still lead a fulfilling life.

This investigation into the inner life of the fully mature human being is one that Seneca continues at intervals throughout the collection. In keeping with Stoic thought, he argues that such a person would not experience longing or anxiety in relation to typical objects of pursuit and avoidance, such as wealth, reputation, or pain. He emphasizes, however, that one can be truly wise and still subject to involuntary reactions such as blushing, shuddering, and shedding tears. These gut reactions are not, properly speaking, emotions, since they do not necessarily register one's deep convictions concerning the significance of some event for oneself. Nonetheless, they are important, for they give evidence that one who is wise can still be sensitive to the inevitable vagaries of human life.

Further, Seneca elaborates on a description of the Stoic wise person's most characteristic affective response. This response, he says, is a deep and heartfelt sensation of joy: a joy that does not come and go, as ordinary pleasures do, but remains with a good person always because it arises from the real and stable goods that belong to the perfected mind itself. In a word, Senecan joy comes from within, from a good person's own character and conduct: it arises from goodness itself and from the right actions one performs. This means that joy will not always be a matter of smiles and laughter, for good actions may be difficult and unpleasant: one may have to accept poverty, endure pain, even die for one's country. A good person does these things only when they are right, and only for that reason, but the doing itself is good and is a reason to rejoice.

Seneca tells us early on that the aim of the Stoic is to live according to nature. It takes him much longer, though, to explain why he believes that excellence of character gives us a life according to nature and why a virtuous life, rather than a life of riches or power or pleasure, should be considered the human good. The most important of his arguments for that point is found in letter 76. There he ties the radical Stoic thesis, "only the honorable is good," to the distinctive nature of the human as a *rational* being, a creature that decides and judges what actions to perform. He notes that every kind of thing has a chief quality or function for which it comes into being and by which it is assessed: in a wine, its flavor; in a hunting dog, its sense of smell. Excellence in its own function is the good for that kind of thing. But the distinction function for human beings is our reasoning ability. Accordingly, the human good consists in perfected reason, also called knowledge or wisdom, which teaches us how to do the right thing in every situation.

Like earlier Stoics, Seneca accepts that such advantages as health, financial security, and physical comfort are in accordance with our nature and worth pursuing, but he also insists that such things are not intrinsically desirable. Similarly, the disagreeable parts of life, such as pain, bereavement, or the loss of one's homeland, are not intrinsically bad. In general, it is reasonable to try to avoid them, but there are times when we should willingly embrace them in order to do what is right. The wise and virtuous will know when those situations arise, and even the person who is still making progress toward virtue can often choose correctly.

Since our knowledge of the world is necessarily derived from experience, it remains to be explained how people can develop a conception of human excellence that is so rarely exhibited in fact. Seneca investigates this issue in some of the latest letters. Such mental operations as analogy and extrapolation must play a role here, for it is not our senses that grasp what goodness is but rather our minds. A puzzle arises, however, when we inquire into the process by which our minds become aware of their own nature. Human beings come under the general rule that every animal has an instinctive sense of "attachment" to its own constitution. But an infant is not yet able to reason, so how can it be attached to the rational nature of a human being? In accordance with earlier Stoic thought, Seneca argues that our constitution changes in the course of our development. We are at first attached only to our animal nature, but as we mature, we transfer our allegiance to the rational capacities that then appear in us.

While Seneca sometimes makes a point of declaring his intellectual independence from earlier representatives of his school, there are only a few instances in which he moves outside the realm of Stoic thought as we know it from other sources. We see in letters 58 and 65 that he has an interest in Plato and Aristotle, although he does not endorse their views on being and causation. Platonic influence is more notable in passages where he speaks of the human mind as a divine power which has descended into the body from above and where he suggests that abstract studies are the means by which this divine spirit can gain escape and immortality. With some justification, he considers this view of the mind to be compatible with a Stoic understanding of divinity and of human wisdom—as long as one does not insist on the soul's immortality, which he does not.

Even though he objects very strongly to Epicureanism as a system of ethics,[5] Seneca is willing to endorse some of Epicurus's views where he feels he can do so without inconsistency. For instance, even though he rejects Epicurus's overall position on natural justice, he agrees with him that wrongdoers are invariably tormented by their misdeeds. More than once we see Seneca take over a point that he knows is Epicurean and adapt it to his own Stoic framework. Thus in letter 11 he is happy to endorse Epicurus's suggestion that each of us should envision some good person as an internal monitor for our actions, but he names Cato and Laelius, both Stoics, as good choices to fill this role. In recounting his visit to the elderly Bassus in letter 30, he admires Bassus's arguments against the fear of death and pain. He finds those arguments comforting and does not feel a need to point out that they are Epicurean in origin.

Teachers and Learners

In keeping with the stated purpose of the letters, but also because of his own literary bent, Seneca shows a strong interest in the activities of teaching through various oral and written forms of discourse. Lucilius, of course, is a learner; but he has pupils

---

5. See for instance 90.35, and compare Seneca, *On Benefits* 4.2.

of his own as well, and Seneca admits that he is still learning himself. Although the youthful enthusiasm he remembers in letter 108 has quieted with age, he does not consider himself too old to sit in a classroom alongside the younger generation. "Why should I not have many characteristics to sort through and either reduce or heighten?" he writes in letter 6. But an equally important aim is to teach others. "If wisdom were given to me with this proviso, that I should keep it shut up in myself and never express it to anyone else, I should refuse it. No good is enjoyable to possess without a companion."

If Seneca in the early letters often expresses appreciation for Epicurean writings—"the other camp," as he calls them—it can only be for their effectiveness in drawing the pupil toward a philosophical way of life. The works of Epicurus and others of his school are valuable because they are full of such well-phrased remarks as "cheerful poverty is an honorable thing" or "anger beyond bounds begets insanity"—points that are easy to memorize and incorporate into one's daily reflections. Epicurus himself had encouraged memorization of epitomes of his teachings, and Seneca considers the method helpful, but only for beginners. In letter 33 he addresses directly the question of whether memorization can ever be an effective means of learning. New recruits may find that isolated sayings take hold easily; one who is beginning to make progress must become a more independent learner. "Let there be some distance between you and the book!" he exhorts. In other words, students must learn to think for themselves and to reason out an appropriate course of action amid the manifold complexities of real situations. Mere familiarity with texts will not do: there must be an increased capacity to make well-reasoned judgments.

For these purposes, an exchange of letters can be a highly effective kind of philosophical writing. Brief and relatively simple, a letter may yet unfold within the mind of the reader, and the back-and-forth of correspondence allows opportunity for the learner's own ideas to develop. So Seneca indicates in letter 38, itself the shortest in the collection. But he recognizes also a need for sequential progress through a more sustained course of reading. A comprehensive study of ethics would be of real value to the student, better than all his own writings to date and much better than the "sophistical arguments" of some teachers, which are merely clever syllogisms purporting to prove an absurd conclusion. For this reason, Seneca means eventually to produce his own comprehensive work on ethics, a book that will be very different from the *Letters on Ethics*. As far as we know, he never completed this project.

A Philosopher at Work

Because they mingle philosophical concerns with a representation of the author's own life, the *Letters* offer an unparalleled opportunity to study the working methods of a philosopher in a Roman setting. We must remember, of course, that what Seneca says about his habits is just the narrative frame that he uses to give a compelling presentation to his material. But we can assume a fair measure of verisimilitude, for the picture had to be recognizable to readers of his own time, who knew his habits and those of other philosophers. In addition, we can sometimes draw inferences that tell us more than our author means to reveal.

At the time Seneca wrote the *Letters on Ethics*, he already possessed a thorough knowledge of many arguments in philosophy, not only the Stoic positions but those of their chief opponents as well. Memory alone would have enabled him to cite standard explanations of doctrine and such definitions as that of mental infirmity in letter 75. Even verbatim quotations might have been supplied from his capacious memory. There are, however, a number of letters in which Seneca supplies an extended discussion of a topic that is not in his usual manner or that he never addresses elsewhere. At these points we should consider the possibility that his information has been drawn in a more immediate way from a specific source, whether oral or written.

Sometimes he tells us directly what book has supplied the material in question. He mentions several specific letters written by Epicurus, naming their recipients and even referring to a date of composition.[6] A long account in letter 90 of the influence of wise individuals in human history repeatedly mentions an unnamed work by the Stoic Posidonius, critiquing Posidonius's views in some detail. These passages are interesting because in them we can observe Seneca's manner of working with a text, even though the texts themselves are no longer available for comparison. We can see how he names the author, quotes passages—sometimes translating directly from the Greek originals—and then goes on to discuss the point, offering specific objections of his own devising.[7] In some instances, though, his discussion mentions more than one earlier work, and it is up to us to infer whether he has read both authors directly or only knows about the earlier author from

---

6. The clearest examples are in letters 9, 18 (which gives a date), 21, and 79.

7. Clear instances of translation from Greek include 9.20 and 97.13.

references in the later one's work. In letter 83, for example, he quotes a syllogism on drunkenness by Zeno of Citium and then an unattributed syllogism refuting it; immediately after- ward, he reports how Posidonius attempted to defend Zeno's argument. Here it is reasonable to conclude that he has before him just one book, that of Posidonius, and knows about both syllogisms from that source.

Another possibility is that the letters may incorporate knowledge gained from oral teaching and live discussion. Seneca mentions attending lectures, and he speaks often of philosophical conversations with friends, including conversations about books: deep reflections on the fear of death with Bassus, a leisurely conversation about metaphysics. Even if these narrated conversations are a literary device, meant to enliven material that the author knows from some written source, it may still be true that some significant part of Seneca's learning has come by oral channels. Just as he must have shared what he knew about philosophy with such friends as Annaeus Serenus and Aebutius Liberalis, so others might have shared their knowledge with him.

A point of particular interest concerns Seneca's knowledge of the philosophical writings of Cicero. One work he certainly knows is Cicero's *On the Republic*, given that he cites it by title in letter 108 and seems familiar with its contents. Unfortunately this treatise, the keystone of Cicero's philosophical reputation in antiquity, now survives only in part, so that Seneca's use of it is hard to assess. Meanwhile, Seneca is strangely silent concerning the philosophical treatises Cicero wrote in 45 BCE, the very ones that give his most extensive treatment to the central concerns of the *Letters on Ethics*. It is surely significant that on some points treated by both authors, Seneca includes details he could not have found in Cicero, and that on others, he omits elements one would have expected him to address.[8] Indeed, it is possible that he did not read these works, or else that he did not consider them important, for he had many Greek treatises available to him, no doubt including ones that Cicero himself had consulted.

The Literary Scene

Throughout the letters, Seneca's knowledge of Roman litera-ture and the current literary scene is much in evidence. He is constantly quoting poetry, especially favoring Virgil's *Aeneid* but also including the *Eclogues* and *Georgics*, the *Metamorphoses* of Ovid, the *Satires* of Horace, and the Epicurean poem *On the Nature of Things* by Lucretius. Comparison with surviving texts of those authors suggests that he quotes from memory, for his quotations are not always exact. On occasion his letters have provided modern scholars with valuable information also about poems in Latin that do not otherwise survive: a passage on Mount Etna by Cornelius Severus, descriptions of dawn and dusk by Julius Montanus, bits of Ennius. He also knows the Greek poets, especially Homer and Euripides. But his

---

8. For instance, in letter 85 (not included here), Seneca discusses the same syllogism as is reported by Cicero in *Tusculan Disputations* 3.18 but also gives the Peripatetic refutation of it. Conversely, in letter 9 Seneca fails to mention the alternative Epicurean accounts of friendship, an egregious omission if he had read books 1 and 2 of Cicero's treatise *On Ends.* It is note-worthy too that Seneca never mentions Antiochus of Ascalon, who plays an important role both in *On Ends* and in the *Academics.* See also the note on 58.6, for the allegedly Ciceronian term *essentia.*

knowledge extends well beyond the poets. He knows a great deal about oratory, both from his own experience as a speaker and hearer and from his reading, for he refers not only to the speeches of Cicero but also to such less-known figures as Papirius Fabianus. Further, he knows something of the writings of contemporary critics and antiquarians, since he is able to comment on methods of interpreting literature and to cite specific anomalies of usage in the manner of the literary scholar.

It was a convention of Roman literary culture to offer a compliment to the literary achievements of one's addressee. Seneca does as much for Lucilius, whose poetic efforts he admires and encourages and whose prose writing he praises in a charming note of thanks (letter 46). There is an implied compliment too in the advice he gives in letter 84 about nurturing one's own literary talent through a varied course of reading. Like the honeybee, Lucilius will find nourishment in many places but will combine what he has taken into "one savor," which is his own distinctive style. By writing, he will give proof of his inner harmony and of his ability to impose order on the world, becoming the "greatly talented man" who "stamps his own form upon all the elements that he draws from his chosen model" (84.8).

This last point applies also to Seneca himself, for it is obvious that he means the *Letters on Ethics* to be a highly literary work. Touches of artistry are noticeable throughout, especially in his detailed descriptions of places, in lively passages of narrative, and in extended metaphors that recall the similes of the epic poets. Passages of satire are frequent, including some that are similar in tone and content to the poetic *Satires* of Horace. In keeping with Roman literary principles, Seneca is careful to vary the subject matter from one letter to the next while still arranging his material in such a way as to suggest connections between letters. His ambitions for his work are also evident in passages where the writing takes on a more elevated style. Such paragraphs as the opening of letter 41, on the majesty of forests and the grandeur of the human mind, leave us in no doubt that Seneca meant the *Letters* to be admired as fine writing. But the intervening passages of plain and sometimes breezy and colloquial style are no less deliberately and artfully composed. His aim, he says, is that the letters should be easy and unstudied, like the conversation of two people walking together: at the same time, however, they should not be "jejune and arid." In his view, "there is a place for literary talent even in philosophy" (75.3).

For Further Reading

The bibliography to this volume gives some indication of the resources available for further study. An especially important work on Seneca's political career, with much information also on his education and writings, is Griffin 1992 (first published in 1976). Shorter works that offer a narrative of Seneca's life include Griffin 2008, Romm 2014, and E. Wilson 2014.

The commentaries by Inwood (2007c) and Edwards (2019) provide more detailed notes on many of the letters contained in this volume. Many specifics concerning Seneca's handling of Stoic philosophy can be found in Inwood 2005 and Wildberger 2006. On Platonic influences, see Reydams-Schils 2010; on Epicurean ones, see Graver 2020. For more information on other important aspects of Seneca's philosophical thought and literary output, readers may consult the overviews in Bartsch and Schiesaro 2015 and Damschen and Heil 2014, or they may pursue the more extensive discussions of particular topics in

Edwards 2018, Graver 2012, Griffin 2007, Inwood 2007a, Schafer 2011, Wilcox 2012, and M. Wilson 2015. Also very useful are the essay collections edited by Bartsch and Wray (2009); Garani, Michalopoulos, and Papaioannou (2020); Volk and Williams (2016); and Wildberger and Colish (2014).

More generally on Stoic philosophy, see Long 2001, Inwood 2003, Brennan 2005, Graver 2007. Most of the ancient evidence for the Hellenistic philosophical schools may be found in English translation either in Long and Sedley 1987 (abbreviated "LS" in our notes) or in Inwood and Gerson 1997. A more extensive collection of material is the four-volume *Stoicorum Veterum Fragmenta* by H. von Arnim (1903–24), abbreviated *SVF* in our notes.

For a brief discussion of the influence of Seneca's *Letters* after the classical period, please consult the introduction to our complete *Letters on Ethics* (Graver and Long 2015), abbreviated *GL* in our notes; in more detail, see Reynolds 1965a, Ross 1974.

Further information about the transmission of the Latin text and about the origins of the readings we adopt will be found in the critical apparatus to Reynolds 1965b or in the editions by Beltrami (1937), Hense (1914), and Préchac (1945–64).

Fifty Letters

Taking charge of your time

From Seneca to Lucilius
Greetings

---

1 Do that, dear Lucilius: assert your own freedom.* Gather and guard the time that until now was being taken from you, or was stolen from you, or that slipped away. Convince yourself that what I write is true: some moments are snatched from us, some are filched, and some just vanish. But no loss is as shameful as the one that comes about through carelessness. Take a close look, and you will see that when we are not doing well, most° of life slips away from us; when we are inactive, much of it— but when we are inattentive, we miss it all. **2** Can you show me even one person who sets a price on his time, who knows the worth of a day, who realizes that every day is a day when he is dying? In fact, we are wrong to think that death lies ahead: much of it has passed us by already, for all our past life is in the grip of death.*

And so, dear Lucilius, do what your letter says you are doing: embrace every hour. If you lay hands on today, you will find you are less dependent on tomorrow. While you delay, life speeds on by. **3** Everything we have belongs to others, Lucilius; time alone is ours. Nature has put us in possession of this one thing, this fleeting, slippery thing—and anyone who wants to can dispossess us. Such is the foolishness of mortal beings: when they borrow the smallest, cheapest items, such as can easily be replaced, they acknowledge the debt, but no one considers himself indebted for taking up our time. Yet this is the one loan that even those who are grateful cannot repay.

4 You ask, perhaps, what I am doing—I, who give you these instructions. I am a big spender, I freely admit, but a careful one: I have kept my accounts. I cannot say that nothing has been wasted, but at least I can say what, and why, and how; I can state the causes of my impoverishment. But it is with me as with many others who have been reduced to penury through no fault of their own: everyone forgives them, but no one comes to their assistance.

5 What of it? A person is not poor, I think, as long as what little he has left is enough for him. Still, I prefer that you, for your part, conserve what you have. And make an early start. For in the words of our ancestors, "Thrift comes late when stocks are low."* Not only is there very little left at the bottom of the jar, but its quality is the worst.

Farewell.

LETTER 2

A beneficial reading program

From Seneca to Lucilius
Greetings

---

1 From your letter and from what I hear, I am becoming quite hopeful about you: you are not disquieting yourself by running about from place to place. Thrashing around in that way indicates a mind in poor health. In my view, the first sign of a settled mind is that it can stay in one place and spend time with itself.

2 Be careful, though, about your reading in many authors and every type of book. It may be that there is something wayward and unstable in it. You must stay with a limited number of writers and be fed by them if you mean to derive anything that will dwell reliably with you. One who is everywhere is nowhere. Those who travel all the time find that they have many places to stay, but no friendships. The same thing necessarily happens to those who do not become intimate with any one author, but let everything rush right through them. **3** Food does not benefit or become part of the body when it is eaten and immediately expelled. Nothing impedes healing as much as frequent change of medications. A wound does not close up when one is always trying out different dressings on it; a seedling that is transplanted repeatedly will never grow strong. Nothing, in fact, is of such utility that it benefits us merely in passing. A large number of books puts a strain on a person. So, since you cannot read everything you have, it is sufficient to have only the amount you can read.

4 "But I want to read different books at different times," you say. The person of delicate digestion nibbles at this and that; when the diet is too varied, though, food does not nourish but only upsets the stomach. So read always from authors of proven worth; and if ever you are inclined to turn aside to others, return afterward to the previous ones. Obtain each day some aid against poverty, something against death, and likewise against other calamities. And when you have moved rapidly through many topics, select one to ponder that day and digest.

5 This is what I do as well, seizing on some item from among several things I have read. Today it is this, which I found in Epicurus—for it is my custom to cross even into the other camp,* not as a deserter but as a spy:

Cheerful poverty is an honorable thing.

6 Indeed, it is not poverty if it is cheerful: the pauper is not the person who has too little but the one who desires more. What does it matter how much is stashed away in his strongbox or his warehouses, how much he has in livestock or in interest income, if he hangs on another's possessions, computing not what has been gained but what there is yet to gain? Do you ask what is the limit of wealth? Having what one needs, first of all; then, having enough.

Farewell.

LETTER 3

Trusting one's friends

From Seneca to Lucilius
Greetings

1 You gave letters to a friend of yours—so you write—to bring to me, and then you advise me not to tell him all your affairs, since you yourself are not in the habit of doing so. Thus in one and the same letter you have said both that he is your friend and that he is not. Well, if you used that word not with its proper meaning but as if it were public property, calling him a friend in the same way as we call all candidates "good men" or address people as "sir" when we don't remember their names, then let it go. 2 But if you think that a person is a friend when you do not trust him as much as you trust yourself, you are seriously mistaken; you do not know the meaning of real friendship.

Consider every question with a friend; but first, consider the friend. After you make a friend, you should trust him—but before you make a friend, you should make a judgment. People who love someone and then judge that person are mixing up their responsibilities: they should judge first, then love, as Theophrastus advised.* Take time to consider whether or not to receive a person into your friendship; but once you have decided to do so, receive him with all your heart, and speak with him as candidly as with yourself.

3 Live in such a way that anything you would admit to yourself could be admitted even to an enemy. Even so, there are things that are customarily kept private; with a friend, though, you should share all your concerns, all your thoughts. If you believe him loyal, you will make him so. Some people teach their friends to betray them by their very fear of betrayal: by being suspicious, they give the other person the right to transgress. He is my friend: why should I hold back my words in his presence? When I am with him, why is it not as if I am alone?

4 There are those who unload their worries into every available ear, telling anyone they meet what should be entrusted only to friends. Others are reluctant to confide even in those who are closest to them; they press every secret to their chest, and would keep it even from themselves if they could. Neither alternative is appropriate—to trust everyone or to trust no one; both are faults, but the former is what I might call a more honorable fault, the latter a safer one.

5 Similarly, there is reason to criticize both those who are

always on the move and those who are always at rest. Liking to be in the fray does not mean that one is hardworking; it is only the hustle and bustle of an agitated mind. Finding every movement a bother does not mean that one is tranquil; it is just laxity and idleness. **6** So let's keep in mind this saying I have read in Pomponius:

> Some flee so far into their dens that they think everything outside is turmoil.*

There should be a mix: the lazy one should do something, the busy one should rest. Consult with nature: it will tell you that it made both day and night.

Farewell.

LETTER 6

Intimacy within friendship

From Seneca to Lucilius
Greetings

1 My understanding is, Lucilius, that what is happening in me is not merely a removal of flaws, but a transformation.* Not that there is nothing left in me to be amended! At this point I don't promise that, nor do I expect it. Why should I not have many characteristics to sort through and either reduce or heighten? This is itself an indication that the mind has reached a better place, when it perceives faults in itself that previously went unrecognized. With some patients, it is cause for congratulation when they realize that they are ill.

2 If only I *could* share such a sudden transformation with you—that's what I would like. In that case, I would begin to have more confidence in our friendship. For it would then be true friendship, such as no hope, no fear, no self-interest can sever. That is a friendship that stays with people until they die—and that people die for. 3 I can name you many people who have friends and yet are without friendship; this is not the case, though, where equal willingness draws minds into a companionship of honorable intentions.* How could it be? For they know that everything they have is held in common, and especially their trials.

You cannot imagine how much progress I see myself making every day. 4 "What remedies are these that have done so much for you?" you say. "Send them to me too!" Indeed, I am longing to shower you with all of them. What gives me pleasure in learning something is that I can teach it. Nothing will ever please me, not even what is remarkably beneficial, if I have learned it for myself only. If wisdom were given to me with this proviso, that I should keep it shut up in myself and never express it to anyone else, I should refuse it. No good is enjoyable to possess without a companion. 5 So I will send you the books themselves; and I will annotate them too, so that you need not expend much effort hunting through them for the profitable bits, but can get right away to the things that I endorse and am impressed with.

But formal discourse will not do as much for you as direct contact, speaking in person and sharing a meal. You must come and see me face-to-face—first of all, because humans believe their eyes much more than their ears, and second, because learning by precepts is the long way around. The quick and effective way is to learn by example. 6 If Cleanthes had merely listened to Zeno, he would not have been molded by him; instead, he made himself a part of Zeno's life, looking into his inmost thoughts and seeing whether he lived in accordance with his own rule.* Plato and Aristotle and the whole crowd of philosophers who would later go their separate ways all derived more from Socrates's conduct than from his words. Metro- dorus, Hermarchus, and Polyaenus were made great men not by Epicurus's formal instruction but by living together with him.* Nor do I summon you to me only for your own benefit. It is for my benefit as well: each of us has much to bestow on the other.

7 Meanwhile, as I owe you the daily dole, I will tell you what pleased me today in the writings of Hecaton:

> Do you ask what progress I have made? I have begun to be a friend to myself.*

Valuable progress indeed: he will never be alone. Believe me, such a person will be a friend to everyone.

Farewell.

LETTER 7

Avoiding the crowd

From Seneca to Lucilius
Greetings

---

1 Do you ask what you should avoid more than anything else? A crowd. It is not yet safe for you to trust yourself to one.

I'll freely admit my own weakness in this regard. Never do I return home with the character I had when I left; always there is something I had settled before that is now stirred up again, something I had gotten rid of that has returned. As with invalids, who are so affected by a lengthy convalescence that they cannot be moved outdoors without taking some harm, so it is with us: our minds are recovering from a long illness; **2** contact with the many is harmful to us. Every single person urges some fault upon us, or imparts one to us, or contaminates us without our even realizing it.

Without doubt, the larger the group we associate with, the greater the danger. Nothing, though, is as destructive to good character as occupying a seat in some public spectacle, for then the pleasure of the sight lets the faults slip in more easily. **3** What do you suppose I mean? Do I come home greedier, more power-hungry, more self-indulgent? Worse than that! I become more cruel and inhumane, just because I have been among humans.

Purely by chance, I found myself at the midday show, expecting some amusement or wit, something relaxing to give people's eyes a rest from the sight of human blood. On the contrary! The fights that preceded turned out to have been downright merciful. The trifling was over: now it was unmitigated slaughter. They are not provided with any protective armor: their bodies are completely exposed, so that the hand never strikes in vain. **4** This is generally liked better than the usual matches between even the most popular gladiators. And why not? There is no helmet, no shield to stop the blade. Why bother with defenses? Why bother with technique? All that stuff just delays the kill. In the morning, humans are thrown to the lions or to the bears; at noon, they are thrown to their own spectators! Those who do the killing are made to submit to others who will kill them; the victor is detained for further slaughter. The only way out of the ring is to die. Steel and flames are the business of the hour. And this is what goes on when the arena is empty!

5 "But one of them committed a robbery! He killed somebody!" So what? He is a murderer, and therefore deserves to have this done to him, but what about you? What did you do, poor fellow, to make you deserve to watch?

"Kill him! Whip him! Burn him! Why is he so timid about running onto the sword? Why does he not succumb more bravely? Why is he not more willing to die? Let him be driven with lashes into the fray! Let them receive each other's blows with their chests naked and exposed!" A break in the action: "Cut some throats in the meantime, just so there will be something going on!" Come, now, don't you understand this, even, that bad examples redound upon those who set them? Thank the gods that the person you are teaching to be cruel is not capable of learning!*

6 The mind that is young and not yet able to hold on to what is right must be kept apart from the people. It is all too easy to follow the many. Even Socrates, Cato, or Laelius could have had their character shaken out of them by the multitude that was so different.* All the more, then, we who are just now beginning to establish inner harmony cannot possibly withstand the attack of faults that bring so much company along. 7 A single example of self-indulgence or greed does a great deal of harm. A dissipated housemate makes one become less strong and manly over time; a wealthy neighbor inflames one's desires; a spiteful companion infects the most open and candid nature with his own canker. What do you suppose happens to the character that is under attack by the public at large? You must either imitate them or detest them.

8 Both are to be avoided: you should not imitate those who are bad because they are many, and neither should you become hateful to the many because they are unlike you. Retreat into yourself, then, as much as you can. Spend your time with those who will improve you; extend a welcome to those you can improve. The effect is reciprocal, for people learn while teaching.

9 There is no reason for you to be enticed into the midst of the people by a prideful wish to display your talent for public recitation or debate. I would want you to do that if you had any merchandise suitable for this populace; as it is, there is nobody capable of understanding you. Perhaps somebody or other will show up, and even that one will need to be instructed, to teach him how to understand you.

"For whom, then, did I learn these things?" You need not fear that your time has been wasted so long as you have learned them for yourself.

10 And so that my own learning today will not be for myself alone, I will share with you three exceptionally fine sayings that come to mind as having some bearing on the point at hand. One shall pay what is due with this letter, and the other two you may credit to my account.* Democritus* says,

> One person counts as a nation with me, a nation as one person.

11 Also well spoken is the remark of whoever it was (for there is some dispute as to the author) who said, when asked why he expended such efforts over a work of art that very few would ever see,

> A few are enough; one is enough; not even one is also enough.

The third is especially good. Epicurus, writing to one of his companions in philosophy, said,

> I write this not for the many but for you: you and I are audience enough for one another.*

12 Take these words to heart, dear Lucilius, so that you may think little of the pleasure that comes from the acclaim of the many. Many people do praise you: does it give you reason to be satisfied with yourself if you are one whom many people can understand? Direct your goods inward.

Farewell.

LETTER 8

Writing as a form of service

From Seneca to Lucilius
Greetings

---

1 "Are you, then, telling me to avoid the crowd, retire, and content myself with my private thoughts? What about those instructions of your school that bid us die in action?"*

Well, do you think this is inaction that I am urging upon you? Here is the reason I have hidden myself away and closed the doors: to benefit the greater number. Not one of my days is spent in leisure, and I claim a part of the nights for study. I have no time for sleep, until it overcomes me; my eyes are exhausted and drooping with late hours, but I keep them to the task. **2** I have withdrawn not only from society but from business, and especially from my own business. The work that I am doing is for posterity: it is they who can benefit from what I write. I am committing to the page some healthful admonitions, like the recipes for useful salves. I have found these effective on my own sores, which, even if not completely healed, have ceased to spread. 3 The right path, which I myself discovered late in life when weary from wandering, I now point out to others.

My cry is this:*

"Avoid those things that please the many, the gifts that fortune brings. Be suspicious; be timid; resist every good that comes by chance. It is by the allurements of hope that the fish is caught, the game snared. Do you think these are the blessings of fortune? They are traps. Any one of you who wants to live in safety must make every effort to shun those baited favors amidst which we, poor creatures, are deceived. We think we have hold of them, when in fact they have hold of us.

4 "That career of yours leads over a cliff. To leave such an exalted life, you have to fall. And once prosperity begins to push us over, we cannot even resist. We could wish to fall only once, or at least to fall from an upright position, but we are not allowed. Fortune does not only overturn us: it upends us, and then smashes us.

5 "Hold therefore to this sound and saving rule of life: indulge the body only to the extent that suffices for health. Deal sternly with it, lest it fail to obey the mind. Let food be for appeasing hunger, drink for satisfying thirst, clothing a protection against cold, a house a shelter against inclement weather. Whether that house is built of sod or of variegated marble from foreign lands is of no significance: believe me, a person can be sheltered just as well with thatch

as with gold. Scorn all those things that superfluous labor sets up for decoration and for show: keep in mind that nothing but the mind is marvelous, that to the great mind, nothing else is great."

6 If I am saying all this to myself and to posterity, do you not think that I am doing more to benefit them than I used to when I was an advocate, going down to post bail or affixing a seal to someone's will or lending my voice and aid to some senatorial candidate? Believe me: those who appear to be doing nothing are doing greater things—they are dealing with matters both human and divine.

7 But now I must make an end; and as has become my custom, I must pay for my letter. This will be done, but not on my own charge. I am still plundering Epicurus, in whose work I today found this saying:

> You should become a slave to philosophy, that you may attain true liberty.*

Those who give themselves in obedient service to philosophy are not put off from day to day: they have their liberty-turn* at once, for this slavery to philosophy is true freedom.

8 Perhaps you will ask me why I mention so many fine sayings from Epicurus rather than from our own school. But is there any reason why you should consider them to belong to Epicurus rather than to the public? So many poets say things that philosophers have said, or that they ought to have said! I need not refer to the tragedians or to the authors of our *fabulae togatae* (for those plays too have a serious element; they are in between tragedy and comedy).* Plenty of highly eloquent verses are to be found even in the mime. Many lines of Publilius are such as would befit not only the writer of comedy but even the tragedian. **9** I will report one verse of his that is relevant to philosophy and indeed to the topic I was just discussing. In it he asserts that things that come by chance ought not to be regarded as belonging to us:

> Whatever comes by wishing is not your possession.*

10 I remember that you yourself expressed the same idea in a much better and more concise way:

> What fortune makes your own is not your own.

Nor will I omit another, even better saying of yours:

> The good that can be given can be taken.*

I am not charging these against your account: they come to you from yourself.
Farewell.

LETTER 9

Friendship and self-sufficiency

From Seneca to Lucilius
Greetings

---

1 You are eager to know whether Epicurus was justified in the criticism expressed in one of his letters* against those who say that the wise person is self-sufficient and for this reason has no need of a friend.* It is a charge made by him against Stilpo* and others who say that the highest good is an impassive mind. 2 (If we choose to express the Greek word *apatheia* quickly in one word and say *impatientia*, we cannot help but create ambiguity, for *impatientia* can also be understood in the opposite sense to what we intend: we mean by it a person who refuses to feel any misfortune, but it will be taken to refer to one who cannot bear any misfortune.* Consider, then, whether it might not be better to speak of the invulnerable mind or the mind set beyond all suffering.) 3 Our position is different from theirs in that our wise person conquers all adversities, but still feels them; theirs does not even feel them.* That the sage is self-sufficient is a point held in common between us; yet even though he is content with himself, he still wishes to have a friend, a neighbor, a companion.*

4 To see how self-sufficient he is, consider this: there are times when he is satisfied with just part of himself. If his hand were cut off in battle or amputated due to gangrene; if an accident cost him an eye, or even both eyes, the remaining parts of himself would be sufficient for him; he will be as happy with his body diminished as he was with it whole. Still, although he does not feel the want of the missing limbs, he would prefer that they not be missing.* 5 He is self-sufficient, not in that he wants to be without a friend, but in that he is able to—by which I mean that he bears the loss with equanimity. But in truth he will never be without a friend, for it rests with him how quickly he gets a replacement. Just as Phidias, if he should lose one of his statues, would immediately make another, so this artist at friend-making will substitute another in place of the one who is lost.*

6 Are you asking how he will make a friend so quickly? I will tell you, provided you agree that my debt is paid herewith, and the account is cleared as concerns this letter. Hecaton says,

I will show you a love charm without drugs, without herbs, without any witch's incantation: love, if you would be loved.*

Moreover, there is great pleasure to be had not only from the practice of an old and established friendship but also from the initiation and acquisition of a new one. 7 The difference between making a friend and having made one is the same as between sowing and reaping. The philosopher Attalus used to say that it is more pleasant to make a friend than to have a friend, "just as it is more pleasurable for an artist to paint a picture than to have painted one."* That focused concentration on one's work is deeply enjoyable in itself; the pleasure one has in the finished product after the work is done does not equal it. Now, the artist is enjoying the result of his art; while he was painting, he was enjoying the art itself. Children are more rewarding when fully grown, but sweeter in infancy.

8 Now let's return to our stated thesis. Even if the sage is self-sufficient, he still wants to have a friend. If for no other reason, he wants to keep such a great virtue from going unused. His motive is not what Epicurus says in this very letter, "to have someone to sit beside him in illness, or to assist him in imprisonment or in need."* Instead, it is to have someone whom he himself may sit beside in illness, whom he himself may liberate from an enemy's capture. He who looks to himself, and comes to friendship for that reason, thinks amiss. As he began, so will he end: he made the friend to gain his assistance in captivity, but he himself will be gone at the first clink of a chain. 9 These are what are commonly called fair-weather friendships. A friend taken on because of his utility will be pleasing only as long as he is useful. That is why those who

are in prosperity have a crowd of friends hanging about, while those who have had a fall are deserted: friends run away just when they have the opportunity to prove their friendship. That is why there are so many terrible stories of people abandoning their friends, or even betraying them, through fear.

Beginnings and endings must agree. He who begins being a friend for the sake of expediency will also stop for the sake of expediency. Some amount of money will be chosen over the friendship if that friendship is valued for anything besides itself. 10 "Why make a friend?" To have someone I can die for, someone I can accompany into exile, someone whose life I can save, even by laying down my own. What you describe is a business deal, not a friendship, for it looks to its own advantage; it thinks in terms of results.

11 No one doubts that the feelings of lovers bear some resemblance to friendship. One could even say that love is a friendship gone mad. So does anyone fall in love in order to make a profit? Or for the sake of ambition, or for glory? Love all by itself, caring nothing for other objectives, inflames the mind with desire for the other's beauty, and hopes the affection will be returned. What shall we conclude? Does a base emotion arise from a more honorable origin?*

12 You say, "Our question is not whether friendship is choiceworthy in itself." On the contrary, that is the point that needs most of all to be established; for if friendship is choiceworthy in itself, then it is possible for one who is self-sufficient to pursue it. "In what way, then, does he pursue it?" As one does any deeply beautiful thing, not drawn by profit, and not cowed by the vagaries of fortune. The grandeur of friendship is diminished when one makes a friend just to better one's lot.

13 "The wise person is self-sufficient." My dear Lucilius,

many people misinterpret this. They pull the sage in on every side, driving him inside his own skin. The fact is, one has to make some distinctions as to what that assertion means and how far it extends. The wise person is self-sufficient as concerns living a good life, but not as concerns living in general. For the latter, there are many things he requires; for the former, only a sound and upright mind that rises superior to fortune.

14 Let me tell you Chrysippus's distinction as well. He says that even though the wise person lacks nothing, he still has a use for many things. "By contrast, there is nothing the foolish person has a use for—since he does not know how to use things—and yet he lacks everything." The wise person has a use for hands and eyes and many other things that are needed for everyday living, and yet lacks nothing. For "lack" implies "need," and the wise person is not in need of anything.*

15 Therefore, even though he is self-sufficient, he does have a use for friends, and wants to have as many as possible. But he does not want them in order to live a good life. He will do that even without friends, for the highest good does not look for instruments outside itself. It is raised in one's own home, and is complete all by itself. If you seek any part of it from outside, it begins to be subject to fortune.

16 "But what sort of life will the wise man have if he is left without friends when in captivity, or stranded in some foreign country, or delayed on some long voyage, or cast away on a desert island?" The kind Jupiter has at that time when the world is dissolved and all gods are mingled into one, when nature ceases its operations for a while and he devotes himself to his own thoughts, and rests in himself. What the sage does is something like that: he retreats into himself and is his own company.*

17 Still, as long as he has the option of arranging his affairs to suit his own preferences, he is self-sufficient, and yet takes a wife; self-sufficient, and yet raises children; self-sufficient, and yet would not live at all if it meant living without other people. What brings him to friendship is not his own expediency but a natural instinct. For just as we innately find certain other things appealing, so it is with friendship. Just as it is inherent in us to shun solitude and seek companionship—just as nature attaches human beings to one another—so also is there an innate prompting to pursue friendships.*

18 All the same, even though the wise person loves his friends very deeply, putting them on a par with himself or, often, ahead of himself, he nonetheless considers every good to be bounded within himself, and will give the same opinion as Stilpo did—that Stilpo who is criticized in Epicurus's letter. Stilpo's homeland fell to invaders; his children were lost, his wife was lost, and he alone survived the destruction of his people. Yet he emerged happy; and when Demetrius, who was called Poliorcetes, or "City-Sacker," asked him whether he had lost anything, he replied, "All my goods are with me."* **19** Here is a brave man, and a tough one: he conquered even his enemy's conquest. "I have lost nothing," he said, and made Poliorcetes doubt whether he had really conquered at all. "All my goods are with me": justice, courage, prudence, and this in itself, the ability to think that nothing is good which can be taken away. We are amazed that some animals can pass through fire without damage to their bodies. How much more amazing is this man, who escaped fire, sword, and devastation, not only without injury but even without loss! You see how much easier it is to defeat an entire people than a single man? Stilpo's saying is shared by the Stoic: he too carries his goods intact through the devastation of cities, for he is self-sufficient. It is by that limit that he defines his prosperity.

20 But you shouldn't think that we are the only ones to speak such noble words. Epicurus himself, for all his criticism of Stilpo, delivered a saying similar to his. Give me credit for it, even though I have already paid up for today. He says,

> Anyone who does not think that what he has is plenty, is miserable, even if he is ruler of the entire world.*

Or, if you think this a better way of expressing it (for our service should be given to thoughts, not words): "Wretched is he who does not believe himself supremely happy, though he rule the world." **21** But to show you that these are widely shared opinions, no doubt dictated by nature, a comic poet supplies the following:

> No one is happy who does not believe himself to be.*

If you think your circumstances are bad, then does it matter what they are really like?

22 "But look," you say. "What about So-and-So, with his tainted money, or So-and-So, master of many and slave of many more? If one of them claims to have a good life, does his opinion make it so?" It is not what he says that counts, but what he thinks—and not what he thinks on any one day, either, but what he thinks over time. Anyway, you need not worry about so great a prize being awarded to one who does not deserve it. Only the wise man is satisfied with what he has: all the foolish are disgusted with themselves, and suffer accordingly.

Farewell.

Blushing

From Seneca to Lucilius
Greetings

---

1 A conversation I had with your promising young friend immediately showed me how much intelligence and talent he has, and indeed how much progress he has already made. He has given us a sample of himself, and the rest of him will be like it, for what he said was not prepared in advance; he was caught off guard. When he began to collect himself, he blushed deeply, for he could not rid himself of that modesty which is such a good sign in a young person.

I suspect he is one who will retain this tendency even when he has fully grown up and has rid himself of every fault—even when he is wise. For natural flaws of body or mind are not removed by any amount of wisdom: what is innate and implanted may be mitigated by treatment but not overcome.*
2 There are people who, though utterly self-contained, still break out in a sweat when they appear in public, just as if they were tired and overheated. Others get weak in the knees when they are about to give a speech, or their teeth chatter, their lips clench, their tongue trips. These things are not eliminated either by training or by any amount of practice; no, nature exerts its force, using these flaws to remind even the strongest of what their nature is. **3** I am sure that blushing is one of these things; for even in the soberest of grown men it still arises, and suddenly too. True, it is seen more in the young, in whom the native heat is greater and the complexion more supple; but it

also affects veteran soldiers and the elderly. Some people are more dangerous when blushing than at any other time; it is as if they had put all their shame into the blush. 4 Sulla was at his most violent when blood had risen to his cheeks. Nothing was softer than Pompey's face: every time he was in company, he blushed, and especially during his speeches.* I remember how Fabianus blushed when called to testify before the Senate; in him, this modesty was strangely becoming.*

5 This does not happen because of any mental weakness but only because of the newness of the situation. People who lack experience of something may be undismayed and yet still affected in this way, if their body's natural disposition tends toward blushing. For just as some people have sluggish° blood, so some have lively, energetic blood that rises swiftly to their faces. 6 As I said, such characteristics are not cast out by any amount of wisdom. If wisdom could erase *all* defects, it would have nature itself under its charge. All contributions made by the circumstances of one's birth and one's bodily temperament will remain with us after the mind has at length managed in large part to settle itself. None of these can be ordered down, any more than they can be summoned at will.

7 Actors imitate the emotions: they portray fear and trembling; they make a show of sadness; but when it comes to bashfulness, their means of indicating it are to tilt the head forward, lower the voice, and fix the eyes on the ground. They cannot make themselves blush, for that can neither be prevented nor induced. Against such things wisdom has no promise to give, no progress to make: they are under their own jurisdiction. They come unbidden and depart unbidden.

8 Now the letter is asking for its closing. Here it is, and a useful and salutary closing too, that I suggest you fix in mind.

We should develop a fondness for some good man and keep him always before our eyes, to live as though he were watching and act in all things as though he could see.*

9 Dear Lucilius, it was Epicurus who gave this instruction. He gave us a guardian and a tutor, and rightly so; for if a witness is present when people are about to commit a wrong, they usually desist. Let the mind have someone it can respect, someone by whose authority it can make even its privacy more reverent.

Blessed is he who improves us not only when present but even when imagined! Blessed too is he who can revere some person so deeply as to bring order and composure to his existence just by remembering that person. One who is capable of such reverence will soon be worthy of reverence himself. **10** Choose Cato, then; or, if you think Cato too stern, choose Laelius, a man of milder temperament.* Choose anyone whom you admire for his actions, his words, even for his face, since the face reveals the mind within. Keep that person in view at all times as your guardian or your example. I repeat: we need a person who can set the standard for our conduct. You will never straighten what is crooked unless you have a ruler.

Farewell.

Visiting a childhood home

From Seneca to Lucilius
Greetings

1 Everywhere I turn I see signs of my advancing age. Arriving at my villa near the city,* I began complaining about my expenditures on the building, which was falling apart. My property manager told me it was not his fault: he was doing everything he could, but the house was old. That villa was put up under my direction! What will become of me, if stonework that is my own age is that decrepit?

2 Annoyed with him, I seized on the nearest excuse to vent my anger. "Those plane trees," I said, "are obviously being neglected. They have no leaves; their branches are terribly gnarled and parched by the sun; their trunks are all discolored and the bark is flaking. This wouldn't be happening if they were kept fertilized and watered."

He swore to me by my ancestral spirit that he was doing all that, and taking care of them in every way, but the trees were getting old. Just between us—I was the one who planted them! When their first leaves came out, I was there to see them.

3 Turning to the door, "Who's that?" I asked. "He's decrepit! You were right to station him by the door—he's on his way out! Where did you get him? Is it some whim of yours to take a corpse off someone's hands?"

But the man said, "Don't you recognize me? I'm Felicio!

You used to bring your trinkets to show me.* I'm the property manager Philostitus's son, your playfellow."

"He's nuts!" said I. "Has he now turned into a little child, and also my playmate? Perhaps so! He's losing teeth enough!"

4 My suburban villa has done me a service; it has brought my age before me at every turn. Let us embrace old age and love it. It is full of pleasure if you know what use to make of it. Fruit is sweetest just before it spoils, boyhood most attractive as it is departing; when one is devoted to wine, it is the last drink that brings the most pleasure—the one that puts you under, giving the final push to inebriation. **5** Every pleasure saves its greatest delights for its last moments. The most pleasurable time of life is on the downhill side, but before the drop-off. Even the time that stands at the very brink has its own pleasures, I believe. Or if not, then it has this instead: one no longer feels the need of any. How sweet it is to have worn out one's desires and left them behind!

6 You say, "It is grievous to have death right before one's eyes." In the first place, death should be under the eyes of the young as well as the old, for we are not summoned according to the census.* Second, no one is so old as to be unjustified in hoping for one more day—and one day is a rung on the ladder of life.

One's entire life consists of parts, large circles enclosing smaller ones. One circle embraces all the rest; this corresponds to the span from birth to one's last day. A second encloses° the years of young adulthood; another binds one's entire childhood in its circuit. Further, a year contains within itself all the time periods which, multiplied, make up one's life. A month is bounded by a tighter circle, a day by the smallest; yet even a day moves from a beginning to an end, from sunrise to sunset.

7 That was why Heraclitus, who got his nickname from the obscurity of his sayings, said,

> One day is equal to every day.*

This is interpreted in different ways. <One person>° says "equal" means "equal in number of hours"; this is true enough, for if a day is a period of twenty-four hours, all days are necessarily equal to each other, since night gains what is lost from daytime. Another says that one day is similar in nature to all other days, for even the longest stretch of time contains nothing that you do not also find in a single day: both light and darkness. The regular alternation of the heavens gives us more nights and more days, but does not change their nature, <although the day is>° sometimes briefer, sometimes more protracted. **8** Every day, then, should be treated as though it were bringing up the rear, as though it were the consummation and fulfillment of one's life.

Pacuvius, who made Syria his own by possession,* used to hold funeral ceremonies for himself, with wine and the ritual meal. After dinner he would have himself carried to bed as his catamites clapped their hands and chanted in Greek, to the accompaniment of instruments, "Life is done! Life is done!" **9** Each and every day he performed his own burial. Let us do the same, not for bad reasons, as he did, but for good. Glad and cheerful, let us say, as we go to our rest,

> I have done living; I have run the race
> that fortune set for me.*

If God gives us a tomorrow, let us be glad to receive it. The happiest person, the most untroubled possessor of himself, is the one who awaits the morrow without anxiety. Anyone who has said, "I have done living" rises profitably each morning, having gained one day.

10 Now it is time for me to bring this letter to a close. "What?" you say. "Is it going to come to me without any payment?" Fear not: it does bring you a little something. But why do I say a little? It brings you a lot. What could be finer than this saying, which I now give to it to convey to you?

> It is bad to live under constraint, but nothing constrains us to live under constraint.*

How could it? The roads to freedom lie open on every side, many of them, and short and easy ones. Thanks be to God that no one can be made to remain alive. We can trample upon those very constraints.

11 "Epicurus said that," you say. "What business have you with another's property?" Whatever is true is my own. I shall persist in showering you with Epicurus, for the benefit of those people who repeat their oaths verbatim and regard not what is being said but who says it. By this they may know that the best sayings are held in common.

Farewell.

Safety in a dangerous world

From Seneca to Lucilius
Greetings

---

1 I admit that a fondness for our body is innate in us; I admit that we are charged with the care of it.* Nor do I hold that one ought not to make any allowances for the body. What I do hold is that one ought not to be its slave. One who is a slave to the body—who is excessively fearful on account of it—who refers all things to it—will be a slave to many. **2** We should behave, not as if the body were the proper reason for our lives, but as if it were merely a necessity for life. Excessive love for it troubles us with fears, burdens us with worries, exposes us to criticism. Honor is cheap to one who holds the body too dear. Take scrupulous care of it, but on condition that when required by reason, or self-respect, or loyalty, it is to be thrown into the fire.*

3 Even so, let us avoid not only danger but also discomfort, as much as we can, and retreat into safety, constantly devising ways of keeping away the objects of fear. If I am not mistaken, those objects are of three kinds. We fear poverty; we fear disease; and we fear the violent deeds of those more powerful than ourselves. **4** Among all these, the one that has most impact on us is the threat from another's power, for this arrives with a great deal of noise and activity. The natural evils I mentioned, poverty and disease, come on in silence; they have no terrors to strike our eyes or ears. But the evil of another makes a great show: it is encompassed with fire and sword, with chains, with packs of wild animals primed to leap upon our human vitals. 5 Imagine here the jail, the cross, the rack, the hook, the stake driven up through the middle of a person and coming out at the mouth, the limbs torn apart by chariots driven in different directions, the garment woven and smeared with flammable pitch, and everything else that savagery has devised. 6 It is no wonder, then, that our greatest fear is of this, since it comes in such great variety and with such frightening equipage. For just as the torturer is most effective when he sets many instruments of pain in view (for some who would have withstood the use of them are broken by the sight), so also among those things that subdue and dominate the mind, the greatest impact belongs to those that have something to display. Those other dangers are no less serious—hunger, I mean, and thirst; festering ulcers; fever burning right down in the gut—but they are unseen. Those have nothing to hold over our heads or before our eyes, while these overpower us, as great wars do, with their panoply and parade.

7 Let us therefore make an effort to avoid giving offense. At one time it is the populace we have to fear; at another, if the state is ruled in such a way that the Senate has charge of most matters, the men of most influence there; at another, individuals in whom is vested the power of the people and over the people. To have all these as friends would require much effort: it is enough if we do not have them as enemies. Thus the wise person will never provoke the anger of those in power, but will steer clear of it, just as one steers clear of a storm at sea. 8 When you were headed for Sicily,* you crossed the strait. The rash helmsman ignores the threatening South Wind (for it is the South Wind that whips up the Sicilian Sea into whitecaps) and does not set a course along the left-hand shore but along the other, where the eddy of Charybdis is quite near.* But the

more cautious helmsman inquires of those who are familiar with that locale what the tides are and how to read cloud patterns, and steers well away from the stretch that is notorious for choppy water. The wise person does the same. He avoids the power that will do him harm, being cautious all along not to be seen avoiding it. For this too is part of safety, to be circumspect in pursuing it, since evasive action amounts to condemnation.

9 So let us look about for ways to be safe from the common crowd. First of all, let us not desire the same objects: strife arises among those who are in competition. Then, let us not possess anything it would be very profitable to steal, and let there be very little on your person that is worth taking. No one goes after human blood on its own account, or very few do.* More act from calculation than from hatred. If a person is naked, the robber passes him by; the poor have peace, even where there is an ambush on the road.

10 Next, we should keep in mind three things that are to be avoided, as the old proverb says: hatred, envy, and contempt.* Wisdom alone will show us how to do this. For it is difficult to balance one thing against another: in seeking to avoid resentment, we have to be careful not to incur contempt, lest while we refrain from trampling on others, we give the impression that we ourselves can be trampled upon. For many, the power to inspire fear in others has produced reasons to be afraid themselves. Let us refrain from both. Being considered superior is just as harmful as being despised.

11 Therefore let us take refuge in philosophy. These studies, like the stoles of priests,* mark one as sacrosanct not only among the good but even among those who are bad in an ordinary way. For eloquence in the courts, or any other kind that stirs the multitude, produces rivals; but this quiet sort that is concerned only with its own business cannot be despised; in fact, it is honored above all arts, even among the worst people. Wickedness will never gain so much strength, nor conspire so much against the virtues, that the name of philosophy will cease to be revered as sacred.

Yet philosophy itself must be practiced calmly and with moderation. **12** "What?" you say. "Do you think Marcus Cato practiced it with moderation, he who stayed a civil war with his word? He who took his stand amid the weapons of furious generals? He who, when some were giving offense to Pompey, others to Caesar, challenged both at once?"* **13** One could at this point dispute whether the wise man was obliged to engage in politics in that situation:*

> What are you up to, Cato? The contest is not for freedom; that was lost long ago. The question is whether Caesar or Pompey will possess the state. What have you to do with such a controversy? It is no business of yours to take sides in it. It is a master that is being chosen: what difference does it make to you who wins? It is possible that the better man will win, but it's not possible to win without being the worse for it.

I have touched on Cato's final stand, but even in his earlier years the times were never such as permit the wise to join in that plundering of the state. What did Cato achieve other than raising his voice—and raising it in vain—when he was on one occasion lifted on the hands of the crowd and so ejected from the Forum, all covered with spit and scandalous abuse?° And on another occasion escorted out of the Senate and into a jail?*

14 But we will investigate later on whether the wise person ought to devote any effort to public service. Meanwhile, I summon you to those Stoics who were cut out of politics and devoted themselves in retirement to the management of life and the establishment of laws for humankind, without offending any of the powerful.* The wise person will not disturb the customs of the public, and neither will he draw public attention by a strange manner of living.

15 "What? Will one who adopts this plan be especially safe?" I cannot promise you that, any more than I can promise that a person of moderate habits will enjoy good health; and yet it is still the case that moderation promotes health. Ships have been known to sink in harbor—but what do you think happens in the middle of the ocean? How much more dangerous would it be to live a very busy and active life, if even a quiet life is not safe? Sometimes the innocent do perish—who denies it?—but more often the guilty. The skill remains, even when one is struck down through one's armaments.* **16** In a word, the wise person considers intention, rather than outcome, in every situation. The beginnings are in our power; the results are judged by fortune, to which I grant no jurisdiction over myself. "But fortune will bring some trouble, some adversity." Death at the hands of a robber is not a condemnation.*

17 Now you are stretching out your hand for the daily dole; I will fill you up with a golden one. And since I have mentioned gold, learn how the use and enjoyment of it may be made more pleasant for you:

He enjoys riches most who has least need of riches.

"Tell me the author," you say. Just to show you how generous I am, I am determined to praise another's material: it is Epicurus, or Metrodorus, or somebody from that shop.* **18** And what does it matter who said it? He said it for everyone.

He who feels the need of wealth also fears for his wealth. But no one has enjoyment from so vexed a good. He is eager to add to it; and while he is thinking about its increase, he is forgetting about its use. He is collecting on his accounts—pounding the pavement of the Forum—flipping through his ledger. He is not master but factotum.

Farewell.

LETTER 15

Exercises for the body and the voice

From Seneca to Lucilius
Greetings

---

1 It was a custom among our ancestors, practiced even into my own lifetime, to add to the opening words of a letter, "If you are doing well, that's good; I am doing well myself."* The right thing for us to say is, "If you are doing philosophy, that's good." For that is the only way one can really be doing well. Without that, the mind is sick; and the body too, even if it has great strength, is sound only as that of an insane or deranged person might be. **2** So care for the mind's health first and foremost, and for the other only secondarily: it will not cost you much, if you have resolved to be truly well.

It is foolish, dear Lucilius, and unbefitting an educated man, to busy oneself with exercising the muscles, broadening the shoulders, and strengthening the torso. You may have great success with your training diet and your bodybuilding, but never will you match the strength and weight of a prime ox. Besides, your mind is then weighed down by a more burdensome body, and is less agile as a result. Restrict your body, then, as much as you can, and give more latitude to the mind.

3 Those who are obsessed with such a regimen incur many discomforts. First, the exercises exhaust the spirit with the effort and leave it with less energy for concentration and intense study. Second, the expanded diet hampers its subtle nature.* Further, one has to take the worst sort of slave as one's master, persons who divide their time between oil and wine, who spend a day to their liking if they work up a good sweat and then make up for the loss of fluids by drink, which has more effect when one is depleted in that way.* Drinking and sweating—a life full of heartburn!

4 There are ways of exercising that are easy and quick, that give the body a workout without taking up too much time— for time is what we have to keep track of more than anything: running, and arm movements with various weights, and jumping, either the high jump or the long jump, or the dance jump, or (not to be class-conscious about it) the fuller's stomp.* Choose whichever you like, and make it easy by practice.° 5 But whatever you do, return quickly from the body to the mind and exercise that, night and day. A moderate effort is enough to nourish it, and its exercise is such as neither cold nor heat will hamper, nor even old age. Tend to the good that gets better with time.

6 I am not telling you to be always poring over a book or tablet: the mind should have some respite, but to relax, not to become lax. Getting out in the sedan chair limbers up the body, and does not preclude study: you could read, or dictate, or speak, or listen. In fact, even walking need not prevent you from doing any of these things.

7 Nor should you neglect to exercise your voice; but I forbid you to practice in scales and rhythms, high notes and low. Why, you might then want to take walking lessons! Once you give an entry to those who earn their bread by inventing new devices, you will find yourself with someone to measure your stride, someone to watch you chew; and they will go boldly on with it for as long as you, in your patience and credulity, lead them on.* Well, then: are you going to start your voice off right away with shouting at the top of your lungs? The natural thing is to raise it by degrees; so much so, in fact, that even in lawsuits the speakers begin in a conversational tone and work their way up to full voice. No one starts out with "Loyalty, O Quirites!"* **8** So no matter how strongly your conviction urges you forward, let your attack on the vices be forceful at some moments, but at other times more gentle, as your voice and your diaphragm° feel inclined; and when you lower your voice again, don't let it drop off, but come down gradually through your in-between volume, not° cutting off with a fierce yelp like an untrained rustic. The point is not to give the voice a workout but for the voice to give the hearer a workout.

9 I have relieved you of quite a bit of work. To that favor let me now add one little payment, one present° from Greece. Here you go, a fine precept:

> The foolish life is ungrateful and fearful; it looks wholly to the future.*

"Who said that?" you ask. The same as said the last. What life do you suppose it is that is being called foolish? That of Baba and Ision?* That's not it: it is our life that is meant. Blind avarice hurls us toward things that may harm and certainly will never satisfy us. If anything *could* satisfy us, it would have already. We do not think how pleasant it is to ask nothing, how great a thing not to depend on chance for fulfillment.

10 So remind yourself often, Lucilius, how much you have achieved. When you see how many people are out ahead of you, think how many are behind. If you want to be thankful to the gods and to your own life, think how many people you have surpassed. But what does it matter about anyone else? You have surpassed yourself.

11 Set a goal that you could not exceed even if you wanted to. Dismiss at last those treacherous goods that are more valuable in expectation than they are in attainment. If there were anything solid in them, we would eventually be sated with them; as it is, they make us thirsty even as we drink. Get rid of the baggage; it is only for looks. As for the future, it is uncertain, at the behest of luck. Why should I beg fortune to give me things rather than demand them of myself? But why should I demand things at all? Just to make a big pile, forgetting how fragile a human being is? Why such labor? See, this day is my last—or if not the very last, still almost the last.

Farewell.

LETTER 16

Daily study and practice

From Seneca to Lucilius
Greetings

---

1 I'm sure you realize, Lucilius, that no one can live a truly happy life, or even a bearable life, without philosophy; also, that while it is complete wisdom that renders a life happy, even to begin that study makes life bearable. But this realization must be confirmed and fixed more deeply through daily rehearsal.* It is more work to follow through on honorable aims than it is to conceive of them. One must persevere and add strength by constant study, until excellent intentions become excellence of mind.

2 So you don't need much verbiage or such lengthy protestations when you are with me. I understand that you have made a lot of progress. I know where these things you write are coming from. You are not making them up, or even touching them up. Still, I will tell you my opinion: I have hopes of you, but as yet no confidence. And if I have my way, you will adopt that same attitude toward yourself, and not be too quick to trust yourself without good reason. Shake yourself out; check yourself over; look at yourself in different ways. Above all, consider whether the progress you have made has been in philosophy, or in life itself. 3 Philosophy is not tricks before an audience, nor is it a thing set up for display. It consists not in words but in actions. One does not take it up just to have an amusing pastime, a remedy for boredom. It molds and shapes the mind, gives order to life and discipline to action, shows what to do and what not to do. It sits at the helm and steers a course for us who are tossed in waves of uncertainty. Without it, there is no life that is not full of care and anxiety. For countless things happen every hour that need the advice philosophy alone can give.

4 Someone will say, "What use is philosophy to me if there is fate? What use is it if God is in charge? What use, if chance has the mastery? For what is certain cannot be changed, and against what is uncertain there is no way to prepare oneself.

Either God has preempted my planning and decreed what I should do, or fortune has left nothing for my planning to achieve." 5 No matter which is true, Lucilius, or even if they all are, we must still practice philosophy. Perhaps the inexorable law of fate constrains us; perhaps God, the universal arbiter, governs all events; perhaps it is chance that drives human affairs, and disrupts them: all the same, it is philosophy that must preserve us.* Philosophy will urge us to give willing obedience to God, and but a grudging obedience to fortune. It will teach you to follow God; to cope with chance.

6 But this is not the time to begin a discourse on the question of what it is that is in our power if providence has dominion, or if a sequence of fated events drags us along in chains, or if spontaneous occurrences hold sway. Instead, I now return to where I was, advising you and exhorting you not to let your mind's endeavor dissipate and grow cold. Maintain it; settle it, so that what is now endeavor may become habit.

7 If I know you well, you have been peeking ahead ever since I began, to see what little gift this letter has brought along. Well, shake it out, and you'll see! But you need not marvel at my good graces, for I am still being generous with another's store. Yet why do I say "another's"? Whatever is said well by anyone belongs to me. This too was said by Epicurus:

If you live according to nature, you will never be poor; if according to opinions, you will never be rich.*

8 Nature's demands are minimal; those of opinion are unbounded. Suppose all the belongings of many rich men were piled upon you. Suppose that fortune were to advance you beyond the means of any private individual, covering you with gold, clothing you with purple, endowing you with luxury and

riches, so much that you could cover the very ground with marble—wealth not only in your possession but even under your feet! Let there be statues too, and paintings, and everything any art has devised to indulge your expensive taste. What will you learn from these things? Only how to desire more. 9 Natural desires are limited; those born of false opinion have no stopping point, for falsehood is inherently unbounded. Those who travel by the road have some destination: wandering is limitless.

So pull back from empty things. When you want to know what it is that you are pursuing, whether it involves a natural desire or a blind one, consider whether there is any place where your desire can come to rest. If it goes far and yet always has further to go, you may be sure it is not natural.

Farewell.

LETTER 18

The Saturnalia festival

From Seneca to Lucilius
Greetings

1 The month is December, and the city is sweating, more than ever. License has been granted to public self-indulgence, and everywhere is a great din of preparations, just as if there were some real difference between a day of Saturnalia and a business day.* But really there is not a bit of difference—so that I agree entirely with the one who said that what used to be the month of December is now the entire year!

2 If I had you here, I'd like to ask your opinion on what our behavior should be. Should we make no alteration at all in our daily routine? Or should we try not to appear at odds with the general custom, and so make our dinners more festive than usual, laying aside the toga? For what never used to happen except in some time of turmoil, some crisis of the state, we now do for pleasure because of the holiday: we alter our mode of dress.*

3 If I know you well, you would stand as intermediary. You would not want us to be exactly like the crowd with the party hats,* but neither would you want us to be completely different. And yet it may be that during these days, one ought more than ever to take charge of one's mind, ordering it to abstain from pleasures just when everyone else is indulging in them. For if it does not proceed and is not enticed into those luxuries which lead to dissipation, it gives a very sure proof of its own strength. 4 The latter is by far the bolder course, to remain cold sober when everyone else is drunk and vomiting. The former is more moderate: not to hold oneself apart or draw attention to oneself, while still not mingling in every respect—to do as others do, but not in the same manner. For one may celebrate the holiday without dissipation.

5 But I am determined to test how firm your mind really is. I will therefore give you the same instructions that great men have given. Set yourself a period of some days in which you will be content with very small amounts of food, and the cheapest kinds, and with coarse, uncomfortable clothing, and say to yourself, "Is this what I was afraid of?" 6 A time when the mind is free of anxieties is the very time when it should prepare itself for adversity: amid the favors of fortune, one should strengthen oneself against the onslaughts of fortune.

The soldier in time of peace goes for a run; he constructs a palisade even when no enemy is at hand, wearing himself out with extra effort so as to be strong enough when effort is required. If you want someone not to be alarmed in a crisis, train him ahead of time.

This was the practice of those who every month used to impose on themselves a time of poverty amounting almost to destitution. The point of it was that if they had schooled themselves in deprivation, they would never be frightened by it. 7 Don't suppose that I mean to recommend the "dinners of Timon," the "paupers' cells," and all the other things that self-indulgence plays at merely because it is bored with riches.* Let your pallet be a real one, your blanket really burlap, your bread actually hard and coarse. Endure it for three or four days, sometimes more, so that it won't be a game but really a trial. Believe me, Lucilius: you will find it exciting to be fed full for a couple of pence; and you will understand that you can be free of anxiety even without the aid of fortune. For even adverse fortune will give you enough to supply your needs. 8 Not that you therefore have reason to think you are doing some great thing. You will only be doing the same thing as many thousands of slaves and poor people. Think well of yourself only in that you are doing it without compulsion, and in that you will find it just as easy to endure this always as to try it occasionally. Let us try some practice bouts; let us make poverty our companion, so that fortune cannot catch us unawares. We will be less anxious in prosperity if we know how trivial a thing it is to be poor.

9 Even Epicurus, the expert on pleasure, used to have certain days on which he would barely satisfy his hunger, just to see whether that would do anything to reduce his complete and maximal pleasure; or if it did, how much, and whether the

difference would be enough to justify anyone in making a great effort over it.* This is surely what he is saying in the letter he wrote to Polyaenus during the magistracy of Charinus.* In fact, he boasts that he can be fed for less than one bronze coin, while Metrodorus, who has not yet progressed to the same point, requires a whole coin.* **10** Do you think a person can be full after that sort of meal? In fact, there is pleasure in it, and not a trivial and fleeting pleasure either; not the kind that keeps having to be refilled but a stable and sure pleasure. For although there is nothing delightful about water and barley gruel or a crust of bread, still it is a very great pleasure to be able to get pleasure even from these things, and to have brought oneself to that state which no adverse fortune can undo. **11** Meals in prison are more generous; the executioner is less stingy with those on death row. How great a spirit it is, then, that submits by choice to a harsher penalty than is assigned to the worst of convicts! That's a way to rob fortune of its shafts!

12 So make a start, dear Lucilius. Follow the custom of those men, and designate certain days when you part from your own property and make scarcity your companion. Begin to have dealings with poverty.

> Make bold, my guest, to rise above mere wealth;
> and shape yourself as well into a likeness
> worthy of God.*

13 No one is worthy of God unless he has risen above wealth. I do not forbid you to possess wealth; I only seek to make you fearless in possessing it. And the only way to achieve that is if you convince yourself that you will be happy even without it—if you look at it as something that might disappear at any moment.

14 Now let's begin rolling this letter up. "First, pay what you owe!" you say. I will refer you to Epicurus; payment is to be made by him.

Anger beyond bounds begets insanity.*

You cannot but know how true this is, since you have had slaves—and enemies.* **15** This emotion flares up against people of every station, as much from love as from hatred, and as much in our business dealings as amid jokes and games. Nor does it matter whether the provocation is great or small: the only thing that makes any difference is the mind that is provoked. It is like fire: what matters is not the size of the flame but what is in its path. Where the material is solid, even the biggest blaze does not ignite it; dry and combustible stuff, though, catches even a spark and makes of it an inferno. That's how it is, dear Lucilius: the outcome of great anger is madness. Hence we should avoid anger, not to keep things in moderation, but to preserve our sanity.

Farewell.

LETTER 20

Consistency
From Seneca to Lucilius
Greetings

1 If you are doing well, and think yourself worthy of someday becoming your own person, I am glad of it. For it will be to my credit if I manage to extricate you from that place where you are now floundering without hope of escape. But this I ask of you, this I urge you, dear Lucilius: let philosophy sink deep into your heart, and test your progress not by speech or writing but by strength of mind and by the lessening of your desires. Prove your words through your actions. **2** They have a different aim, those declaimers who seek to win the agreement of an audience; a different aim, those speakers of the present day, who merely set out to produce a prolix and varied rant for the entertainment of young men without enough to do. Philosophy teaches us to act, not to speak. Its demands are these: each person should live to the standard he himself has set; his manner of living should not be at odds either with itself or with his way of speaking; and all his actions should have a single tenor. This is the chief task of wisdom, and the best evidence of it too: that actions should be in accordance with words, that the person should be the same in all places, a match for himself. "Is there any such person?" Not many, but there are some. It is indeed difficult. And I don't mean, even, that the wise person always walks the same steps, but only that he walks a single road.

3 So take stock of yourself. Is your manner of dress out of line with your house? Are you generous with yourself, but stingy with your family? Do you dine frugally, but spend extravagantly on your building projects? Adopt once and for all some single rule to live by, and make your whole life conform to it. Some people cut back at home only to extend themselves in public, and live large. This discrepancy is a fault, a sign that the mind is vacillating and does not yet hold to its own character.

4 Moreover, I will tell you where that inconsistency comes from, that difference between action and intention. No one fixes his mind on what it is that he wants; or if he does, he fails to persevere and so falls away, not just altering his ways but actually regressing, returning to the very behavior he had forsworn. **5** Let me then set aside the old definitions of wisdom and give you one that takes in a whole method of human existence. Here's one I can be content with. What is wisdom? Always wanting the same thing, always rejecting the same thing. You do not even have to add the proviso that what you want should be right: only for the right can one have a consistent wish.

6 Hence people don't know what it is they want except in the very moment when they want it. No one has made an all-round decision as to what he wants or does not want. Their judgment varies day by day, changing to its opposite. Many people live life as if it were a game. So press on with what you have begun. Perhaps it will take you to the top; or if not that, then to a point that you alone know is not yet the top.

7 You say, "What will happen to my flock of dependents if the family does not have an income?" Once you stop feeding that flock, it will feed itself. Or else poverty will teach you what you cannot teach yourself: your real, true friends will stay by you even then, while anyone who was not clinging to you but to something else will depart from you. Should we not love poverty for this if for nothing else? It will show you who your friends are. O, when will that day come when no one will lie to you for the sake of the office you hold!

8 Therefore leave every other prayer in God's hands, and direct your thoughts, your cares, your wishes, to this alone: contentment with yourself and with the goods that come from yourself. What prosperity could be nearer at hand? Trim yourself back to that small fortune that chance cannot take away.

And to make that easier for you to do, this letter's remittance will make reference to it. I'll deliver that immediately. 9 Although you may complain, my payments are still to be made, quite willingly, by Epicurus:

> Believe me, your speech will be more impressive on a pallet and in shabby clothing. Then, you won't only be speaking; you'll be proving what you say.*

I certainly hear the words of our friend Demetrius* differently after seeing how he slept: not only without a mattress but even without a blanket! He doesn't just preach the truth; he gives testimony to it.

10 "What's this? Can't one despise wealth while it is in one's pocket?" Why not? There is greatness of spirit also in the person who sees wealth heaped up around him and laughs long and loud for sheer amazement that it has come to him. Others tell him it is his; on his own he scarcely realizes it. It is a great thing not to be corrupted by living amid riches; great is the man who is a pauper in his wealth.

11 You say, "I do not know how such a man would bear poverty if he should come into it." Nor do I know, Epicurus, whether your boastful° pauper would scoff at wealth if he should come into it. So we must evaluate the mind of each, and examine them to see whether the one relishes his poverty and whether the other declines to relish his wealth. Otherwise the pallet and shabby clothes are but little proof of good intent, if it is not also apparent that the person is enduring them by preference rather than of necessity. 12 But it is a promising sign when a person does not rush out to get them as if they were better clothes, yet still prepares himself for them as easy enough to bear. And it is easy, Lucilius; in fact, when you have

rehearsed for it long before, it is enjoyable too. For there is something in such garments without which nothing else is enjoyable: there is tranquility.

13 So I think it is really necessary to do what I told you in my letter great men have often done: set aside some days when by making a pretense of poverty we train ourselves for the real thing.* We should do it all the more since we are steeped in luxuries, and think everything harsh and difficult. Better to wake the mind from sleep; pinch it, and remind it of how little our nature actually requires. No one is born rich: everyone who comes forth into the light is ordered to be content with milk and a bit of cloth. From such beginnings do we come, and yet now whole kingdoms are not big enough for us!

Farewell.

LETTER 21

How reading can make you famous

From Seneca to Lucilius
Greetings

---

1 Do you think your business is with those people you wrote about? Your business is most of all with yourself: it is you that are the problem. You don't know what you want. You admire honorable conduct more than you imitate it; you see where happiness lies, but you dare not go after it.* So, since you have little insight into what it is that holds you back, I will tell you.

You suppose that the things you are about to leave behind

are important; and just when you have set your eyes on that tranquility toward which you are headed, you linger over the gleam of this life you are leaving behind, like one who is to go down into mire and darkness. 2 You are mistaken, Lucilius. Passing from this life to that one means going up! You know the difference between a glow and a gleam, how one gives off light from its own sure origin, the other reflects light from something else. There is the same difference between this life and that. This life is suffused by a brightness that comes from outside itself, so that anyone who stands between will cast it into thick darkness; that life is radiant with a luster of its own.

Your studies will make you famous. I will report an example from Epicurus. 3 When he was writing to Idomeneus, calling him back from a life of fine appearance to a reliable and constant glory (though Idomeneus was at that time an aide to a powerful king, charged with great matters), he said,

> If glory matters to you, my letters will make you more famous than all those things you are attending to and that make others attend on you.*

4 Was he not telling the truth? Who would have known about Idomeneus if Epicurus had not happened to write to him? All those potentates and satraps, even the king who granted Idomeneus his title, all are buried deep in oblivion. It is the letters of Cicero that prevent the name of Atticus from perishing. It would have profited him nothing that Agrippa married his daughter and Tiberius his granddaughter, or that Drusus Caesar was his great-grandson.* Among such great names, his own would no longer be spoken, had Cicero not made him an addressee.°* 5 Deep is the abyss of time that will close over

us. A few talented minds will raise their heads above it, and although they too must eventually depart into silence, yet for long will they resist oblivion and assert their freedom.*

What Epicurus was able to promise his friend, I promise to you, Lucilius: I shall find favor with posterity, and I can bring others' names along with me, so that they will endure as well. Our poet Virgil promised eternal remembrance to two people, and gives it to them too:

> Fortunate pair! If there is anything
> that poems of mine can do, no future day
> will ever erase you from the memory
> of ages, while Aeneas's line shall dwell
> on the unmoving rock, the Capitol,
> and while the Roman father still holds sway.*

6 Those whom fortune has thrust into the midst of things, who have been the members and partakers of others' power, have great prestige and many visitors—while they are on their feet: the moment they are gone, they cease to be remembered. But minds of talent are held in growing esteem, and this extends not only to the authors themselves but to anything that is associated with their memory.

7 Now, I'm not going to let Idomeneus into my letter for free! He can make the payment for it himself. It was to him that Epicurus wrote that fine sentence urging him to enrich Pythocles in no common or ambivalent way. He says,

> If you want to make Pythocles rich, what you must do is not add to his money but subtract from his desires.*

8 This saying is too clear to need interpretation, and too well phrased to need improvement. My only addition is to remind

you not to refer it only to wealth: its import will be the same wherever it is applied. If you want to make Pythocles honorable, what you must do is not add to his accolades but subtract from his desires. If you wish to make Pythocles experience constant pleasure, what you must do is not add to his pleasure but subtract from his desires. If you wish to make Pythocles live a long and complete life, what you must do is not add to his years but subtract from his desires. **9** You need not regard these sayings as belonging to Epicurus: they are public property. I think philosophers should adopt senatorial practice. When someone has stated a judgment that pleases me in part, I ask him to divide his opinion, and I follow the part I approve.*

These splendid sayings of Epicurus also serve another purpose which makes me even more willing to mention them. They prove to those people who take refuge in him for base motives, thinking to find cover for their faults, that they need to live honorably no matter where they go.* **10** When you arrive at Epicurus's Gardens, and see° what is written there:

HERE, GUEST, WILL YOU BE WELL ENTERTAINED: HERE
PLEASURE IS THE HIGHEST GOOD—

then the keeper of that house will be ready to receive you and, being hospitable and kind, will serve you a plate of porridge and a generous goblet of water and say to you, "Is this not a fine welcome?" "These gardens," he will say, "do not stimulate appetite; they appease it. They do not give drinks that make one thirstier, but quench thirst with its natural remedy, which comes free of charge. This is the pleasure in which I have lived to old age."

11 I am speaking to you now of those desires that are not alleviated by soothing speech, desires that must be given something to put an end to them. For about those superfluous desires that can be put off, rebuked, or suppressed, I remind you only of this: such pleasure is natural but not necessary. You do not owe it anything: anything you do devote to it is voluntary. The belly does not listen to instructions: it merely demands and solicits. Still, it is not a troublesome creditor. You can put it off with very little, if you just give it what you owe rather than what you can.

Farewell.

LETTER 23

Real joy is a serious matter

From Seneca to Lucilius
Greetings

---

1 Do you think I am going to write to you about how leniently the winter has dealt with us (and it *was* a short and mild winter), how harsh and unseasonably cold is the spring, and all the other nonsense people write when they are short of things to say? No, I'll write something that will benefit both you and me. What will that be? What else, but to exhort you toward excellence of mind? Would you like to know what it is that such excellence is founded upon? It is this: don't rejoice in empty things.*

2 Did I say it was the foundation? The pinnacle, rather. Reaching the heights means knowing what to rejoice in— finding prosperity in that which no one else can control.

Anyone who is enticed by hope is anxious and unsure of himself, even if hope is for something close at hand or not difficult to get, even if the things one hoped for never prove disappointing.

3 Do this above all, dear Lucilius: learn how to experience joy.* Do you now suppose that because I am removing from you the things of fortune and think you should steer clear of hopes, those sweetest of beguilements, I am taking away many pleasures? Not at all: what I want is that gladness should never be absent from you. I want it to be born in your own home—and that is what will happen if it comes to be inside of you. Other delights do not fill the heart; they are trivial feelings that merely smooth the brow. Surely you don't think that every person who smiles is rejoicing! The mind must be energetic and confident; it must be upright, superior to every trial. 4 Believe me, real joy is a serious matter. Do you think that it is with a relaxed expression—or, as the self-indulgent say, *avec le sourire**—that one despises death, opens his home to poverty, reins in pleasure, and rehearses the endurance of pain? One who is pondering such things is experiencing a great joy, but hardly a soft or seductive one. This is the joy I want you to possess: you will never run out of it, once you learn where it is to be found. 5 Shallow mines yield but a little; the most precious lodes are hidden deep in the earth, and it is these that will repay the effort of digging with ever greater abundance. The pleasure that is in the amusements of the many is slight and superficial. And any joy lacks foundation when it has been imported from elsewhere. The joy of which I am speaking, to which I seek to direct you, is solid through and through, and has its widest scope within.

6 There is only one course of action that can make you

happy. I beg you, dearest Lucilius, to do it: cast aside those things that glitter on the outside, those things that are promised you by another or from another, and trample them underfoot. Look to your real good, and rejoice in what is yours. What is it that is yours? Yourself; the best part of you. As for your paltry body, it is true that nothing can be done without it, but think of it as a necessary thing rather than as something great.* The pleasures it accumulates are empty, short, and regrettable; besides, unless tempered with a good deal of self-control, they soon turn into pleasure's opposite. Yes, pleasure stands at the edge of a cliff, and tips toward pain if it does not keep within its bounds. But it is difficult to keep within bounds when you believe something to be good.

Greed for what is truly good is sure of satisfaction. 7 "What is that?" you ask, or "Where does it come from?" I will tell you: it comes from a good conscience, from honorable counsels, from right action, from despising the things of fortune, from a calm and steady mode of life that walks a single road. For how can people have anything sure, anything they can rely on, when they themselves jump around from one plan to another? Or if they don't even do that, but are merely blown about by every breeze of chance, hovering and flitting through life? 8 There are few who make deliberate arrangements for themselves and their possessions. The rest are like objects floating in a river: they are not advancing but only moving with the current. One ripple is gentler, and carries them easily along; another sweeps them away more roughly; one flows languidly and deposits them near the shore; yet another is a raging flood and hurls them out to sea. Let us decide, then, what it is that we want, and persevere in that.

9 Here is the place for paying my debt. I can give you a saying of your dear Epicurus* in payment of this letter's bond:

It is wearisome to be always beginning one's life.*

Or, if this is a better way to express the thought,

They live badly who are always starting to live.

10 "Why?" you ask. The saying requires an explanation. It is because for them, life is always unfinished: a person who has just begun to live cannot stand ready for death. We must endeavor to have enough of life, and no one achieves that when he is just at the point of laying out his life's project.

11 Nor do you have cause to believe that such people are rare: practically everyone is like this. In fact, some people are just beginning right when it is time to quit. If you think this remarkable, I will add something to amaze you even more: some people quit living long before they begin.

Farewell.

LETTER 30

An Epicurean on his deathbed

From Seneca to Lucilius
Greetings

---

1 I have seen Aufidius Bassus,* a fine man, who has had a stroke and is wrestling with the advance of years. He is fighting still, but this is a hold he will never break, for age has pressed its great weight on him at every point. You know that he has always been scrawny and weak in body. He has held it together for a long time—or rather, to put it more accurately, has kept it going. But suddenly his strength has failed.

2 It's like when a boat takes on water: you stop up one leak, then another; but once it begins to open up and give way at many places, there's no way to fix it; it's just a leaky vessel. So it is with an aging body. Stopgap measures can sustain it for a while, but when every joint is giving way like the seams of a dilapidated house, when you cannot take care of one thing without something else giving out in the meanwhile, then it is time to look around for the exit.

3 Yet our friend Bassus is as lively as ever in his mind. Philosophy does this: it enables a person to be cheerful within sight of death, and brave and cheerful no matter what condition his body is in, not giving up just because the body is giving out. A great captain sails on, even with his canvas in tatters; even if he has jettisoned the ship's equipment, he keeps the remnants of his vessel on course. That's what our Bassus is doing. He looks on his own end with such a calm expression that if he looked so on another's, you would think him uncaring. **4** It's a great thing, Lucilius, a lesson of many years—when the hour of no escape arrives, to depart in peace.

Other ways of dying have an admixture of hope. An illness abates; a fire is extinguished; a collapsing building lowers to the ground the people it might have crushed. Those swallowed up by the sea have been cast out unharmed just as forcibly as they were swept away; the soldier has withdrawn his sword from the very throat of the condemned. But he whom old age draws toward death has nothing to hope for; he alone cannot be rescued. It is the gentlest form of death, but also the slowest.

5 It seemed to me that our Bassus was attending his own funeral—laying out his body for burial—living on after himself, and bearing his loss (that is, the loss of himself) as a philosopher should. For he speaks much about death, and tries hard to convince us that if there is anything unpleasant or frightening in this business, it is the fault of the person dying and not of death itself, and that there is no more discomfort in the moment of death than there is afterward. **6** A person would be crazy to fear something that's not going to happen to him, and it is equally crazy to fear something you won't feel. Or does anyone believe that he *will* feel death, when in fact it is through death that he ceases to feel anything else? "For that reason," he says, "death is so far removed from every evil that it is beyond every fear of evil."*

7 All this, I know, has often been said, as indeed it should be; but it never did me as much good when I read it in books, or when I heard it from people who were not themselves in any danger. This time, though, the impact on me was very great, since the man was speaking about a death that was very near. **8** I will tell you my opinion: I think the person who is at the point of death is braver than one who is merely in the vicinity. For when death is at hand, it inspires even the untrained to face what cannot in any case be avoided. Thus the gladiator who has been terrified throughout the contest will offer his throat to his opponent and guide the wavering point home. But when death is only near at hand, though sure to come, it requires an unyielding mental strength. This is less often found, and can only really be exhibited by the wise person.

9 So I was very glad to listen to him passing judgment, as it were, on death, and telling me what it is like when one has seen it close up. I imagine that if someone who had experienced death were to come to life again and tell you that death is not an evil, you would give him great credence and authority. In the same way, your best informants on the distress that accompanies the near approach of death will be those who have stood right next to it, who have not only seen it coming but even greeted it. **10** Among those you may count Bassus.

He did not want us to be deceived. Fearing death, he said, is as foolish as fearing old age; for just as age follows youth, so death follows age. "He who is unwilling to die never wanted to live, for life is given to us with death as a precondition. Death is where we are headed, and for that reason one would be mad to fear it. It is uncertainty that frightens us; when things are certain, we simply await them. **11** Death is a requirement that is imposed equitably and unavoidably. Who can complain about being under the same restrictions as everyone else? The first element in equity is equality.

"But I need not plead nature's case at this time. It is not nature's will that we should have any law but its own: what it has assembled, it breaks down; and what it breaks down, it assembles again. **12** If it should happen that old age releases a person gently, not tearing him suddenly away from life but letting him slip away gradually, then that person should give thanks to all the gods. He should indeed, for he had his fill before being taken to his rest, a rest that is necessary for mortal beings, and welcome to the weary.*

"You see some who long to die, who indeed insist on it more firmly than people usually ask to live. I don't know which ones I find more inspiring, those who ask for death or those who meet death with calm cheerfulness. For such requests sometimes come of madness or some sudden fit of outrage, while such tranquility comes of a settled judgment. There are people who come to death out of anger; there is no one who sees death coming to him and offers it a cheerful welcome, unless that person has been long resigned to it."

13 So I have to confess that although I had many reasons to visit Bassus often (he is after all a dear friend), I wanted in particular to see whether I would find him the same each time: would his mental energy diminish as his body grew weaker? But it kept growing, just as one often sees excitement building in a chariot team when it is in the seventh lap, with the palms of victory in sight. **14** In fact, he used to say, in conformity with Epicurus's teachings, "First of all, I hope there will be no pain in that last breath; but if there is, it will be short, and that itself is some comfort. For severe pain is never of long duration.* But if there is torment in the moment when mind separates from body, I will console myself thus: after that pain, I can no longer experience pain. For no doubt my aged breath is only barely clinging to my lips and needs no great force to draw it from my body. A fire that is well supplied with fuel needs water to put it out and sometimes the collapse of the entire building; one that has exhausted its fuel gives out of its own accord."

15 My dear Lucilius, I am glad to listen to these words. It's not as if they were new, but it is as if they have become a present reality to me. Why? Have I not watched many people reach their life's end? Yes, I have, but they make a greater impression on me when they come to death with no hatred for life, when they let death in rather than reaching for it.

16 In fact, he used to say that the torment we feel comes about through our own agency, because we become alarmed when we believe that death is close at hand. But isn't it close to everyone, ready in every place and every moment? "Let us keep in mind," he said, "that in the moment when some cause of death seems to be drawing near, there are others, even nearer, that we don't fear. A man had received a death threat from an enemy—and a digestive ailment got there first. **17** If we are willing to draw some distinctions among the causes of our fear, we will find that some are real, others only apparent. It is not death we fear but the thought of death, for death itself is always the same distance away from us. So if death is ever to be feared, it is to be feared at all times. For what time is there that is not subject to death?"

18 But I should be afraid that you will hate such long letters even *worse* than death! So I'll stop. As for you, if you want never to be afraid of death, think about it always.

Farewell.

LETTER 31

Our mind's godlike potential

From Seneca to Lucilius
Greetings

---

1 I recognize my Lucilius! He is beginning to make good on his promises. Keep it up! For you had the force of character to pursue every excellence, trampling underfoot the goods that are popularly esteemed. Great and good as I want you to be, it is no more than you were striving for. The foundations you have laid cover a wide area; now make the result as grand as your endeavor. Bring your design to full completion!

2 In a word, you will be wise to close your ears. But wax will not be enough to stop them up; you need some tighter seal than what Ulysses is said to have used on his crew.* That voice they feared was alluring, but it was not the voice of the public. This voice that you should fear does not sound from a single crag; it echoes around you from every direction and from every land. Sail on, then, not past a single spot where treacherous pleasures threaten, but past all the cities of the world. Turn a deaf ear to those who love you most: their intentions are good, but the things they are wishing for you are bad.* If you want to be truly prosperous, entreat the gods that none of the things they want for you may happen. **3** Those are not goods that they wish to see heaped upon you. There is but one good, and that is both the cause and the mainstay of happiness: trust in oneself.

But if you are ever to attain to it, you must think nothing of hard work, counting it as one of those objects that are neither good nor bad. For it cannot be that any one thing is bad at one time and good at another, or light and easy to bear at one time and terrifying at another. **4** Work is not a good. So what is? Not minding the work. For that reason, I am inclined to fault those who expend great effort over worthless things. On the other hand, when people strive toward honorable goals, I give them my approval, and all the more when they apply themselves strenuously and do not let themselves be defeated or thwarted. I cry, "Better so! Rise to the occasion! Take a deep breath, and climb that hill—at one bound, if you can do it!"

5 Noble spirits are nourished by hard work. Hence there is no reason for you to choose your wish, your aim, from among the things your parents prayed long ago for you to have. And in general it is shameful for a man who has achieved great things to be still bothering the gods. Why do you need prayers? Make your own prosperity! And you will do so if you have well understood that anything mingled with virtue is good, anything conjoined with bad conduct is shameful. Nothing shines unless it has some admixture of light; nothing is black unless it contains some darkness or has absorbed some kind of murk; nothing is hot without the assistance of fire, nothing cold without air.* In just the same way, it is association with virtue or vice that makes a thing honorable or shameful.

6 What, then, is good? Knowledge of the facts. What is bad? Ignorance of the facts. The man who is truly wise and skilled will exercise avoidance or choice in accordance with circumstances; but he does not fear the things he avoids nor admire the things he chooses, not if he has a great and unconquerable spirit.*

I forbid you to abase yourself; I forbid you to be downcast. Not refusing labor is too little: ask for it. **7** "But what if the work is demeaning?" you say. "What if it is unnecessary or is demanded for frivolous reasons? Isn't such work bad?" No more so than labor expended on attractive objects. Your very endurance shows spirit, when you urge yourself on toward difficult tasks, saying, "Why the delay? A real man is not afraid of sweat."

8 Besides, complete virtue consists in the evenness and steadiness of a life that is in harmony with itself through all events, which cannot come about unless one has knowledge and the skill of discerning things human and divine. This is the highest good; if you obtain it, you begin to be an associate of the gods and not a suppliant.*

9 You ask, "How do I get there?" You need not scale the Alps, at either the Pennine or the Graian Pass, or navigate the Syrtaean shoals, or traverse the mountain fastness of Illyria; you need not approach the straits where Scylla and Charybdis are; and yet you passed through all of these for no more reward than your paltry governorship.* No, the road is both safe and pleasant, and is one for which you have been equipped by nature. Nature has given you certain gifts, and if you do not abandon them, you will mount up equal to a god.

10 Money will not make you equal to a god: God owns nothing. A tunic bordered with purple will not do it; God is naked. Fame will not do it, and neither will self-display and spreading one's name far and wide: no one has personal acquaintance with God, and many think ill of him with impunity. Nor will a troop of slaves bearing your sedan chair through the streets, in the city and abroad: God, the greatest and most powerful god, is himself the bearer of everything. Not even beauty and strength can confer blessedness on you; neither endures the onset of age. **11** You must devote your efforts to that which does not deteriorate over time, and which no obstacle can bar. What is that? It is the mind—but specifically this mind, which is upright, great, and good. What else would you call it but God dwelling in a human body? This mind can be found just as well in a freedman or even a slave as in a Roman of equestrian status.* For what is a Roman equestrian, or a freedman, or a slave? Those are names born of ambition or of unfair treatment. One may leap up to heaven even from a chimney corner. Rise, then,

> and shape yourself as well into a likeness
> worthy of godhead.

But you will not make that likeness from gold or silver: from such materials no likeness can be made that truly resembles God. Bear in mind that in the days when the gods were well disposed, their images were of clay.*

Farewell.

The use of philosophical maxims

From Seneca to Lucilius
Greetings

---

1 You request that I should close these letters, as I did the earlier ones, with quotations, and that I should take them from the leaders of our own school. *They* did not busy themselves with flowery bits of speech: their entire fabric is masculine.* Where what is noteworthy stands out from the rest, you can be sure the quality is uneven. A single tree excites no wonder when the entire forest rises to the same height.

2 Poems are stuffed with sayings of that sort, and historical writings too. So I do not want you to think of them as belonging to Epicurus: they are public property, and especially *our* property. But in him they attract more attention, just because they occur infrequently, because they are unexpected, because it is surprising that anything courageous should be said by a man who professed effeminacy. That, at least, is what most people think about him; to my mind, though, Epicurus is indeed brave, even if he did wear sleeves.* Courage, hard work, and a mind fit for war can be found among the Persians just as well as among those who wear a belt.

3 And so you have no cause to demand excerpts and quotations. The kind of remark that is excerpted from other authors can be found without intermission in the writings of our school. Thus we do not have the eye-catchers you have in mind; with us, the buyers are not disappointed by entering the shop and finding nothing more than was hung up outside. We let them choose the display items from any point in the text they happen to prefer. 4 Just suppose we did want to separate a few individual sayings from the throng: To whom would we attribute them? To Zeno? To Cleanthes? To Chrysippus? To Posidonius? To Panaetius? We are not under a monarch. Each of us asserts his own freedom. Among the Epicureans, anything Hermarchus said, or Metrodorus, is attributed solely to one individual; in that camp everything anyone says is said under the guidance and auspices of one man.* We, however, have such a number of resources, all equally fine, that we cannot separate out just one, even if we try. I repeat, we cannot:

only the pauper keeps count of his herd.*

Wherever you cast your eyes, you will read something that could have been outstanding if the remainder were not equally good. 5 For this reason, you must give up hope that you will ever be able to take just a quick sampling from the works of the greatest men. You must read them as wholes, come to grips with them as wholes. The subject matter is treated along the lines that are proper to it, and° an intellectual product is devised from which nothing can be removed without a collapse. Still, I have no objection to your studying the individual limbs, provided you retain the actual person. A beautiful woman is not the one whose ankle or shoulder is praised but the one whose overall appearance steals our admiration away from the individual parts.

6 But if you insist, I will not be stingy with you, but will deal them out by the fistful. There are piles of them lying about; one only has to pick them up; there is no need to collect them. They come not by dribs and drabs but in a steady flow, all interconnected.

I'm sure these do a great deal for beginners and for listeners from outside the school. For individual sayings take hold more easily when they are isolated and rounded off like bits of verse. 7 That is why we give children proverbs to memorize, and what the Greeks call *chreiai*: they are what a child's mind is able to encompass, not yet having room for anything larger.* It is shameful, though, when a man who is making definite progress seizes on flowery bits or props himself up with a handful of commonplaces he has memorized. Let him stand on his own feet! Let him say these things for himself, not recall what he has memorized. For shame, that an old person, or one nearly old, should get his wisdom from a textbook! "This is what Zeno said": what do you say? "Cleanthes said this": what do you? How long will you march under another's command? Take charge: say something memorable on your own account; bring forth something from your own store.

8 So I feel that all those people who are never authors but always interpreters, concealing themselves in the shadow of another, have nothing noble in them, for they have never dared to put into action what they have been so long in learning. They have trained their memories on other people's words; but remembering is one thing, knowing is something else. Remembering is keeping track of something you have committed to memory; knowing, by contrast, is making all those things your own, not having to depend on a model or to keep looking to your teacher for instructions. 9 "Zeno said this, and Cleanthes that." Let there be some distance between you and the book! How long will you be a pupil? Now, be a teacher as well. Why should I listen to things I can read? "It makes a big difference when things are spoken aloud," he says. Not when the speaker is only borrowing someone else's words, as a copyist might do!

10 And there is another issue concerning these people who never take charge of their own lives: they begin by following their leaders on subjects where everyone else has declared independence; then they follow them in matters that are still subject to investigation. Nothing will ever be found out if we rest content with what has been found out already! Anyway, followers never find anything; no, they never even look for anything.

11 How about it, then? Will I not walk in the footsteps of my predecessors? I will indeed use the ancient road—but if I find another route that is more direct and has fewer ups and downs, I will stake out that one. Those who advanced these doctrines before us are not our masters but our guides. The truth lies open to all; it has not yet been taken over. Much is left also for those yet to come.

Farewell.

LETTER 38

Fewer words achieve more

From Seneca to Lucilius
Greetings

---

1 You are right to insist that we exchange these letters more frequently.* The reason dialogue is highly beneficial is that it works its way into the mind bit by bit. Speeches prepared in advance and delivered before a crowd make for more noise, but less intimacy. Philosophy is good advice, and no one gives advice in ringing tones. There are times when one does need to deliver a campaign speech, if I may call it that, when someone is hesitating and needs a push. But when the aim is not to motivate learning but that the person should actually learn, then one has to revert to these less strident utterances. They get in more easily, and they stick; for one does not need a great number of words, but words that are effective.

2 They should be scattered like seeds.* A seed is just a little thing, and yet when it lands in the right spot, it unfolds its resources and expands into a great and growing plant. Reasoning does the same: when you examine it, it is of small extent; but when you put it into effect, it grows. Only a few words are said, but if the mind receives them well, they become tall and strong.

I say it again: words work like seeds. Though tiny, they achieve much. Only, as I said, the mind that receives them has to be suited to them, and has to absorb them. Then it will itself reproduce them, and many more than it received.

Farewell.

LETTER 40

Oratory and the philosopher

From Seneca to Lucilius
Greetings

1 I am grateful to you for writing so often, for you are showing me yourself, in the only way that you can. It never fails: I receive your letter, and right away we are together. If portraits of absent friends are a delight, refreshing our memory and easing the pain of separation with a kind of comfort, though false and empty, how much more delightful are letters, which bring us real traces, real news of an absent friend! For what is sweetest about seeing someone face-to-face is also to be found in a letter that bears the imprint of a friend's hand—a moment of recognition.

2 You write that you heard the philosopher Serapio when he made a stop in your vicinity.* "It is his way to deliver a great onrush of words, not releasing them one at a time° but driving them on in stampede. For so many come that one voice is hardly enough!" I do not approve of this in a philosopher. A philosopher's manner of speaking should be well regulated, just as his life should be, but nothing is orderly if it is all in a rush. That is why, in Homer, the rapid and uninterrupted speech that is "like a snowstorm" is given to the younger orator,° while the gentle flow of speech "sweeter than honey" belongs to the elder.*

3 Believe me, then, that the copious flow of words you told me about is more suited for the lecture circuit than for someone who has serious, important work to do and to teach. It's not that I want a slow drip and dribble of words, any more than I want a flood. A speaker should neither weary our waiting ears nor overwhelm them. For a meager, impoverished way of speaking makes the audience less attentive, since they grow bored with a slow and halting delivery; all the same, we learn more easily from what keeps us waiting than from what goes flying past us. Besides, we say that precepts are "imparted" to the pupil. Running away with something is not imparting it!

4 Moreover, speech that aims at the truth should be unaffected and plain. This popular style of speaking has nothing to do with truth; it seeks to stir the crowd, to steal upon unguarded ears and carry them by storm. It does not expose itself to scrutiny, but is off at once. But how can speech supply us

with discipline if it is itself undisciplined? Bear in mind that this kind of speech, which is intended to bring healing to the mind, has to get deep inside us. Remedies that do not stay in the system cannot be effective. 5 Anyway, the popular style is largely vacuous and inane, more sound than substance. I need the speech to calm my terrors, curb my temper, dispel my illusions, curtail my self-indulgence, and rebuke my greed. Which of these things can be done in a hurry? What doctor cures the sick while in transit?

Indeed there is not even any pleasure to be had from such a tumult of words, hurtling on without any effort at selection. 6 In general when something has happened that you thought was impossible, you are satisfied to learn of it a single time. So also with these people who put words through their paces: a single hearing is plenty. For what is there in such speeches that anyone would want to learn or to imitate? What judgment is one to make about the speaker's mind when his speech is disorderly, out of control, unstoppable? 7 Just as people running downhill cannot stop where they meant to but are carried° farther than they intended by the momentum of their bodies, so this rapidity of speech is not in command of itself and not well suited to philosophy. Philosophy ought to place its words, not spew them out; it should go forward one step at a time.

8 "What do you mean? Shouldn't it sometimes take wing?" Of course it should—but in such a way as to preserve its dignified character. Excessive vehemence strips that away. Philosophy should have great strength, but a strength that is under control; it should be an ever-flowing stream, not a flood.

I would scarcely permit even an advocate to use such a rapid rate of speech. For it forges ahead without discipline and cannot be called back. How is the juror to follow it? Especially since jurors are sometimes inexperienced and untrained. Even when the advocate is eager to show off or is carried away by his emotions, he should restrict his pace and his accumulation of ideas to what the ear can take in.

9 You will be right, then, to disregard those who care about how much they say rather than how well, and to prefer, if you must, to speak haltingly, like Publius Vinicius.° When someone asked Asellius how Vinicius's speech went, he said, "Bit by bit." For as Geminius Varius said, "I don't know how you can call that man an orator; he can't string three words together."* Yet why should you not choose to speak as Vinicius does? 10 So what if some jokester comes your way like the one that heard Vinicius when he was groping for words as if he were dictating rather than speaking, and said to him, "Say, are you going to say something?"° For although Quintus Haterius was highly renowned as an orator in his day, his swift speaking is just what I would want the person of sense to avoid.* He never hesitated, never took a breath; he began but once, and left off only at the end.

11 I suppose also that some things are either more or less suited to certain peoples. In Greeks you would put up with such license; we Romans make it a habit to put in the punctuation, even when we write.* Cicero too, the wellspring of our Roman eloquence, went forward one step at a time. Roman speech has more circumspection; it sets a value on itself, and lets others make their assessment as well. 12 Fabianus was a fine man both in his manner of living and in his depth of knowledge, and eloquent as well, although that is of lesser importance.* He used to lecture efficiently rather than energetically. One could say that he exhibited a facility with language, but not that he had great speed of delivery. I allow that this

may be a characteristic of the man of wisdom, though I do not make it a requirement. By all means, let his speech issue forth without impediment. But it is one thing to deliver, another to gush; I prefer delivery.

13 Another reason I have to dissuade you from that contagion is that you cannot employ that style of speaking except by losing your sense of shame. You have to coarsen your sensibilities and never listen to yourself. That heedless dash will bring with it many expressions that you would wish to criticize. 14 I repeat: you cannot achieve it without losing your sense of propriety.

Besides that, you need to practice every day, and that means putting your energy into the words rather than the content. And even if a rapid flow of words comes easily to you, requiring no effort, still you should keep it in check. For just as a man of wisdom should be modest in his manner of walking, so should his speech be restrained, not impetuous.

The sum of all my summing up, and my command, is this: speak slowly.

Farewell.

LETTER 41

God dwells within us

From Seneca to Lucilius
Greetings

1 You are doing what is best and most beneficial for you if, as your letter says, you persevere in moving toward excellence of

mind. How silly it is to pray for that! It is a wish you yourself can grant.

You need not raise your hands to heaven; you need not beg the temple keeper for privileged access, as if a near approach to the cult image would give us a better hearing. The god is near you—with you—inside you. 2 I mean it, Lucilius. A sacred spirit dwells within us, and is the observer and guardian of all our goods and ills. However we treat that spirit, so does the spirit treat us. In truth, no one is a good man without God. Or is there anyone who can rise superior to fortune without God's aid? It is God who supplies us with noble thoughts, with upright counsels. In each and every good man

resides a god: which god, remains unknown.*

3 If you happen to be in a wood dense with ancient trees of unusual height, where interlocking branches exclude the light of day, the loftiness and seclusion of that forest spot, the wonder of finding above ground such a deep, unbroken shade, will convince you that divinity is there. If you behold some deeply eroded cavern, some vast chamber not made with hands but hollowed out by natural causes at the very roots of the mountain, it will impress upon your mind an intimation of religious awe. We venerate the sources of great rivers; we situate an altar wherever a rushing stream bursts suddenly from hiding; thermal springs are the site of ritual observance; and more than one lake has been held sacred for its darkness or its measureless depth. 4 So if you see a person undismayed by peril and untouched by desire, one cheerful in adversity and calm in the face of storms, someone who rises above all humankind and meets the gods at their own level, will you not be overcome with reverence before him?

Will you not say, "Something is there that is so great, so exalted, that we cannot possibly believe it to be of the same kind as that paltry body it inhabits. **5** A power divine has descended on him. That eminent and disciplined mind, passing through everything as lesser than itself, laughing at all our fears and all our longings, is driven by some celestial force. Such magnitude cannot stand upright without divinity to hold it up. In large part, then, its existence is in that place from which it has come down. Even as the sun's rays touch the earth and yet have their existence at their point of origin, so that great and sacred mind, that mind sent down to bring us nearer knowledge of the divine, dwells indeed with us and yet inheres within its source. Its reliance is there, and there are its aim and its objective: though it mingles in our affairs, it does so as our better."*

6 So what mind is this? It is one that shines with a good that is its own. Do we praise a person for qualities belonging to someone else? What could be sillier than that? Do we marvel at possessions that can be transferred to another at a moment's notice? What could be more foolish? A golden bridle does not improve the horse. The tamed lion with his gold-encrusted mane, harried into submission and loaded down with trinkets, is goaded on by his handlers: how different is the spring of the wild lion, whose spirit is unbroken! Surely he, fierce in the attack, as nature intended—he, with his rugged splendor that has no ornament but in the terror of the beholder—is superior to that other languid, gilded creature!

7 No one should glory except in what is his own. We commend the vine only if its branches are laden with grapes, if it bears so heavily that the stakes cannot support it. Would anyone really prefer the vine that is hung with golden fruit and golden leaves? Fruitfulness is the distinctive excellence of the vine; similarly in a human being we should praise that which belongs to him. So what if he has attractive slaves, a lovely home, vast plantations, substantial investments? All these things surround him; they are not in him. **8** Praise in him that which nothing can take away and nothing can confer—that which is distinctive about the human being.*

Do you ask what that is? It is the mind, and rationality perfected within the mind. For a human being is a rational animal. Hence his good is complete if he fulfills that for which he is born. But what is it that this rationality requires of him? The easiest thing of all: to live in accordance with his own nature. It is our shared insanity that makes this difficult: we push one another into faults. And how can we be recalled to health, when all people drive us forward and no one holds us back?

Farewell.

LETTER 46

A book by Lucilius

From Seneca to Lucilius
Greetings

---

1 Your book arrived as promised.* I opened it, thinking to read it later at my convenience, and meaning for the moment only to take a taste; then the work itself seduced me to continue. How eloquent it was you may learn from this fact: it seemed light to me, though its bulk would seem at first glance to be that of Livy or Epicurus, not of your writings or mine.* Yet with such sweetness did it hold me and draw me on that I read it through without delay. The sunshine beckoned—hunger nagged—a storm threatened—and still I read it through to the end. **2** It was not only delight that it gave me: it was joy.

What talent it showed—what spirit! I would have said, "What impact!" had there been in it any quiet stretches—had it roused itself only at intervals. But as it was, it was not impact but a steady state. The style is masculine and chaste; nonetheless, there came in from time to time that note of sweetness, that just-right gentle moment. You are tall, upright—this I would have you keep; this is how you should walk. The subject matter has also contributed something, which is why one should choose a fertile subject that will engage and motivate one's talent.

3 I will write more about the book when I have been over it a second time; at present my judgment is hardly settled. It is as if I had heard these things rather than read them. Allow me to ask some questions as well. You have nothing to fear—I shall tell you the truth. Happy man! You have nothing that would give anyone cause to lie to you, even from so far away— except that nowadays we lie even when there is no cause, just out of habit.

Farewell.

The evils of slavery

From Seneca to Lucilius
Greetings

---

1 I am pleased to learn from those who have been with you that you live on familiar terms with your slaves.* This is becoming in a person of your good sense and education.

"They are slaves." No, they are human beings.

"They are slaves." No, they are housemates.

"They are slaves." No, they are lowborn friends.

"They are slaves." Fellow slaves, rather, if you keep in mind that fortune has its way with you just as much as with them.

2 For that reason, I laugh at those who think it is beneath them to share a meal with their slaves. Why not? There is but one reason: it's one of the traditions of arrogance for the master to eat his dinner with a crowd of slaves standing in a circle around him. He eats more than he can hold, immense greed loading his distended stomach—a stomach that has forgotten its proper function—merely so that he can expend more effort on vomiting than he did on ingestion. **3** Meanwhile, the poor slaves aren't allowed to move their lips even to speak—every murmur is curtailed by the rod. Not even a sneeze, not even a chance cough or a hiccup, is exempt from the lash; if the silence is broken by any sound of the voice, they pay a terrible price for it. All night they stand there, mute and famished. **4** The result is those same slaves who cannot speak in their master's presence are ready to speak about him to others.* But in the old days, when they not only spoke in the master's presence but actually conversed with him, slaves never had their lips sewn shut and yet were ready to risk their necks for him, to turn dangers that threatened him on their own heads. They spoke during dinner parties but were silent under torture. **5** It was later that the proverb began to go around, coming of that same arrogance: "Count your slaves and you count your enemies." They are not our enemies just by being there: we make them so.

I can hardly list all the cases of cruel and inhuman treatment such as would be abusive to beasts of burden, let alone human beings. While we recline at dinner, one is wiping up gobs of spit; another crawling under the couch to pick up the scraps the drunkards let fall. **6** A third carves the expensive fowl, his trained hand separating out perfect slices from the breast and from the thigh. Unhappy he, who lives for this alone—the proper carving of poultry! Or he would be if it were not worse to be the one who teaches him to do it. He learns because he has to; the other teaches at the behest of pleasure. **7** Another is the cupbearer, decked out like a woman and struggling against his years. He cannot escape boyhood—he is made to revert to it. Already he carries himself like a soldier, yet his cheeks are smooth, every hair shaved away or plucked out. He is on duty all night: his first shift is devoted to his master's drinking, his second to his lust—for he is a boy only at the party: in the bedroom he's the man. **8** Yet another has been assigned to evaluate the guests. It is his unhappy task to stand there and observe which ones are the flatterers, which cannot control their gluttony or keep a watch on their tongues. These are the ones who will be invited again the following day. In addition there are the arbiters of gourmandizing, who possess a fine-tuned awareness of the master's tastes: which foods stimulate his palate, which please his eye, which are new to him and may prove attractive

even when he is queasy, which he has come to hate because
they are served too often, and what he has a hankering for on
that particular day. Such are the persons with whom he cannot
bear to dine, thinking it beneath his dignity to come to the
same table as his own slave. Heavens, no!

Yet how many masters might he have among them! 9 Once
at the doorway of Callistus* I saw Callistus's own former master standing in attendance. He who had given up the man
for sale, who had auctioned him off among the worn-out
slaves, could not even gain admission, though others could.
That was the thanks he got from the slave he had thrown in
with the first lot, the ones the auctioneer warms up with. Turn
and turn about: now it was Callistus's turn to write him down
for exclusion—now it was Callistus who judged the man unworthy to cross his threshold. That master sold Callistus; now
Callistus made him pay the price.

10 Reflect, if you will: that man whom you call your slave
was born of the same seeds as you—enjoys the same sky—
breathes, lives, dies, just as you do. It is possible that you will
see him a free man, and equally possible that he will see you
enslaved. At the time of Varus's disaster, many highborn nobles
were laid low, men who looked forward to a senatorial career
after their military service. Luck made one of them a shepherd,
another the guardian of a hut.* Go now and scoff! The fortunes
of those you despise may come upon you at any time.

11 I don't want to get carried away with some long speech
about the treatment of slaves. We are indeed most haughty,
cruel, and demeaning toward them. But all my instructions
can be summed up in this: live with an inferior the same way
you would want a superior to live with you. Each time you remember the extent of your power over a slave, remember also

that your own master has that same amount of power over you.
12 "But I have no master," you say. You're still young—perhaps
someday you will. Don't you realize how old Hecuba was when
she became a slave? Don't you realize how old Croesus was?
The mother of Darius? Plato? Diogenes?*

13 Live mercifully with your slave, amicably, even; and include him in your conversation, in your planning, and in your
meals. At this point, the whole order of sybarites will cry out
against me. "Nothing is more degrading than that! Nothing is
more humiliating!" Yet I will catch these same men kissing the
hands of other people's slaves.

14 Don't you people know what our ancestors did to eliminate resentment toward masters and abuse toward slaves? They
used the name "father of the household" for the master, and
"household members" for the slaves—a term that still persists
in stage mime. They instituted a holiday when masters would
share a meal with their slaves—not that they did so only at
that time, but that it was the custom on that day in particular.
They allowed slaves to hold offices and pronounce judgments
within the house, for they considered the house to be a polity
in miniature.

15 "What are you saying? Shall I admit all my slaves to my
table?" No, no more than you admit all who are free. But you're
wrong if you think I am going to exclude some on grounds that
their work is less clean—the stable-hand, say, or the cowherd. I
will evaluate them not by their jobs but by their character. Jobs
are assigned by chance; character is something each person
gives himself. Let some dine with you because they are worthy
of that distinction, others to make them worthy. For if there is
something slavish in them, owing to their life among the lowly,
sharing meals with more honorable people will get rid of it.

16 My dear Lucilius, you need not look for friends only in the Forum or in the Senate House. If you look closely, you will find them in your household also. Good materials often go to waste for lack of a skilled craftsman: try them out and you will see. Just as one would be foolish to consider buying a horse when one hasn't inspected the animal itself but only its saddle and bridle, so it is extremely foolish to judge a human being by his clothing and his position in life. For position is only one more garment that surrounds us.

17 "He is a slave." But perhaps his mind is free. "He is a slave." Is that going to hurt his chances? Show me who isn't! One person is a slave to lust, another to greed, a third to ambition—and all are slaves to hope; all are slaves to fear. I will give you an ex-consul who is a slave to a little old lady, a wealthy man who is a slave to a servant girl. I will show you young men of the best families who are the vassals of pantomime dancers.* No servitude is more shameful than the kind we take on willingly.

So why be afraid of those snobs? Show your slaves a cheerful demeanor, above them and yet not haughty. Let them respect you rather than fear you. **18** At this point someone will say I am calling for emancipation and for knocking down masters from their exalted position, just because I said, "Let them respect you rather than fear you."* "What's this?" he says. "Should they respect you as clients, as morning callers?" He who says this has forgotten that what suffices for a god cannot be insufficient for slave owners. One who is respected is also loved, and love and fear do not mix. **19** Thus I think you are doing the right thing when you prefer not to be feared by your slaves and when you correct them only with words. Whips are for training speechless animals.

Not everything that offends us is harmful to us. It is our indulgences that make us go into a frenzy, becoming enraged at anything that doesn't suit our whim. We put on airs as if we were kings. **20** For kings too forget their own power and the weakness of others, and so become enraged, just as if they sustained some injury—from which experience they are quite safe, thanks to the magnitude of their fortunes. And they are well aware of that fact, and yet in their pettishness they grasp at any opportunity to hurt others. They consider themselves wronged just so they can do a wrong themselves.

21 I don't wish to keep you any longer, for you need no encouragement. One thing about good character is that it is content with itself and so persists over time. A bad one is fickle: it changes frequently, not for the better but just for the sake of changing.

Farewell.

LETTER 49

Remembering old times

From Seneca to Lucilius
Greetings

---

1 Quite right, dear Lucilius: one is negligent and indeed remiss if one remembers a friend only when reminded by some particular locale. But sometimes familiar spots do awaken a yearning that has been hidden in our mind, not rekindling a memory that had gone out but stirring up one that was at rest.* It's like the way a family's grief, though mitigated by the passage of time, is renewed by the sight of some slave child, or some garment or house, that was a favorite of the one who is gone.

Here's Campania—and it's incredible how this region, and above all Naples and your dear Pompeii, have made me wish for your presence all over again.* Every bit of you is before my eyes. I am leaving you even now. I see you blinking back tears—struggling in vain against emotions that cannot be suppressed. It seems only just now that I lost you.

2 For remembrance makes everything "just now," doesn't it? Just now I was a boy, sitting in the house of Sotion the philosopher;* just now I began to argue cases; just now I stopped wanting to argue them; just now I ceased to be able. The rapidity of time is boundless—and is more evident when one looks back. For though it goes at breakneck speed, it glides by so smoothly that those who are intent on the present moment fail to notice it passing.

3 Do you ask the reason for this? All the time that has passed is in the same place; we look on it all at once. All things are dropping into the same abyss. Besides, there cannot be long intervals within something that is brief overall. Our life span is a pinpoint—even less than a pinpoint. But nature has mocked even this infinitesimal point with a specious show of longer extent, making one element in it our infancy; another our childhood; another our youth; another a sloping course, as it were, between youth and age; another old age itself. That's a lot of steps for such a narrow span! 4 It was only just now that I saw you off, and yet that "just now" covers a fair portion of our lives. Let us keep in mind how brief those lives are, and how soon they will run out. Time never used to seem so swift; now its speed amazes me, whether because I perceive the finish

line approaching, or because I have begun to pay attention and compute what I have lost.

5 Thus I am all the more indignant that although even the most careful stewardship of time cannot make it last long enough for our needs, there are some who spend the better part of theirs on superfluities. Cicero says that twice his lifetime would not be time enough for him to read the lyric poets.* Well, I put the dialecticians in the same category, only they are more severe in their foolishness. The poets are frivolous by design; these logicians think they are accomplishing something. **6** I am not saying one should not give such things a look—but it should be only a look, a greeting from the doorway, just enough to make sure we are not taken in by them, thinking there is some deep and arcane value in what they do.*

Why are you going to rack and ruin over that question? You would show more cleverness by scoffing at it than by solving it. Delving into minutiae is for one who has nothing to worry about—who travels by his own schedule. When the enemy is harrying your retreat, when the army is ordered to the march, then necessity discards what peace and leisure had collected. **7** I have no time to spare for chasing down ambiguous terms and exercising my ingenuity on them.

> Behold the assembled peoples, the high walls
> Sharpen their weapons, and the gates are shut.*

The clash and clatter of war are sounding all around me; I need courage to heed them. **8** Everyone would think I was crazy—and they would be right—if, in the midst of siege, while women and old men are carrying stones up to the battlements, while young men are massed inside the gates waiting, even begging for the signal to sortie, while enemy spears come flying within the gates and the ground beneath our feet quakes with tunneling and sapping, I should sit there, idly posing little conundrums like this:

What you have not lost, you have.
But you have not lost horns.
Therefore you have horns.

That, or some other intellectual lunacy along the same lines!

9 Yet you have my permission to think me just as crazy as they are if I spend time on such things. For in fact I am under siege at this moment. In the other case, it would have been an external danger threatening me; there would have been a wall between me and the enemy. As it is, deadly perils are right here with me. I have no time to waste on such foolishness: a great business is afoot.

What am I up to? Death is after me; life is on the retreat. Teach me something I can use against that! **10** Don't let me run from death any longer; don't let life run away from me! Encourage me to face what is difficult; give me the serenity° to accept what I cannot avoid. Expand the narrow confines of my remaining time. Teach me that the goodness of a life depends not on how long it is but on how it is used; and that it is possible—in fact quite common—for a person to have a long life that is scarcely a life at all. Say to me before I sleep, "It's possible you will not wake up," and when I rise, "It's possible you will never sleep again." Say to me when I go out, "It's possible you will not return," and when I return, "It's possible you will never leave. **11** You are wrong if you think it is only aboard ship that 'life is but an inch away from death.' The interval is the same wherever you go. There death is in full view, but everywhere it is just as close to us."

Dispel these shades for me, and you will find it easier to teach me the lessons I have been preparing myself to learn. Nature created us susceptible of instruction; it endowed us with reason, which, though imperfect, can yet be perfected. **12** Lecture to me on justice, on devotion, on frugality, on modesty—both kinds of modesty, the kind that keeps back from another person's body and the kind that takes care of one's own. Just don't sidetrack me, and I will get where I'm going much more easily. For as the tragic poet* says,

Straightforward is the speech of truth—

—and that is why we ought not to complicate things. Those are just verbal traps. Nothing could be less suitable for minds of great endeavor.

Farewell.

LETTER 53

A bad experience at sea

From Seneca to Lucilius
Greetings

---

1 What can I not be talked into? This time I was persuaded to take a trip by boat!* The sea was calm when I set out. To be sure, the sky was heavy with mottled clouds, the kind that usually resolve themselves into rain or squalls; but I thought the mileage was so short from your town of Parthenope to Puteoli* that I could get away with making the trip, even in uncertain and threatening weather. So I tried to get done with it quickly by heading through the deep water directly toward the isle of Nesis, intending a shortcut past all the inlets.

2 The moment I got to where it made no difference whether I went on or turned back, the calm surface that had enticed me was no more. It was not yet a storm but sloping seas, with the waves ever more frequent. I began asking the helmsman to let me off somewhere on shore; he said, though, that the coastline was rugged and without anchorage, and that in a storm the land was the very thing he feared the most. 3 But I was in too bad a way to have any use for danger. I had that persistent seasickness that brings on nausea but does not relieve it by vomiting. So I forced the issue with the helmsman and required him to head for shore whether he wanted to or not.

As we drew near I did not wait for any of the instructions in Virgil to be carried out, for them to "turn the bow seaward" or "cast the anchor from the bow."* Remembering my abilities (for I have long been a swimmer), I threw myself into the sea as a cold-water enthusiast should, wearing my mantle. 4 Just imagine how I suffered as I staggered forward through the breakers, seeking a way, forcing a way. I understood then that sailors have reason to fear the land. It is unbelievable how much I endured just because I could not endure myself! Let me tell you, the reason Ulysses had shipwrecks everywhere was not so much that he was born to an angry sea; no, he was just prone to seasickness. I too will take twenty years to get wherever I am going if I have to get there by ship!

5 As soon as I had settled my stomach—for you know it takes longer to escape from seasickness than from the sea—and as soon as I had applied some oil to refresh my body, I began to reflect on how easily we forget our imperfections. We

forget even our obvious bodily defects, which give us constant reminders; but still more do we forget those that do not show on the outside—and the worse they are, the less we can see them. **6** A slight fever can deceive a person, but when it increases and becomes a genuine illness, even the toughest and most enduring are forced to admit it. There's pain in the feet, a prickling sensation in the joints; we pretend it isn't there, saying we've twisted an ankle or worn ourselves out by some exertion. As long as there is doubt, as long as the disease is in its early stages, we invent some specious name for it; but when it begins to cramp up the lower leg and cause distortion in both feet, we have no choice but to admit that it is arthritis. **7** It is the opposite with those infirmities that affect the mind.* With these, the worse one is afflicted, the less he is aware of it. There's nothing surprising in that, dear Lucilius. When one is just barely asleep, one has impressions in accordance with that state of rest and is sometimes even conscious of being asleep; deep sleep, though, blots out even our dreams, drowning the mind so deep that it has no awareness of itself at all. **8** Why do people not admit their faults? Because they are still in the midst of them. Dreams are told by those who are awake; admitting to one's faults is a sign of health.

Let us wake up, then, so that we will be able to recognize our mistakes. But philosophy is the only thing that will awaken us; the only thing that will rouse us from our deep sleep. Devote yourself entirely to philosophy. You are worthy of it, and it of you: embrace one another. Refuse every other claim on you, boldly and openly: there is no reason you need to do philosophy only in your spare time. **9** If you were ill, you would take a break from your responsibilities at home. Your career concerns would drop away; no one's defense case would be so important to you that you would go back down to the Forum while still anticipating a relapse. All your efforts would be devoted to freeing yourself from disease as soon as possible. What about it, then? Will you not do the same thing now? Get rid of everything that stands in your way; make time for excellence of mind. No one gets there while occupied with business.

Philosophy asserts its power. It grants us time; it does not merely accept what we give to it. Philosophy is a full-time job, not a hobby; it is our supervisor, and orders us to appear.° **10** Alexander once said to a town that promised him part of its arable land and half of all its production, "My purpose in coming to Asia was not to receive any gifts you might give, but to allow you to keep anything that I might leave."* Philosophy says the same thing, but in every situation. "I am not going to accept just the time you have left over; rather, you will have what I reject."

11 Turn your entire mind to philosophy. Sit by philosophy and serve it, and you will be much above other people. Mortals will all be far behind you, and the gods not far ahead. Would you like to know what difference there will be between you and the gods? They will have a longer time of existence. But to encompass a complete whole in a miniature work of art—that is indeed the sign of a great craftsman. For the wise, a lifetime is as spacious as all of time is for God.* Indeed, there is a way the sage surpasses God. It is by gift of nature that God is without fear; the sage gives that same gift to himself. **12** Here indeed is a great achievement: to retain our human weakness and yet have the tranquility of God.

It is amazing what power there is in philosophy to beat back all the assaults of chance. No weapon lodges in its flesh; its defenses cannot be penetrated. When fortune's darts come

in, it either ducks and lets them pass by, or stands its ground
and lets them bounce back against the assailant.

Farewell.

LETTER 54

A near-fatal asthma attack

From Seneca to Lucilius
Greetings

---

1 Ill health had given me a long respite; then suddenly it assailed me again. "What was the trouble?" you ask—and well
you may, for there is no illness with which I am unacquainted.
But there is one that has me in its charge, so to speak. Why
should I use its Greek name?* I can call it wheezing; that fits
well enough.

Its attack is quite brief, like a squall; it is usually over within
the hour. No one can be at last gasp for very long! 2 Every
bodily discomfort, every peril, has passed through me; and
nothing, I think, is harder to bear. How could it not be? Anything else is just being sick; this is pushing out one's life breath.
For this reason doctors call it "the rehearsal for death": the con-
striction sometimes achieves what it has so often attempted.
3 Do you think that I am glad to be writing these things to you,
glad that I escaped? If I delight in this cessation as if it were a
return to health, I am as laughable as the person who thinks he
has won his case just because his hearing has been postponed.

Yet even as I was suffocating, I did not fail to find peace in
cheerful and brave reflections. 4 "What is this?" said I. "Does

death make trial of me so many times? Let it—I have made trial of it as well,° long ago. "When?" you ask. Before I was born. Death is just nonexistence. I know already what that is like: what will exist after me is the same as existed before me.* If there is any torment in this thing, then there must have been torment also before we saw the light of day. Yet we did not feel any discomfort at that time.

5 I ask you this: wouldn't you say a person was quite stupid if he thought that a lamp was worse off after it was extinguished than before it was lighted? We too are extinguished; we too are lighted. Betweentimes there is something that we feel; on either side is complete lack of concern. Unless I am wrong, dear Lucilius, our mistake is that we think death comes after; in fact, it comes both before and after. Whatever was before us is death. What difference is there between ending and simply not beginning? Both have the same result: nonexistence.

6 With these encouragements, and others in the same vein, I did not cease to encourage myself—without speaking, of course, since I had no breath to spare. Then, gradually, my wheezing, which had already given way to panting, began to come at greater intervals, then slowed and finally steadied. Even yet, though the attack is over, my breathing does not come naturally; I feel a kind of catch in it, a hesitation.

So be it, as long as I am not sighing on purpose! **7** Here is my pledge to you: I shall not tremble at the end; I am already prepared; I am not thinking at all about my overall span of life. The person you should praise—and imitate—is the one who enjoys living and yet is not reluctant to die. For what virtue is there in departing only when you are cast out? Yet there is virtue here too: I am indeed being cast out, and yet it is as if I am making my departure.

For that reason, the wise person too is never cast out, for being cast out is being driven away from a place you are unwilling to leave. The sage does nothing unwillingly: he escapes necessity in that he wishes to do what necessity will in any case require.

Farewell.

LETTER 56

Noisy lodgings above a bathhouse

From Seneca to Lucilius
Greetings

---

1 I swear it—silence is not as necessary to a scholarly retreat as you might think. Here is cacophony sounding all about me—for I am living right upstairs from the bathhouse.*

Call to mind every sort of awful noise that grates on the ears. When the stronger men do their exercises, swinging their hand weights about and straining with the effort (or pretending to), I hear the grunts each time they exhale, their rasping and gasping for breath. When I get some idle fellow who's happy with an ordinary man's massage, I hear the hands slapping his shoulders and the change of sound when they strike with the cupped hand or with the palm. Then if a ballplayer shows up and starts counting how many he catches, I'm done for! **2** Now add the quarrelsome type—and the one caught stealing—and the one who likes to hear himself sing in the bath chamber—and also the ones who jump into the swimming pool with a great splash. Besides all these, who are at least using their normal voices, imagine the tweezer man screeching over and over in his shrill falsetto, just to attract attention: he is never silent unless he is plucking someone's armpits and making him cry out instead. Now add the cries of the drink man, the sausage man, the bakery man, and all the different sellers of cooked foods, singing out their wares in their distinctive tones.

3 "You must be made of steel," you say, "or deaf, to retain your concentration amid so many varied and discordant sounds! Why, our own Crispus° was driven to the point of death merely by a constant stream of visitors!"* Yet for me, in truth, the racket is of no more concern than waves or falling water. I've heard, though, of a race of people who relocated their city solely because they could not stand the tumult of one of the cataracts of the Nile.

4 I think a voice is more distracting than any din; for the one engages our mental faculties, the other merely fills the ears with its reverberations. Among the noises that sound around me but do not distract me, I count passing carriages, a carpenter somewhere in the building, a nearby saw grinder, and that fellow who demonstrates flutes and trumpets near the Meta Sudans, not so much playing them as bellowing.* 5 Even now I find noises that recur at intervals more bothersome than a continuous drone. But I have inured myself to all such sounds to such an extent that I could even put up with hearing that horribly shrill cry that a coxswain uses to give the beat to his rowers. You see, I force my mind to pay attention to itself and not to be distracted by anything external. It does not matter what is making a noise outside, so long as there is no turmoil inside—as long as there is no wrangling between desire and fear, as long as greed is not at odds with self-indulgence, one carping at the other.

For how does it help to have silence in the neighborhood, when one's emotions are in tumult?

6 All things were settled in night's restful calm.*

It's a lie: there is no restful calm but that which is settled by reason. Night doesn't take away our cares; rather, it exposes them to view, exchanging one anxiety for another. For even when we are asleep, our dreams may be as tumultuous as waking life. Only as the mind develops into excellence do we achieve any real tranquility.

7 Look at a person who yearns for sleep in the quiet of a household laid to rest. Not one sound assails his ears: all his mob of slaves is hushed; they creep on tiptoe past his room. Yet all the same, he rolls to one side and the other, dozing fitfully amid his sorrows, and complains of sounds he did not really hear. **8** What do you suppose is the reason? His mind is noisy: he must put that to rest, must quell its insurrection. You need not think the mind is at rest just because the body is lying still. Sometimes quiet is itself unquiet. So when we are oppressed with idleness, let us rouse ourselves to action or busy ourselves with cultural pursuits. For idleness has no patience with itself. **9** Great generals, when they see the troops grow restive, assign them some labor and fill their time with marches: if they are kept busy, they find no leisure for insubordination. And nothing is more certain than that the faults of inactivity are dispelled by activity.

Many a time our weariness with affairs of state and second thoughts about an unrewarding and thankless job have induced us to go into retreat. Or so we thought; and yet, within that den where tiredness and fear have driven us, ambition all the while is festering anew. It has not been cut away; it has not ceased to trouble us; it was only fatigued or indeed only vexed that things did not go its way. **10** Of self-indulgence I say the same. It seems at times to be in remission; then, when we are pledged to modest living, it harries us again, and in the midst of our economy goes after pleasures we had not in fact renounced but only abandoned. And it pursues them all the more energetically the more they are kept under cover. For all our failings are milder in the open. Even the infirmities make the turn toward healing once they emerge from hiding and exhibit their full force.* Thus when greed, ambition, and other maladies of the human mind subside into apparent health, that is when you can tell they are at their deadliest.

11 We seem to be at leisure, but we aren't. For if we truly are—if we have really sounded the retreat—if we have turned our back on things that merely glitter, then, as I was saying, nothing will distract us. No chatter of men, no song of birds will interrupt our thoughts—excellent thoughts, and now sure and solid too. **12** It is a lightweight mind and one not yet devoted to introspection that stirs at a voice or at chance occurrences. It has within some anxiety, some element of panic, that makes it uneasy. Our poet Virgil says,

> And I, who long endured the hurtling darts
> unmoved, the Achaeans massed in threatening ranks,
> now fear the wind, now start at every sound,
> trembling alike for my companion and my load.*

13 The earlier case is that of the wise person, who is not alarmed by the hurtling arrows, the ranks of armed men in close formation, the clamor of a city under siege; the latter is the one without experience, who fears for his own affairs and trembles every time he hears a thump. Every voice seems to him a menacing roar; the slightest movement throws him into a panic. His baggage makes him fearful. **14** Choose any one of those prosperous persons, those who have much to carry and much in their train, and you will see him "trembling alike for his companion and his load."

Therefore you may be sure that your mind is settled only when no outcry reaches you, when no voice distracts you from yourself, whether with blandishments or with threats or just with meaningless noise.

15 "What is it you're saying, then? Isn't it easier sometimes to be away from the racket?"

Yes, I grant that, and that's why I'm going to leave this place. I wanted to test myself, give myself a workout. But why should I be tormented any longer, when Ulysses found his companions such an easy solution?* That was effective even against the Sirens!

Farewell.

LETTER 57

A dark tunnel

From Seneca to Lucilius
Greetings

---

1 When I had to leave Baiae and head back to Naples, I did not attempt to go again by boat.* They said there was a storm, and I was easy to convince! But there was so much mud all along the road that you might think I had floated my way there after all.

That day I had the whole of the athletic regimen to put up with, for we went right from the mud into the dust of the Naples tunnel.* 2 Nothing is longer than that dungeon, nothing gloomier than those torches, which only enabled us to see the darkness, not to see through it. Even if there were any light in that place, the dust would have blocked it out. Dust is a terrible annoyance even out in the open; what do you suppose it was like there, where it billows up onto itself and, enclosed in a space with no exchange of air, sinks back on those who stir it up? Thus we endured two contrary discomforts at once: on the same road, the same day, we struggled both with mud and with dust.

3 Still, the darkness did give me something to think about. For I felt a kind of impact on my mind and, though without fear, a change, brought about by the newness and unpleasantness of the unfamiliar circumstance. And now I am not speaking about myself—for I am far from being even a tolerable human being, let alone a perfect one—but about that person over whom fortune no longer holds sway. His mind too will be struck; his color will change.* 4 For there are some things, dear Lucilius, that no virtue can escape: nature gives the virtuous person a reminder of his own mortality. So he will change expression at sad events, and shudder at sudden events, and grow dizzy when looking down from a great height. This is not fear but a natural reaction which cannot be assailed by reason. 5 Thus some who are brave and very ready to shed their own blood cannot look at that of others; some grow faint when handling and inspecting a fresh wound, others at an old and infected wound; and there are yet others who can bear the stroke of a sword more easily than the sight of one. 6 What I felt, then, was, as I said, not an emotion but only a change. As

soon as I got back to the light of day, my cheerfulness returned without thought or bidding from me.

Then I began the old conversation with myself, about how foolish we are to fear some things more and some less, when all of them have the same ending. What difference does it make whether a person is crushed under a falling balcony* or under a rockslide? You'll find there is none. Yet some people fear the rockslide more, though both are equally fatal. For fear looks to the cause rather than the effect.

7 You think I am talking about the Stoics, who hold that the soul of one who is crushed by a great weight cannot persist through that event and, since it has no immediate egress, is scattered in an instant. But that's not what I am doing. In fact, I think those who say this are mistaken.* 8 Just as a flame cannot be crushed (for it escapes around whatever presses upon it) and just as air is not harmed by the punch of a fist or the crack of a whip, nor is it even split up, but merely swirls around whatever stirs it, so the mind, being made up of a very rarefied material, cannot be caught or broken up within the body, but owing to its fine texture passes through the very things that press upon it. As lightning strikes and flashes over a wide area yet finds its way back through a tiny opening, so the mind, which is even more thin-textured than fire, can escape through each and every body.*

9 Hence we should make some inquiry as to whether the mind can be immortal. But of this, at least, you may be sure: if it does survive the body, it cannot by any means be crushed. For there is no sort of immortality that admits of exceptions, and there is nothing that can harm what is eternal.

Farewell.

A conversation about Plato

From Seneca to Lucilius
Greetings

---

1 The great poverty, indeed the destitution, of our language has never been more evident to me than it was today. We happened to be talking about Plato, and a thousand things came up for which we needed a word but could not find one.* For some of them, in fact, a word did exist at one time but had been lost because of the fastidious standards we now uphold.

Destitute, and yet fastidious! It is intolerable. **2** What the Greeks call an *oestrus*—the stinging fly that drives herds pell-mell, scattering them all over the mountainside—used to be called in our language *asilus*. You may have Virgil for your authority on that:

> There is a fly, frequent in Alburnus
> and in the green oak grove near Silaris;
> *asilus* is its Roman name; the word in Greek
> is *oestrus*. Fierce it is, its high-pitched whine
> scatters the panicked herd all through the woods.*

3 I believe one can conclude that the former term is no longer in use. But let me keep this brief. Some words that now have prefixes were at one time used without them. For instance, people used to say "terming with the sword" rather than "determining with the sword." Again, Virgil will demonstrate this to you:

Tall men, born in all corners of the earth,
meeting amongst themselves and termining with
the sword.*

Nowadays the use of that word without a prefix has been lost. 4 The ancients used to say "if I order" for "if I will have ordered."* You need not believe me on that! Believe Virgil:

The other troop should join with me to march
wherever I order.

5 My point in all this pedantry is not to show how much time I have wasted among literary scholars but to make clear to you how much of the vocabulary of Ennius and Accius has fallen into disuse, since even in Virgil, whom people read thoroughly every day, there are some terms that have been lost to us.*

6 "What is the purpose of these preliminaries?" you ask. "What is your objective?" I won't conceal it from you. I want, if possible, to make your ears receptive to the word *essentia*—and I'll say it in any case, even if it offends your ears! I have Cicero as my guarantor for the term; his resources surely are ample. If you are looking for someone more recent, I can give you Fabianus, an author of great facility and elegance, whose speech was pure enough even for our current standards.*

What else can I do, dear Lucilius? How will I render *ousia*? For that is a necessary item: nature that comprises the basis of all things.* So I am asking your permission to use this word. Still, I will try to be as economical as I can in using the privilege you have granted. It may be that I will content myself with being allowed to use it.

7 You indulge me, but what's the use? There's no way I can express in Latin the concept that induced me to take our lan-

guage to task. You will object to our Roman limitations even more than I do when you learn that the word I am incapable of rendering is just one syllable. Would you like to know what it is? It's *to on*.* You're thinking that I'm not very bright, and that a possible translation is right under my nose; namely, *quod est*, "that which is." But on my view, "that which is" differs considerably from *to on*. I am forced to use a verb in place of a noun; but if I must, I'll write "that which is."

8 Our friend, who is a very learned person, was saying today that *to on* is used by Plato in six ways.* I will explain all of them; first, though, I must state that there is such a thing as a genus and also a species. Now, at present we are looking for that primary genus on which all the remaining species depend, from which arises every division, and in which all things are included. We will find it if we take things one at a time and work backward, for in this way we will be led back to what is primary. **9** "Human being" is a species, as Aristotle says; "horse" is a species; "dog" is a species. Therefore we must look for some shared feature that is the link between all of them—something that encompasses them and has them subordinate to itself. What is that? It is "animate creature." Thus there begins to be a genus of all those items I just listed: "human being," "horse," "dog"—namely, "animate creature."

10 But some things have life° and yet are not animate creatures, for it is generally agreed that *anima*, the animating principle, inheres also in trees and bushes—which is why we say that they both live and die. Hence "living things" will occupy a higher place, since both animate creatures and plants are in this class.

But there are also things that are not living, for instance rocks; thus there will be something prior to living things, namely, "body." I will divide this genus as follows: all bodies are either living or nonliving.

11 Yet there is still something higher than "body," for we say that some things are corporeal and some incorporeal.* So what will that genus be from which these things are drawn? It will be the one to which we assigned the not entirely apposite name "that which is." This genus will be divided into species in this way: "that which is" is either corporeal or incorporeal. **12** This, then, is the first and primary genus, the generic genus, if I may call it that; all the others are genera, yes, but specific genera. For example, "human being" is a genus, since it has within itself species that are nations (Greeks, Romans, Parthians) or colors (white, black, yellow); it also has individuals—Cato, Cicero, Lucretius. Thus it counts as a genus in that it contains multiple things, but as a species in that it is subordinate to something else. "That which is," the generic genus, has nothing above it; it is the beginning of things; all others are subordinate to it.

13 The Stoics want to place above this yet another, still more primary genus. I will say something about that in a moment, but first I want to point out that the genus I already described is rightly given pride of place, since it contains all things. **14** I divide "that which is" into species as follows: corporeal or incorporeal; there is no third species. How do I divide "body"? So as to say that bodies are either living or nonliving. Again, how do I divide "living things"? Like this: some have mind, some only life; or like this: some have the capacity for impulse—they walk and move from one place to another; some are implanted in the ground and are fed through their roots and grow. Again, into what species do I divide animate creatures? They are either mortal or immortal.*

15 Some of the Stoics hold that the primary genus is the "something." I will include here their reason for holding this view. They say, "There are some things in the world's nature that are and some things that are not; but even the things that are not are included in the world—things that occur to the mind, such as centaurs, giants, and whatever else is devised by fictive thinking and begins to have some image, although it does not have substance."*

16 Now I return to the topic I promised you: how Plato makes a sixfold division of the things that are.* The first "that which is" is not apprehended by sight or touch or any sense; it is the thinkable. "That which is by genus," for instance the generic human, does not present itself to the eye, but the specific does, such as Cicero and Cato. "Animate creature" is not seen, it is thought; what one sees are its species, horse and dog.

17 What Plato posits as the second of the things that are is that which exceeds and surpasses all other things; this, he says, is "preeminent being." The word "poet" is used commonly, since this is the name for all who make verses; but among the Greeks, it has by now come to refer only to one: when you hear "poet," you understand "Homer." What is this, then? Obviously it is God, since it is greater and more powerful than everything else.*

18 The third kind is of things that are said to be in the strict sense; these are innumerable, but are beyond our sight. Do you ask what these are? They are the distinctive accoutrements of Plato; he calls them Ideas (*ideas*).* From them everything we see comes into being, and everything is shaped in accordance with them. They are immortal, unchangeable, incorruptible.

19 As for what an Idea is—or rather, what Plato thinks an

Idea is—listen: "An Idea is the eternal model of those things which come naturally into being."* To this definition I will add some interpretation so as to make the subject plainer to you. Suppose I want to make a portrait of you. I have you as a model for the picture: from that model, my mind receives a certain configuration to impart to its work. Hence that which instructs and informs me—your appearance, from which the imitation is derived—is an idea. The world's nature includes countless models of this sort: models of human beings, of the various fishes and trees. All things that must come into being by nature's agency are formed according to these models.

20 The fourth position will be occupied by the *eidos*, or form. As for what this *eidos* is, you must pay attention, and blame Plato, not me, for the difficulty of the subject. But without difficulty there is no fineness of distinction. A moment ago, I used the image of a painter. That painter, when he wanted to depict Virgil with his pigments, looked at the man himself. Virgil's appearance, the model for the work that was to be, was the Idea; that which the artist derived from it and imparted to his work is the *eidos*. **21** Do you ask the difference? One is the model, the other is the form derived from the model and imparted to the work. The artist imitates the one but makes the other. A statue has an appearance; this is the *eidos*. The model itself, the one the craftsman looked at when he made the statue, has an appearance; this is the Idea. Still another way of making the distinction, if you feel you need one, is that the *eidos* is in the work, the Idea outside the work, and not only outside the work but prior to the work.

22 The fifth kind is of those things that exist commonly.* These begin to relate to us. Here are "everything," "people," "farm animals," "things."

The sixth kind is of those things that quasi-exist, like void and like time.

Everything we see or touch is excluded by Plato from those things which on his view "are" in the strict sense. For they are in flux and are constantly decreasing and increasing. Not one of us is the same in old age as he was in youth; not one of us is the same in the morning as he was the day before. Our bodies are carried away like rushing streams. Anything you see is passing as time passes; not one of the things we see stays put. I myself, even as I tell you of these changes, have changed.

23 This is what Heraclitus means when he says, "We step into the same river twice and not at all."* The name of the river remains the same; the water has passed on. This is more evident in a river than in a human being; but a current sweeps us along as well, and it is no less swift. For that reason I am amazed that we are so far out of our minds as to love a thing that is so fleeting—the body—and that we are afraid ever to die, when every moment is the death of our previous condition. Why be afraid of something happening once when it is happening every day?

24 I have spoken of how the human being is matter in flux, perishable and subject to every influence. The universe as well, though enduring and undefeated, changes and does not stay the same. For though it contains everything it had before, it contains those things in a different way; it changes their arrangement.

25 "What have I to gain," you say, "from these fine distinctions of yours?" Nothing, if you ask me. But just as the engraver, tired from a long period of close work, turns his eyes away to rest and, as we say, to "nurture" them, so should we sometimes relax our minds and refresh them with some amusement. Still, even one's amusements should become worthwhile endeavors:

if you put your mind to them, you will derive something potentially beneficial.

26 That's my own custom, dear Lucilius: I take every thought, no matter how far removed from philosophy, and try to extract something from it and turn it to good use. What could be more distant from the reform of character than those matters I explained just now? How can the Platonic Ideas make me a better person? What am I going to get out of them to check my desires? Or is it just this: that all those things that minister to our senses, that entice and arouse us, are not accepted by Plato as things that truly exist? 27 Thus they are figments and present an appearance only for a time. None of them are stable or solid, and yet we desire them as if they were to exist forever, or as if we were to possess them forever.

Weak and fluid ourselves, we stand in the midst of illusions. So let us direct our minds toward things that are eternal. Let us fly upward and gaze in wonder at the forms of all things, and at God, who dwells among them. Since God could not make his created things immortal (for matter prevented it), in his providence he gives us this way to defend against death and through reason to overcome the deficiencies of the body.* 28 For all things last not because they are eternal but because they are defended by the concern of their ruler; if they were immortal, they would not need a guardian. The craftsman preserves them, by his power overcoming the fragility of the material. Let us spurn all those things which are so far from being valuable that it is in doubt whether they exist at all.

29 At the same time, let us reflect on this: if providence preserves the universe itself from danger, which is just as mortal as we are,* then our own providence can also procure a somewhat longer life span for this paltry body of ours, as long as it

enables us to govern and control those desires that are usually the cause of death. **30** Plato preserved himself into old age by careful management. True, he was strong of body and blessed with good fortune, and it was his broad chest that gave him his name.* But the perils of seafaring had reduced his strength greatly; still, by frugal living, taking good care of himself and limiting those things that arouse the appetites, he made it to old age despite many obstacles. **31** For I suppose you know that thanks to his careful management, Plato completed eighty-one years of life and died on his birthday, not a day short. For that reason, some Persian soothsayers who happened to be in Athens made burnt offerings to him after his death, believing that since he had completed the most perfect number (which they get by multiplying nine times nine), his fate was of more than humankind. Well, I expect you would not mind giving up a few days from that total, and the sacrifice as well. **32** But frugal living *can* prolong old age; and although I don't think old age is something to hanker after, it's not to be turned down either. It's pleasant to be with yourself as long as you possibly can—provided you have made yourself worth being with.

So now I will give an opinion on the point you raise, whether it is appropriate to spurn extreme old age, not waiting for the end but making an end by one's own act. It's the next thing to cowardice when one merely waits in idleness for death to come, just as one must be excessively devoted to wine if he drains every drop from the vat and guzzles even the lees. **33** My question, though, is this: is the last part of life really the lees, or is it the finest, purest part? That is, provided the mind is without impairment, the senses intact and of use to the mind, and provided the body is not crippled and moribund before its time. For it matters a great deal whether one is prolonging life or prolonging death. **34** Yet if the body can no longer perform any service, why should it not be appropriate to release the suffering mind?

Perhaps what is called for is even to act a little before you must, lest when the time comes you should be unable. The risk of living in misery is worse than that of dying swiftly—and that being so, it's foolish not to use a small amount of time as coin to buy off a huge gamble. Rarely does a prolonged old age deliver anyone to death without impairment; on the contrary, people are frequently confined to their beds without use of their limbs. Do you think it is any more cruel to lose something of your life than it is to lose the privilege of ending it?

35 Don't be unwilling to hear me, thinking that this opinion relates immediately to yourself. Assess what I'm saying on its own merits. I will not abandon old age as long as it allows me to keep my whole self—that is, the whole of my better part. But if it begins to attack my mind and lop off parts of it—if it keeps me alive without allowing me a life, then I will fling myself from the decayed and collapsing edifice.* **36** I will not die to escape sickness, provided it is curable and no impediment to the mind. I will not lay hands on myself because of pain: such a death is defeat. But if I know I will have to endure the pain without intermission, I will depart, not because of the pain itself, but because it will hinder me from everything that makes life worth living. He who dies merely because of pain is weak and lazy; he who lives merely for pain is a fool.

37 But I am carrying on at length. There is material besides this, enough to make a day of it. But how will a man be able to end his life, when he cannot even end a letter? Farewell, then—a word you will be happier to read than this unremitting talk of death!

Farewell.

Consolation for the death of a friend

From Seneca to Lucilius
Greetings

1 I am sorry your friend Flaccus has passed away, but I want you not to grieve excessively.*

Not grieve at all? That I will not venture to ask of you, though I know it would be better. Such firmness of mind belongs only to the person who has risen high above misfortune. And even he will feel a twinge at something like this, but only a twinge. As for us, we may be forgiven our tears, if there are not too many, and if we do regain control. Having lost a friend, you should not be dry-eyed, but neither should you drown in weeping; you should cry, but not wail.

2 Does my rule seem strict to you? And yet the greatest of the Greek poets allowed just one day for lawful mourning. And he says that even Niobe thought of food.*

Do you ask where lamentations come from? What is the source of weeping beyond measure? We are trying by our tears to prove our sense of loss: it is not that grief forces us but that we are exhibiting grief to others. People are not sad just for themselves. Hapless idiocy! Even in grief there is competition.

3 "What then?" you ask. "Shall I forget my friend?" It's not very long that you are promising to remember him if your memory lasts only as long as your grief. The time is at hand when some chance thing will brighten your face with a laugh; very soon, I say, your pangs will subside, even the sharpest, and every feeling of loss will be eased. The minute you stop watching yourself, your look of sadness will be gone. Right now you are guarding your grief, but even so it is escaping. The more severe it is, the sooner it ends.

4 Let us try to make the memory of those who are gone a pleasant one. If the thought brings torment, one does not willingly return to it, and so here: we are bound to feel a biting when the names of loved ones come to mind.* But even this has its own pleasure. 5 Our friend Attalus* used to say,

> The memory of friends who have died gives a pleasure like that of apples that are both tart and sweet, or like the pleasing acidity of an old wine. After a time, though, all that pains us is extinguished, and only the pleasure remains.

6 If we are to believe him,

> Thinking of friends safe and sound is cakes and honey; remembering those who are gone is bittersweet. Yet who would deny that sharp and even bitter flavors are sometimes to our taste?

7 My experience is different: to me, the thought of friends who have died is sweet, even comforting. For when I had friends, I had them as one who would lose them; now that I have lost them, I am as one who still has them.

And so, dear Lucilius, do what suits your sense of fairness. Stop misinterpreting what fortune has done for you. Fortune has taken something from you, but it was fortune that gave.

8 Because we cannot be sure how long we will have our friends, let us eagerly enjoy them now. Let us consider how often we have gone on some long trip and left them behind, how often we failed to see them even when living in the same place: we will then understand that we lost more time with

them while they were alive. Some people are careless about their friends while they have them, then grieve terribly for them when they are gone. **9** Will you put up with this? They have to lose people in order to love them! They are afraid there may be some doubt whether they really loved them, and this makes their grief even more effusive. They are looking for some delayed signs of their own affection.

10 If we have other friends, we give them little credit and hardly merit their esteem if we do not find in them a valuable consolation for the one who has passed away. If, on the other hand, we have no other friends, then we are doing a worse injury to ourselves than fortune has done to us: fortune took one person from us, but we are taking from ourselves every person we do not make our friend. **11** Moreover, anyone who cannot make friends with more than one person does not love even that one very much. If someone who had lost his only tunic were to weep and wail, rather than look about for something to put over his shoulders to keep himself warm, wouldn't you think he was an idiot? The one you loved has passed away: find someone to love. Replacing the friend is better than crying.

12 I know that what I am about to add is a well-worn saying, but I am not going to leave it out just because everyone else has said it.

Time puts an end to grief—

even if you did not choose to put an end to it yourself. One does become tired of grieving—but a thoughtful person should be deeply ashamed to let that be the means of healing. Better you should abandon your grief than it should abandon you. Given that you cannot continue very long even if you want to, you should stop as soon as you are able.

13 Our forefathers established one year as the period of mourning for women, not that they should mourn that long, but that they should not mourn longer than that. For men there is no legal period, since no period is honorable.* Yet even among women, and those women who can hardly be dragged away from the bier—the ones we have to pry away from the corpse—even among them I defy you to show me one whose tears have lasted an entire month. Nothing becomes hateful as quickly as grief. When fresh, it brings sympathy and visits of consolation; once it grows old, it draws nothing but mockery. And rightly, for by then it is either stupid or feigned.

14 And I am writing these things to you—I, who wept for my beloved Annaeus Serenus* so unrestrainedly that I myself may serve, most unwillingly, as an example of one conquered by grief. But today I censure my own behavior. I understand, now, that the main reason I felt such grief was that I had never thought it possible that his death should precede my own. I kept in mind only that he was younger than I, much younger. As if birth order determined our fate!

15 So let us remember mortality, in ourselves as well as our loved ones. I ought to have said, back then, "My dear Serenus is younger than I, but what difference does that make? He ought to die after me, but he could die before." Because I did not do this, fortune struck me suddenly and unprepared. Now I keep in mind not only that everyone and everything must die, but that they die according to no determinate law. If it can happen at all, it can happen today.

16 And so, most dear Lucilius, let us reflect that we too will soon be going where the one we mourn has gone. And perhaps the tales of philosophers are true, and there is a place that receives us.* If so, then the one we think is gone has only gone on ahead.

Farewell.

LETTER 65

Some analyses of causation

From Seneca to Lucilius
Greetings

1 Yesterday I shared the day with illness: it claimed the morning for itself but left me the afternoon.* At first I tested my breath with a little reading; when it stood up to that, I ventured to demand more of it—or rather to allow it more leeway. I did some writing; indeed, I wrote more intensely than usual, as I was contending with a difficult subject and did not want to be beaten by it. Finally some friends came by, so as to restrain me by force, like some unruly invalid. 2 Conversation took over from the pen, and out of that conversation I will convey to you the part that is still in contention. We have called on you to adjudicate the matter.

It's more work than you think: the case is threefold. As you know, the adherents of our Stoic school say that in the world's nature there are two things from which everything comes into being: cause and matter. Matter lies inert, a thing open to all possibilities, which will remain inactive unless moved by someone else. But cause—that is, reason—shapes matter and turns it in any direction it wants, producing from it various works.* Hence for any given thing there has to be something out of which it is made and something by which it is made: the latter is the cause, the former the matter.

3 Every skill is an imitation of nature; so transfer what I was saying about things in general to those that have to be made by a human being. A statue has both material for the craftsman to work on and a craftsman to impose some appearance on the material. Thus in the case of the statue, the material is the bronze and the cause is the artisan. The same specification applies to all things: they consist of that which is made and that which makes.

4 The Stoics hold that there is just one cause, that which acts. Aristotle's view is that the word "cause" is used in three ways.* "The first cause," he says, "is the material itself, without which nothing can be created; the second is the artisan; the third is the form that is imposed upon each and every work, just as it is upon the statue." This is what Aristotle calls the *eidos*. "There is also a fourth cause," he says, "in addition to these; namely, the purpose of the work as a whole." **5** I will explain what that is. Bronze is the first cause of the statue, for it would never have been made if that from which it was cast or forged had not existed. The second cause is the craftsman, for the bronze could not have been worked into the shape of a statue if his skilled hand had not been added. The third cause is the form, for that statue would not be called a "spear bearer" or "youth tying a headband" if that appearance had not been imposed upon it.* The fourth cause is the purpose of making it; for if this had not been there, it would not have been made. **6** What is the purpose? It is what motivated the craftsman, what he was after in making it. Either it was money, if he crafted it to sell; or reputation, if he wanted to make a name for himself; or reverence, if he fashioned it as a gift for a temple.

Therefore this too is a cause for its being made—or don't you agree that something without which a thing would not have been made should be counted as one of its causes?

7 To these causes Plato adds a fifth, the model, which he calls the Idea.* This is what the craftsman had in view when he made what he intended to make. It does not matter whether he has an external model to cast his eyes upon, or an internal one that he himself has conceived and set up within. These, the models of all things, God holds within himself, and encompasses in his mind the numbers and measures of everything that is to be achieved. He is full of those shapes that Plato calls Ideas—deathless, changeless, tireless. Thus while human beings indeed perish, humanity itself, according to which a human being is molded, remains; and although human beings suffer and die, humanity is unaffected.

8 There are, then, five causes on Plato's account: that from which, that by which, that in which, that according to which, and that because of which. Last of all, there is that which comes of these. For instance, in a statue (to continue in my previous vein), that from which is the bronze, that by which is the craftsman, that in which is the form that is applied to it, that according to which is the model that the person who makes it is imitating, that because of which is the maker's purpose, and that which comes of these is the statue itself. 9 By Plato's account, the world too has all of these: the maker—this is God; that from which it is made—this is matter; the form—this is the condition and order of the world that we see; the model—which is to say, that according to which he made such a vast and supremely beautiful piece of work; the purpose—his aim in making it. What aim does God have, you ask? Goodness. That is definitely what Plato says: 10 "What was the cause of

God's making the world? He is good; one who is good is not parsimonious with any good; he made it, then, to be the best world he could make."*

You be the judge, then, and make your ruling. Whose account seems to you most likely to be true? Not who gives the truest account, for that is as far above us as truth itself.

11 This host of causes posited by Aristotle and by Plato encompasses either too many things or too few. For if their view is that whenever the removal of something would make it impossible for some item to be made, that thing is a cause of its making, then they have named too few things. They should count time as a cause, for nothing can be made without time. They should count place: if there is nowhere in which a thing can be made, once more it will not be made. They should count motion: without motion, nothing is either made or destroyed; without it, there is no craftsmanship and indeed no changing.

12 We, however, are looking now for the primary and generic cause. This must be simple, for matter too is simple. Are we asking what this cause is? Unquestionably, it is productive reason, that is, God.* For all these things you have mentioned are not multiple individual causes but are dependent on one, the one that makes. **13** You say that form is a cause? Form is what the craftsman imposes on his work; it is part of the cause but not the cause itself. The model is not the cause either but a necessary instrument of the cause. The model is necessary to the craftsman in the same way as the chisel and the pumice stone: without them his craft cannot go forward, and yet they are not parts of the craft, and neither are they causes. **14** Someone says, "The aim of the craftsman—the purpose for which he came to make something—is a cause." Even supposing it is a cause, it is not the efficient cause but a supervenient cause.

And such causes are innumerable; what we are looking for is the generic cause. As for their claim that the entire world in all its fullness is a cause, there they speak with less than their usual sophistication. For there is a big difference between a work and the cause of that work.

15 Either make your ruling, or do what is easier in this sort of case: say you find no clear solution and tell us to go home.

"What is the attraction for you in frittering away your time on these matters which do not eliminate any of your passions nor drive out any desires?" In fact I do go after those more important things;° I do engage in those studies by which the mind is calmed. I examine myself first, and then this world of ours. **16** Even now I am not wasting time, as you suppose. For as long as such studies are not beaten to death, nor dragged off down pointless pathways of scholarly sophistication, they do elevate the mind.* They lighten that burden under which it labors, longing to get free and to return to its origins. For this body is the weight and penalty of the mind: while thus oppressed, it is in chains, unless philosophy comes to its aid, bidding it gaze upon the world's nature and so draw breath, releasing it from earthly things to things divine. This is its freedom, its diversion: it gets away for a while from the prison-house where it is confined, and finds refreshment in the skies.* **17** Just as craftsmen, when they are engaged in some intricate task that strains the eyes and the light is indirect and poor, come out into the open and visit some place devoted to public recreation, there to refresh their eyes with the free light of day; even so does the mind, shut away in this somber, dark apartment, emerge whenever it can into the open and relax in the contemplation of the universe. **18** The wise person, and likewise the seeker after wisdom, abides indeed within his body, yet with his better part is absent, turning his thoughts to things above. Like one sworn into the service,* he thinks himself well paid if he but remains alive, and due to his training has neither love of life nor hatred of it but endures this mortal time, though he knows of richer things to come.

19 Do you forbid me to gaze upon the universe? Do you pull me back from the whole, and confine me to the part? Am I not to ask what are the beginnings of all things? Whose is the hand that shaped the world? When all things were merged into one and weltering in inactive matter, who separated them? Shall I not ask who is the craftsman of the universe itself? By what plan such vastness came to be ordered and regulated? Who collected what was scattered, separated what was mingled, apportioned visible form to all that lay in one vast and shapeless mass? What is the source of the mighty light that is shed on us? **20** Was it fire, or something brighter than fire? Shall I not ask these things? Am I not to know whence I have descended? Whether I shall see this world but once, or be born many times? Where I shall go when I depart? What abodes are waiting for my spirit when it is released from the slavery of human life? Do you deny me my share of heaven—which is to say, do you bid me live with eyes cast downward?

21 Too great I am to be slave to my body; too great is that for which I was born. I regard the body as nothing but a shackle fastened around my freedom. Therefore I set it in the way of fortune as a hindrance, and do not allow any hurt to pass through it to me. This is the only thing in me that can suffer injury: in such vulnerable quarters does my free mind dwell. **22** Never will this flesh compel me to cowardice; never to pretenses unworthy of a good person; never will I tell a lie merely to honor this paltry body of mine. When I see fit, I will break off my alliance with it; and even now, while we adhere to one another, that alliance will not be of equal standing: the mind will draw every privilege to itself. Disregard for one's body is certain liberation.*

23 But let me get back to my stated objective. This freedom is greatly abetted by that contemplation we were just talking about. It's like this. All things in the universe are made up of matter and God. God controls them, and they are his followers, ranged about him as their ruler and guide. But that which makes—which is God—is more powerful and valuable than matter, which is acted upon by him. **24** Now in a human being, the mind performs the same role as God performs in the world, and what matter is in the world is in us the body. So let the inferior parts serve the better: let us be brave against the strokes of fortune; let us not tremble at injuries, or wounds, or fetters, or want.

What is death? Either an end or a crossing over. I am not afraid to come to an end (for that is the same as never having started), and neither am I afraid to cross over. For nowhere will I be as constricted as I am here.

Farewell.

LETTER 70

Ending one's own life

From Seneca to Lucilius
Greetings

1 After a long interval, I have seen Pompeii, your hometown.* It took me back within sight of my youth. I felt as if I could still do the things I did there as a young man, and in fact as if it were only a short while since I did them. **2** Lucilius, we have skirted the shores of life. When one is at sea, as our poet Virgil says, "lands and cities drop away";* and it is just the same with us on this voyage of speeding time. First we lose sight of our childhood, then of our youth, then of the entire interval between youth and age, and then of the best years of old age as well. Finally there comes into view that ending shared by the entire human race. **3** We think it is a rock—but that's insane: it is the harbor. Sometimes we need to steer for it, but never away from it. One who has been carried there early in life should not complain any more than a sailor whose voyage has gone quickly. For as you know, one traveler is held back by lazy winds that play games with him and weary him with the boredom of a completely flat calm; another is driven swiftly on by an ungovernable gale. **4** Imagine the same thing happening to us. Life rushes some people toward where we are all headed, no matter how we try to delay; others it leaves to steep and simmer.

As you know, life is not always something to hang on to. Our good does not consist merely in living but in living well. Hence the wise person lives as long as he ought to, not as long as he can. He considers where he will be living, and how, and with whom, and what he will be doing. He is always thinking about the quality of his life, not the quantity. **5** If he encounters many hardships that banish tranquility, he releases himself.* Nor does he do so only in the extremity of need; rather, as soon as he begins to have doubts about his fortunes, he makes a careful assessment to determine whether it is time to quit. It is a matter of indifference to him whether he brings things to an end himself or only accepts the end that comes, and whether it happens later or sooner. He does not fear that end as if it were some terrible loss: no one can lose much when what he has is only a driblet. **6** Whether one dies sooner or later is not the issue; the issue is whether one dies well or badly. And dying well means that one escapes the risk of living badly.

For that reason I think it was quite unmanly what that fellow from Rhodes said, the one who had been thrown into a cage by a tyrant and was being fed like some wild animal.* When someone urged him to stop eating, he replied, "While life endures, all hopes remain." **7** Even if that is true, life is not worth buying at every price. Some things may be important— may even be certain of attainment—and yet I would not attain them through a base admission of weakness. Am I to think that fortune can do everything to a person as long as he remains alive? Rather, fortune can do nothing to a person as long as he knows how to die.

8 And yet there are times when even if certain death awaits and he knows that his sentence has been predetermined, he still will not lend a hand in his own execution. Only if it were in his interests would he do so. It is foolish to die merely through fear of death. Someone is coming to kill you? Wait for him. Why the rush? Why are you the stand-in for someone else's cruelty? Do you begrudge your executioner his task? Are you sparing him the trouble? **9** Socrates could have starved himself to death, choosing lack of food over the poison. Yet he spent thirty days in prison waiting for death, not because he thought that anything might still happen (as if such a long time had room for many possible outcomes), but so that he might submit to the laws and give his friends the benefit of Socrates's last days.* To despise death but fear poison: what could be more foolish?

10 Scribonia, a serious woman, was the aunt of Drusus Libo, a young man who was as stupid as he was wellborn.* He was very ambitious, more so than anyone could be in that period, and more than he should have been in any period. He was sick, and had been carried from the Senate in his litter. (Mind you, he was not well attended! All his relatives had shamelessly deserted him, for by that point he was the deceased rather than the defendant.) He then began to take counsel whether he should commit suicide or whether he should wait. Scribonia said to him, "Why does it please you to do another's business?" She did not persuade him; he laid hands on himself, and not without reason. For when one is bound to die in three or four days at an enemy's behest, then remaining alive *is* doing another's business. **11** Therefore you may not be able to make any overall pronouncement about what to do when death is predetermined by an external power, whether to go ahead with it or wait. For there are many considerations that could draw you in one direction or the other.

If one is a death with torture and the other easy and uncomplicated, why not put out your hand and take the latter? If I were getting ready to sail, I'd pick out a ship; if I were getting ready to move in somewhere, I'd pick out a house; just so, if I were about to die, I would choose my manner of death. **12** Besides, in the same way as long duration does not of itself make life better, so long duration does make death worse. In death, even more than in other things, we ought to make allowances for temperament. Let a person make his exit according to his own inclination. Whether he prefers the sword or the noose or some poison that spreads through the bloodstream, let him go forward with it and break the bonds of servitude.

A person's life should be pleasing not only to himself but

also to others; his death need only please himself. The best death is the one he prefers. **13** It is foolish to think, "One person will say I did not act courageously enough; a second will say I was too rash; a third will say another kind of death was braver." Remember, if you will, that reputation has no bearing on the decision you now have in hand. There is only one consideration: to escape fortune's grasp as quickly as you can. Otherwise you will have people showing up to raise objections to your action.

14 You will find some people, even some committed philosophers, who say that one should never take violent measures against one's own life, feeling that it is wrong to become one's own murderer. They say one should wait for the end that nature has decreed.* Those who say this do not realize that they are blocking the road to freedom. Of all the things the eternal law has done for us, this is the best: we have one way into life, but many ways out. **15** Am I to wait for the cruel action of disease, or of a person, when I could pass through the midst of my torments, shake off my adversities, and depart? This is the one reason why we cannot complain about life: life does not hold anyone by force. The human condition is well situated in that no one is miserable except by his own fault. If it suits you, live; if not, you are allowed to return to where you came from.

16 You have often endured bloodletting in order to relieve a headache; people sometimes sever a vein as a way of losing weight. There is no need of a huge wound that splits open the chest. A lancet opens the way to that great freedom; a nick buys your tranquility. What is it, then, that makes us idle and reluctant? There is not one of us who thinks of the time when he must leave this apartment. We are like aging tenants, who even when mistreated still allow themselves to be detained by habit and by their fondness for the place. **17** Do you want to be free as concerns your body? Dwell in it as one who will move on. Keep in mind that you must someday be deprived of this habitation; you will then face your eviction more courageously.

But how can people take thought for their own end if they desire all things without end? **18** We need rehearsal for this more than anything else. With other things, we will perhaps turn out to have practiced them in vain. We have prepared our minds against poverty, and our wealth has remained. We have steeled ourselves to disregard pain and have been lucky enough to have sound and healthy bodies that never demanded any proof of our courage. We have taught ourselves to be brave in facing the loss of those we love, and fortune has kept our loved ones alive. Yet for this, and this alone, the day that will put our preparations into effect cannot fail to come.

19 You need not suppose that only great men have been strong enough to break the bonds of our human slavery. You need not think that it can only be done by Cato, who extracted with his hand the breath that his dagger had not released.* People of the lowest rank have managed by extreme effort to escape to safety. When they were not accorded any convenient way of dying, and could not choose the means of death to suit them, they seized whatever was at hand, and by forcible endeavor made things into weapons that were not dangerous by nature. **20** Recently at the wild-animal games, one of the Germans went off to the latrine during the preparations for the morning show*—it was the only private moment he had without a guard—and there took the stick with a sponge attached that is put there for cleaning the unmentionables and stuffed the entire thing down his throat, closing off his airway.

That was indeed offering insult to death. He went right ahead, unsanitary and indecent as it was: how stupid to be fussy about one's way of dying!

21 What a brave man! He was worthy to be granted a choice in his fate. How boldly he would have used a sword; how courageously he would have thrown himself over some jagged cliff, or into the depths of the sea! With no resources from anywhere, he still found a way to provide his own death, his own weapon. From this you may know that there is but one thing that can delay our dying: the willingness. Each of us may decide for himself as to the merits of this ferocious man's deed—so long as we all agree that death, even the most disgusting, is preferable to slavery, even the cleanest slavery.

22 Since I have started using unsavory examples, I'll keep on with it: each person will demand more of himself if he sees that even the most contemptible people could hold this thing in contempt. We think that the Catos, the Scipios, and the others whose deeds we habitually admire have been elevated beyond imitation; yet I will now demonstrate that such courage is exemplified just as often in the wild-animal games as in leaders of the Civil War.* **23** Not long ago, a man consigned to the morning spectacle was being conveyed there in a wagon surrounded by guards. Feigning sleepiness, he let his head sink lower and lower until he could get it between the spokes of the wheel, and then held himself down against his seat long enough for the wheel to come around and break his neck. Thus he used the very wagon that was carrying him to punishment as his means of escape.

24 If what one wants is to break free and get away, there is nothing to prevent that. Nature keeps us in a prison without walls. If circumstances permit, we may look about for a gentle way out; if there are many instruments at hand with which to assert our claim to ourselves, we may ponder the matter and choose the best means of liberation. But if a person is in a difficult situation, let him seize on whatever is nearest and think that best, even if it is strange and unheard of. Ingenuity will not fail him if only determination does not. **25** Don't you see how even very watchful guards can be deceived by the meanest of chattel slaves, once pain goads them into action? The great man is not the one who merely commands his own death but the one who actually finds a death for himself.

But I promised you some more examples from the same offering. **26** During the second staged naval battle, one of the barbarians took the lance he had been given to use against his opponent and sank the whole of it into his own throat. "Why did I not escape long ago," he cried, "from every torment, every ridicule? Why? Why am I waiting for death when I have a weapon?" It made the show more worth watching, since from it people learn that dying is more honorable than killing.

27 Well, then. If desperate characters and criminals have such spirit, won't people also have it who have been prepared against misfortune by long practice and by reason, the ruler of all things? Reason teaches us that there are many ways of getting to our fate, but that the end is the same, and that since it is coming, it does not matter when it begins. **28** That same reasoning advises you to die in the way you prefer if you have that opportunity, but if not, to do so in whatever way you can, grasping any available means of doing violence to yourself. It is wrong to steal the means of living, but very fine to steal the means of dying.

Farewell.

What it means to make progress

From Seneca to Lucilius
Greetings

1 You complain that I am expending less care on the letters I send you. So I am, for who expends care over a conversation? Only one who deliberately adopts an affected manner of speaking. I wish my letters to be like what my conversation would be if you and I were sitting or walking together: easy and unstudied. They have in them nothing forced, nothing feigned. **2** If it were possible, I would prefer to show you what I think rather than tell you. Even if I were delivering a speech, I would not stamp my foot or gesture with my hands, and I would not raise my voice. I would leave those things to the orators and be content to convey my thoughts to you in a manner that is neither ornate nor haphazard.

3 The one impression I would want to make upon you is that I feel every one of the things I say; indeed, that I love them as well as feel them. People kiss a lover in one way and their children in another; yet even in that chaste and restrained caress there is a sufficient show of affection. It is not—by heaven—that I want what is said about such great themes to be jejune and arid (for there is a place for literary talent even in philosophy); still, it is not proper to expend a great deal of effort over the words. **4** Let this be the whole of our intention: let us say what we feel, and feel what we say; let the conversation be in harmony with how we live. What is it to fulfill one's promise? It is for the person we see and the person we hear to be one and the same. It is then that we see what sort of person it is who has promised, and how big a person he is; for then he is just one person.

5 Our words should provide benefit rather than delight. Still, if eloquence can be achieved without effort, if it comes easily or costs but little, then let it come and attend on the most beautiful of subjects. But let it be such as will show off the subject rather than itself. Other arts are entirely concerned with one's talent; what is at issue here is the business of the mind. **6** The sick person does not go looking for an eloquent doctor, although if the person who has the ability to cure him also happens to be able to speak in a polished manner about the measures to be taken, he considers it a plus. Even so, he has no reason to congratulate himself on having found a doctor who is also an orator: it is of no more importance than when a skilled helmsman is also good-looking.

7 Why are you tickling my ears? Why be so entertaining? There is other business at hand. What I need is to be cauterized, operated on, given a restricted diet. This is what you are summoned to do. Your responsibility is to cure a long-term illness which is both serious and widespread. It is as big a job as a physician's in an epidemic. Are you preoccupied with words? Be glad all along if you do not fail in the deed.

So many things to know: when will you learn them? When will you fix them in your mind so that they cannot be forgotten? When will you try them out? For these are not like other objects of study. With these, memorization is not enough: you must put them into effect. The happy person is not the one who knows them but the one who performs them.

8 "But look: are there no levels below that person? Is it just wisdom and then a sudden drop-off?" No, I don't think that.

The one who is making progress is indeed counted among the foolish, and yet he is separated from them by a considerable interval. And even among progressors there are important distinctions to be made.*

According to some, they are divided into three types. **9** First are those who do not yet possess wisdom but have set their feet in that vicinity, for being nearby is still being outside. Do you ask who these people are? They are those who have put aside their emotions and their faults, but whose loyalty is still untried. They do not yet possess their good in such a way as to use it; nonetheless, it is no longer possible for them to fall back into those things they have left behind. They are now in that place from which there is no backsliding, but they do not yet realize this about themselves. As I remember writing in one of my letters, "They do not know that they know."* Already it is their lot to enjoy their good, but not yet to be confident of it.

10 Some authors delimit the aforementioned category of progressors in such a way as to assert that they have now rid themselves of the infirmities of mind* but not yet of the emotions, and that they are still in danger, since no one has gotten beyond peril of vice until he has shed it altogether, but no one has shed it altogether unless he has put on wisdom in its place. **11** The difference between infirmities of mind and emotions is something I have explained more than once. I will remind you now as well. The infirmities are faults that have become ingrained and hard, like greed and ambition. These are conditions that bind the mind much more tightly and have begun to be permanent afflictions. To give a brief definition, an infirmity is a persistent judgment in a corrupted person that certain things are very much worth pursuing that in fact are only slightly worth pursuing. Or, if you prefer, we can define it this way: it is being overly concerned with things that one ought to pursue either casually or not at all, or considering something to be of great value when in fact it is either of some lesser value or of no value at all. **12** The emotions are unjustifiable movements of the mind that are abrupt and agitated.* These, when they occur frequently and do not receive any treatment, cause the infirmity, just as a single cold in the head, if it is not protracted, brings on nothing more than a cough; but if it happens repeatedly for a long time, it brings on the wasting disease. Hence those who have made the most progress have gotten beyond the infirmities, but they still experience emotions, even though they are very near perfection.

13 The second category comprises those who have put aside both the worst of the mind's failings and the emotions, but not in such a way as to have a secure grasp on their tranquility: they are still liable to relapse.* **14** The third category is beyond many serious faults, but not all. They have escaped greed, but still experience anger; they are not troubled by lust, but are still subject to ambition. They no longer experience desire, but they still experience fear. Even in fear they are steadfast against some things but yield to others: they are unconcerned about death but still terrified of pain.

15 Let us give some thought to this matter. It will be well for us if we can join the last group. By great natural gifts and constant studious application, one may attain to the second; the third stripe, however, is not to be despised. Think how many ills you see around you—how no wrong is unexampled, how much depravity advances each day, what misdeeds are committed both publicly and in private—and you will realize that it is sufficient achievement for us if we are not among the worst.

16 "I hope I can gain a higher rank," you say. That would be my wish for us; but it is a wish, not a promise. We have already been taken over: we are in the grip of faults even as we strive for virtue. I am ashamed to say it, but we seek honorable conduct only in our spare time. And yet if we make a clean break from the things that preoccupy us and from our faults that cling so closely, how great is the reward that awaits us! It will not be desire that drives us, nor fear. **17** Untroubled by any anxiety, undefiled by pleasure, we shall fear neither death nor the gods. For we shall know that death is not an evil, that the gods mean us no harm. That which does harm is as feeble as that which suffers harm: the best things have no capacity to harm at all.

18 What awaits us, if ever we emerge from this murky depth to the lofty regions above, is tranquility of mind and the freedom and independence that come when all error has been expelled. What is freedom, you ask? To fear no human being and no god, to want neither what is base nor what is excessive, to have absolute power over oneself. Just being one's own person is wealth beyond measure.

Farewell.

LETTER 76

Only the honorable is good

From Seneca to Lucilius
Greetings

---

1 You swear you will become my enemy if I don't inform you about every one of my day's activities.* See how forthright I am in my life with you. I will share even this: I am taking philosophy lessons! Today is the fifth day I have gone to school to hear the philosopher lecturing from two o'clock onward.

"What, at your age?" Why not? What could be more foolish than failing to learn a thing simply because you haven't learned it earlier?

2 "So I'm supposed to take after the youthful squires?"* I'm doing quite well by my advancing years if I don't shame them any more than that. Here is a school that admits people at any age.

"Is this what old age is for—to go chasing after the young?" Shall I go to the theater in my old age; shall I ride in my sedan chair to the Circus, be present at every gladiatorial match, and yet blush to visit a philosopher? **3** You should keep learning as long as you lack knowledge; or, if we believe the proverb, as long as you live. And that is just what this learning is for: you should keep learning how to live for as long as you live. On that point I have something to teach as well. "What's that?" you ask. It is that even the old have something to learn.

4 But every time I enter the school, I am ashamed for the human race. As you know, I have to pass right by the theater of Naples on my way to the house of Metronax.* The theater is packed. A cheering crowd decides who is a good flutist; the trumpeter has a following, and so does the announcer. But in the place where the question is who is a good man, where one learns what a good man is, the seats are almost empty, and the general opinion is that those who are there have nothing better to do. People call them useless drones. Well, I don't mind that sort of ridicule: the criticism of ignorant people is not something to get upset about. One whose aims are honorable should scorn their very scorn.

5 Make haste, then, Lucilius. Move quickly, lest what happened to me should happen to you, and you become a pupil in your old age. But the real reason you should make haste is that the study you have embarked upon is one you can scarcely learn thoroughly even if you do become an elderly learner.

"How much progress can I make?" you say. As much as you attempt. **6** What are you waiting for? No one attains wisdom merely by chance. Money will come of its own accord; public office will be conferred on you; popularity and influence will perhaps be accorded you without any action on your part; virtue, though, will not just happen to you. The work it takes to recognize it is neither easy nor short; but the effort is worth making, for by it one will take possession of every good at once. For there is but one—the honorable. You will find nothing real, nothing sure, in those things that reputation favors.

7 I will now explain why the honorable is the sole good, since you judge that I failed in my earlier letter to achieve that end, praising the thesis rather than proving it. Here, then, is a concise version of what has been said on the subject.*

8 Each thing is so constituted as to have its own excellence. Fertility commends the vine; flavor the vintage; swiftness the stag. About a mule, you ask how strong its back is, for the only function of a mule is to carry burdens. In a dog, the chief quality is keenness of scent if it is to track the game; speed of foot if it is to chase the game down; and boldness if it is to dart in and harry. In each, its best quality ought to be that for which it is born and by which it is assessed. **9** What, then, is the distinctive property of a human being? Reason. It is by reason that the human surpasses animals and is second to the gods. Therefore perfected reason is the human's distinctive excellence; everything else is shared with animals and plants.

The human is strong; so are lions. He is beautiful; so are peacocks. He is swift; so are horses. I am not remarking that he is surpassed in all these attributes: my inquiry is not what attribute is greatest in humans but what it is that is particular to humans. The human has a body; so do trees. He has the capacity for impulse and voluntary movement; so do beasts, and worms too. He has a voice—but how much louder is the barking of dogs; how much higher the cry of the eagle; how much deeper the bellow of bulls; how much sweeter and more melodious the trilling of the lark! **10** What is special about a human being? Reason. When that is set straight and made complete, it achieves the blissful fulfillment of human nature.

Therefore if each thing is worthy of praise and arrives at the culmination of its own nature when it perfects its own particular good, and if the particular good for a human is reason, then if a person perfects his reason, he is worthy of praise and has attained the culmination of his own nature. This perfected reason is called virtue, and is also the same as the honorable.

11 Hence the one thing that belongs solely to the human is the sole good of the human. For we are now asking not what the good is but what the human good is. If nothing but reason belongs solely to the human, this will be his sole good. But this good must be weighed in with all other attributes: if anyone proves to be bad, he will be blamed; if good, he will be approved.* Hence that by which a human being is approved and blamed is his primary and only distinctive attribute.

12 You do not doubt that this is a good; you doubt whether it is his sole good. If someone should be found who has all other advantages—health, riches, a fine family tree, an entry hall crowded with visitors—but it is agreed that he is a bad person, you will criticize him. Conversely, if someone has none of those things I listed—neither money, nor throngs of clients, nor noble birth, nor a long line of ancestors—but it is agreed that he is a good person, you will approve of him. Hence this is indeed the sole good of the human, since one who has it is to be praised even if he is lacking in other advantages, while one who does not have it is condemned and rejected even if he is well supplied with other advantages.

13 The situation is the same for humans as for things. What we call a good ship is not the one decorated with expensive paints, nor the one whose prow is tipped with gold or silver, nor the one whose hold is ornamented with ivory, nor the one laden with royal treasure and the bursaries of nations, but rather the steady vessel, stoutly made with joints that keep the water out, sturdy enough to withstand every assault of the sea, swift and unfazed by the wind. **14** What we call a good sword is not the one with a gilded baldric, nor the one whose sheath is studded with gems, but the one whose cutting edge is keen and whose point will slice through every kind of defensive armor. With a ruler, you do not ask how pretty it is but how straight it is. Everything is praised for that feature which is distinctive of it and for which it is obtained. **15** So in a human too, the pertinent consideration is not how much land he has under the plow, not how much capital he has to invest, not how many clients attend him, not how expensive a bed he lies in, not how transparent his drinking goblet is but how good a person he is. Yet he is good only if his reason is fully developed, straight and right, and adapted to the intent of his nature. **16** This is called virtue; this is the honorable and the sole good of the human being. For since only reason perfects a human, only reason makes him perfectly happy. But that by which alone he is made happy is his sole good.

We say too that those things which proceed from virtue and are connected with it—that is, all the activities of virtue—are themselves goods. Still, virtue is the sole good, because there is no good without it. **17** If every good inheres in the mind, then whatever strengthens, exalts, enlarges the mind is a good. But virtue makes the mind stronger, loftier, and more expansive. For other objects of our desire also lower the mind and weaken it, and when they seem to elevate us, they are actually puffing us up and deceiving us with empty wind. The sole good is therefore that by which the mind is made better.

18 All the actions of an entire life are governed by consideration for what is honorable and what is base; reasoning about what to do or not do is guided accordingly. Let me explain. A good man will do what he believes is honorable, even if it is arduous, even if it is dangerous. Conversely, he will not do what he believes is base, even if it brings money, or pleasure, or power. Nothing will frighten him away from what is honorable; nothing will entice him toward what is base. **19** So it is only if there is no good other than virtue and nothing bad except what is shameful that he will pursue the honorable unconditionally and avoid the base unconditionally, and will look to those two in every action of life.

If virtue alone is unperverted and it alone maintains its own condition, then virtue is the one good that cannot turn out to be anything other than good. It escapes all risk of change. Foolishness creeps toward wisdom; wisdom does not relapse into foolishness.

20 I have said (as perhaps you remember) that there are some who by unconsidered impulse have trodden beneath their feet those objects the common crowd either wants or dreads. Examples can be given of one who threw away his wealth, one who set his hand on fire, one whose smile did not abate under torture, one who shed not a tear at the funeral of his children, one who met death without dismay, all because love, anger, or desire drove them to court such dangers. If a brief steeling of the mind can do so much when roused by the spur of the moment, then virtue can achieve all the more, being rigorous not on some sudden impulse but equally on all occasions, constant in its strength. **21** It follows that those objects that are scorned quite often by the imprudent, and always by the wise, are neither good nor bad. Virtue itself, then, is the sole good, which walks proudly between opposite fortunes with lofty scorn for both.

22 If you accept the view that something besides the honorable is a good, then every virtue will have a hard time. For no virtue can be maintained if it looks to anything beyond itself. If that is the case, it is contrary to reason,* on which the virtues depend, and to truth, which does not exist without reason. And any view that is contrary to truth is false.

23 You admit that the good man must of necessity be supremely respectful toward the gods. For that reason he will calmly tolerate anything that happens to him, for he knows that it has happened through the divine law by which all events are regulated. If that is the case, then in his eyes honorable conduct will be the sole good; for that includes obedience to the gods, neither raging against the shocks of fortune nor complaining of one's own lot but accepting one's fate with patience and acting as commanded.* **24** If there is any good other than the honorable, then we will be dogged by lust for life and for life's equipment—and that is intolerable, unending, ill-defined. Thus the sole good is the honorable, which has a limit.

25 We said that if things in which the gods have no share, like money and public office, are goods, then human life will be more blessed than the lives of the gods. Now add this consideration: if indeed our souls linger on when released from the body, a happier condition awaits them than while they are embodied. But if those things that we use through the body are goods, they will be worse off after their discharge, and that is contrary to our intuition that souls that are free and released into the universe are happier than souls locked up under siege. **26** I had also said that if those things are goods that pertain no more to humans than to animals devoid of speech, then animals too will partake of happiness, and that is impossible.

For the sake of the honorable, one ought to put up with absolutely anything; but if there were some good besides the honorable, there would be no such obligation.

27 I pursued these topics at greater length in my earlier letter; here I have compressed them, giving a brief overview. But a view of this kind will never seem to you to be true unless you raise your mind to a higher level. Ask yourself this: if circumstances should require you to die for your country, purchasing the lives of all its citizens at the cost of your own, would you stretch out your neck not just willingly but even gladly? If you would, then there is no other good, for you are abandoning everything to have this.

See what great power there is in the honorable: you will die for the state, even if you realize the need only just before you are to do it. **28** Sometimes from an extremely beautiful object one experiences great joy even in a tiny space of time; and although no profit from the act performed accrues to the one who is deceased and removed from human life, still there is satisfaction in the very contemplation of the deed ahead. A just and courageous man, when he envisions the benefits of his death—the freedom of his homeland, the safety of all those for whom he lays down his life—is at the height of pleasure, and is gladdened by his own danger.* **29** But if one is deprived even of this joy that the doing of this greatest, last deed provides, even then one will still plunge down into death, finding satisfaction in acting correctly and with due devotion. Confront him with many reasons to be dissuaded; say to him, "Your act will soon be forgotten and will win hardly any gratitude or esteem from the populace." He will reply, "Everything you are saying is external to my task. My concern is with the task itself. I know that task is honorable, and so I follow wherever it summons me to go."

30 This, then, is the sole good, as recognized not only by the perfect mind but also by the mind that is nobly born and of good natural disposition. Other things are fleeting and changeable. Possessing them is an anxious matter: even when a kindly fortune piles them on, they weigh heavily on their owners. Always they are a burden; sometimes they are even a mockery.

31 Not one of those whom you see wearing the purple is fortunate, any more than actors are fortunate when assigned to bear the scepter and royal robes on stage, when they parade before the audience in wide garments and platform shoes, then immediately go off, remove their footgear, and resume their proper stature. Not one of those whom wealth and public office have taken to the top is truly great. Why does he appear great? You are including the pedestal in his measurement. A dwarf is not tall even if he stands on a mountain; a giant will keep his height even if he stands in a pit. **32** This is our mistake; this is how we are fooled: we do not assess people by what they are but add to them the trappings of their station. Yet when you want to make a true assessment of a person and know what he is like, strip him naked. Let him shed his inheritance, his offices, and all of fortune's other lies. Let him take off even his body. Contemplate his mind and see what is his quality and what his stature: is he great through his own store or someone else's? **33** If his gaze is steady as he looks upon the flashing swords, if he knows it makes no difference to him whether he breathes his last through his mouth or through his opened throat, then call him happy—if, when he hears of prison and exile and all the needless terrors of human thoughts, he feels no concern but says,

> "No aspect of these labors,
> Sibyl, arises new or unforeseen
> by me: I grasped it all before this day,
> and in my mind I faced and finished all.*

You, Aeneas, make such proclamations on this day only; I make them always to myself, and since I am human, prepare myself for human events."

34 Misfortune's blow falls lightly when the mind is prepared for it. But the foolish and those who put their trust in fortune find that every aspect life presents is new and unexpected. For inexpert minds, a large portion of their misfortune lies in the novelty of it. **35** Evidence of this is that when they have grown used to the circumstances they had considered harsh, they endure them more patiently. For this reason the wise man accustoms himself to misfortunes that are yet to come: he takes what others make light through long endurance and makes it light through long reflection.* We sometimes hear the voices of the inexpert saying, "I knew this was waiting for me." The wise man knows that everything is waiting for him. No matter what happens, he says, "I knew it."

Farewell.

A trip around Sicily brings thoughts of glory

From Seneca to Lucilius
Greetings

---

1 I am looking forward to a letter from you describing what new information you have discovered on your sailing trip around Sicily; and in particular, some definite facts about Charybdis itself.* For I am well aware that Scylla is only a promontory, and not especially dangerous to navigation; Charybdis, though, I would like to have described to me in writing. Is it like the Charybdis of legend? If you happen to have made any observations—and it is well worth the trouble—then fill me in. Is there only one wind that makes it billow up, or does every squall stir up the sea in the same way? And is it true that anything that is drawn into the whirlpool there at the strait is carried many miles underwater until it surfaces near the beach at Taormina?

2 If you write to me on these points, my next request will be a bold one: climb Etna too, in my honor. Some say that the summit of that mountain is being eaten away and is gradually diminishing in elevation. This is an inference from the fact that it used to be visible from farther out at sea; but that might not be because the height of the peak is diminishing but because its fires are becoming fainter, spewing out less violently and in lesser amounts, as is the smoke during the day. Neither explanation is implausible. It could be that the mountain is shrinking, being consumed from within day by day; but it could also be that it remains the same, since the fire is not burning the mountain itself but welling up from some recess deep within the earth. In that case, the actual peak is not its source of supply but only a channel. 3 In Lycia there is a famous district, called by the inhabitants Hephaestion, where there are a number of holes in the ground surrounded by harmless flames that do no damage to the vegetation. The area is grassy and fertile, for the flames do not burn anything but merely flicker lazily in one place. 4 But let's save those inquiries until after you have written to me about the others. How far is it from the crater to the patches of snow? They are well sheltered from the heat—even in summer they do not melt.

No, don't charge this effort you are making to my account. In your fevered state, you'd have done it anyway, even if no one had requested it. 5 How much would I have to pay to keep you from touching on Mount Etna in your poem—Etna, the hallowed theme of every poet! Was Ovid prevented from writing about it just because Virgil had already covered it? Was Cornelius Severus deterred by either of them?* Anyway, it is fertile ground for everyone. The earlier writers have not, I think, exhausted the possibilities; rather, they have opened up the way. 6 It makes a big difference whether you take up a spent subject or one that has merely been treated before. A topic grows over time; invention does not preclude inventiveness. Besides, the last to come has the best of it: the words are all laid out for him, but a different arrangement lends them a fresh appearance. Not that he takes them up as belonging to someone else: they are public property. 7 If I know you at all, you are absolutely drooling over Etna, wishing to write something great to equal your predecessors. For modesty does not permit you to hope that you might surpass them. So great is your respect for those who have gone before that if the opportunity should arise for you to defeat them, I think you would rather curb your talent.

8 One of the good things about wisdom is that no one can be beaten at it by another except during the ascent. Once you reach the heights, everything is on a level; there is no room for increase; it is a stopping point. Does the sun increase in size? Does the moon wax beyond the full? The level of the oceans does not rise; the world maintains its shape and its condition. **9** Whatever has attained its proper stature cannot exceed itself; everyone, therefore, who becomes wise will be on an equal footing. Each individual among them will have his own gifts: one will be more genial, another more quick-witted; one more fluent in his orations, another more elegant; but our concern is with the source of their happiness, and that is the same in all. **10** Whether Mount Etna could ever collapse onto itself, whether that lofty peak, visible far out at sea, is shrinking from the constant force of its fires, I do not know. What I do know is that no flame, no devastation will ever bring down the exalted nature of virtue. This is the one greatness that knows no diminishment. It can neither be heightened nor reduced; its magnitude is fixed, like that of the heavenly bodies.*

Let us endeavor to advance ourselves to that condition. **11** Much of the work has already been done. No, not much, if truth be told: merely being better than the worst is not goodness. Does a man boast of his eyesight just because he is able to tell that it is daytime? When the bright sun cuts through his fading vision, he is relieved to have escaped the darkness for a while, but he does not yet have the benefit of that light. **12** We will have no reason to congratulate ourselves until our weltering in the dark is over and our mind emerges not to squint at the brightness but to gaze full upon the light of day; to be restored to heaven from whence it came; to claim the place that is its birthright. Its origins summon it upward. It will be there even before it is released from this prison-house, as soon as it sheds its faults and flashes upward, pure and light, toward godlike contemplation.*

13 Dearest Lucilius, how glad I am that we are doing this— that we are pressing on in this direction with all our strength, even if few people ever know; even if no one knows. Glory is the shadow of virtue; it accompanies virtue even when it is not wanted.* But just as a shadow sometimes goes before, some- times behind, so is it with glory: sometimes it is out ahead, presenting itself to view; sometimes it falls the other way and is all the greater for coming later, when envy has receded. 14 How long a time was Democritus thought to be insane!* How nar- rowly Socrates escaped oblivion! How many years was Cato unknown to his country! It rejected him and did not under- stand him until it had lost him. The innocence and courage of Rutilius would never have come to light but for the injustice done to him; once wronged, he became a beacon.* Surely he must have been grateful for the chance to embrace his life in exile.

I have been speaking of those on whom adverse fortune conferred distinction; for many, though, their moral progress became known only after they were gone. And how many more have not been greeted by renown so much as exhumed by it! 15 Look at Epicurus: it is not only educated people who are amazed at him but even the ignorant masses; yet his existence was unknown even in Athens, in whose environs he had se- questered himself. Hence in one of his letters, after a hymn of gratitude remembering his friendship with Metrodorus (who had died many years before), he remarked at the end that amid such great blessings, it never did either of them any harm that Greece, that well-known land, not only failed to recognize them but scarcely even heard of them. **16** Surely, then, he must have been discovered only after he had ceased to exist; surely it was only then that his reputation became illustrious. Metrodorus too admits in one of his letters that he and Epicurus were not very well known, but says that those who were willing to follow in their footsteps would have a great name prepared for them.*

17 No instance of virtue lies hidden forever. If it has remained so for a time, it has lost nothing: though buried for a while in oblivion, suppressed by the resentment of its own generation, a day will come that will make it famous. One who thinks only of his contemporaries is born for but a few. There are many thousands of years to come, many thousands of peoples: look to them. Even if all those who live with you are silent because of jealousy, others will come who will judge your merits with neither malice nor favoritism. If fame is any reward for virtue, then that reward will never perish. To be sure, the speeches of posterity will be nothing to us; yet those speeches will attend us unawares.

18 In life or in death, the pursuit of virtue never goes unrewarded, as long as one has followed it in earnest, not with hairstyle and makeup but with a character that is the same on the surprise visit as on the planned occasion. Pretense is of no avail. Few are deceived by the face that is just painted on: one's true identity goes right to the core. Deceits have nothing solid about them. A lie is a tenuous thing, and on close inspection, transparent.

Farewell.

Heavy drinking

From Seneca to Lucilius
Greetings

---

1 You tell me to describe every one of my days from start to finish. You must think well of me if you suppose there is nothing in them that I would hide from you. Our lives should indeed be like that, lived as if in the sight of others. Even our thoughts should be conducted as though some other person could gaze into our inmost breast. For there is someone who can. What use is there in keeping a secret from human beings? Nothing is hidden from God. God is in our minds; God enters into the midst of our thoughts. I say enters—as if he had ever left!

2 So I will do as you tell me, and write to you willingly of what I am doing, all in order. I will observe myself straightway, and conduct an inquiry of my day. It is a very useful practice. What makes us terrible people is that no one looks back over his life. We ponder what we are about to do (though not as often as we should); we do not ever reflect on what we have done. Yet plans for the future depend on the past.

3 Today has been a solid block of time. No one has taken any of it from me; the entire day has been split between resting and reading. Only a little has been devoted to bodily exercise, and on that account I am grateful to old age: it costs me but little. As soon as I stir myself, I am tired, but that is the aim of exercise even for the strongest people. **4** Would you like to know about my regimen? A single trainer is enough for me. It is Pharius, a mere child, as you know, and a lovable one. But he will be replaced: I am now looking for someone even younger. To be sure, he says that we are at the same point in our lives—both losing our teeth! But already I can hardly keep up with him in running, and in a few days I won't be able to. You see what daily exercise is doing for me! The distance between two people increases quickly when they are moving in opposite directions. He is climbing even as I descend, and you know well how much more quickly the second happens. I misspoke: our time of life is not a descent but a free fall.

5 But would you like to know the outcome of our race to-day? Something that rarely happens in running—a tie. After this flurry of activity (one can hardly call it a workout), I got down into a cold bath—for "cold" is the word I use when the water is just barely warm. And I used to be such a cold-water enthusiast! On the first of January, I used to pay my respects to the Canal. Just as I used to read or write or say something on that day, so also was it a ritual of mine to greet the new year with a dip in the Maiden.* But then I moved my encampment, first to the Tiber, and now to this tub, where—when I am at my bravest, and all indications are good—the water is warmed only by the sun. I can hardly manage a cold bath anymore.

6 Next it is dry bread, a meal without a table, after which I need not wash my hands. I sleep hardly at all. You know my habits: I take just a very brief nap, a mule team's rest, as it were. It's enough for me if I doze off for a moment. Sometimes I know I have slept, and sometimes I only guess.

7 Listen—you can hear the noise from the crowds at the races. Some sudden cry rises from every throat to assail my ears, but my thoughts carry on undisturbed, unbroken even.

The roar does not bother me at all: many voices mingled into one are to me as waves on the shore or wind among the trees or any other meaningless sound.

8 What, then, do I have to occupy my mind? I'll tell you. Yesterday's reflections have left me wondering what certain very intelligent men were thinking when they made their proofs of important points so trivial and confusing. Even if what they say is true, it seems more like falsehood. 9 Zeno, who is the greatest of men and the founder of our very brave, very chaste school of philosophy, wishes to dissuade us from drunkenness. Listen to how he proves that a good man will not become drunk:

> No one entrusts a secret to one who is drunk.
> But one does entrust a secret to a good man.
> Therefore a good man will not be drunk.*

In mockery of this, one could use similar reasoning to prove the exact opposite. Here's how—taking just one example:

> No one entrusts a secret to one who is asleep.
> But one does entrust a secret to a good man.
> Therefore a good man does not sleep.

10 Posidonius takes up the cause of our master Zeno in the one way he can, though even then the position seems to me untenable.* He says that "drunk" has two meanings: one is when a person is loaded with wine and not in control of himself, the other is when he is in the habit of becoming drunk and is susceptible to this fault. The latter, he says, is what Zeno has in mind—the one who is in the habit of becoming drunk, not the one who is drunk right now. This is the person to whom no one will entrust a secret, lest he blurt it out when he is drinking.

11 But that's false: the first syllogism posits one who is drunk, not one who will be so in the future. For you will grant that there is a big difference between a person who is drunk and a drunkard. A person who is drunk could be drunk for the very first time, without having acquired the habit. Conversely, the habitual drunkard can sometimes be free of drunkenness. For that reason, I understand the word in its usual signification, especially since it is employed by one who makes some claim to precision and who scrutinizes words. Besides, if Zeno understood the word one way but meant us to take it in another, then he made the ambiguity of a term the occasion for deceit, and one ought not to do that when truth is one's object. **12** But suppose he did mean that. What follows is false, that one does not entrust a secret to someone who has a habit of getting drunk. Think how many soldiers are entrusted with information that their commanders, tribunes, and centurions need to keep quiet. Yet soldiers are not models of sobriety. The plan to assassinate Caesar (I mean the Caesar who was in power after the defeat of Pompey) was disclosed to Tillius Cimber* as well as to Cassius. Cassius drank water all his life; Tillius Cimber was besotted with wine and a troublemaker too. He himself told a joke about it. "How can I have any tolerance for people," he said, "when I don't have any for wine?"

13 Each of us could name people who cannot be trusted with wine but can be trusted with a secret. I will recount just one example that occurs to me so that it won't be forgotten. Life should be well supplied with exemplary anecdotes so that we don't always have to go back to the old ones. Lucius Piso,* the commander of the city watch, got drunk once and was continually so thereafter. **14** He spent most of the night at parties, then slept until noon; noon was daybreak, as far as he was concerned. Still, he attended scrupulously to his responsibilities, on which depended the safety of Rome. The divine Augustus trusted this man with secret instructions when he appointed him to a command in Thrace, which he subdued; then Tiberius did the same as he was departing for Campania, since he was leaving much resentment and many causes for suspicion behind him in Rome. **15** I believe it was because Piso's drunkenness had yielded such good results that Tiberius later appointed Cossus as his urban prefect—a serious, well-disciplined man but positively soaked in wine, to the point that once when he had come directly to the Senate from a party, he had to be carried out because he had fallen asleep and could not be awakened. Nonetheless, Tiberius used to write to him with his own hand on matters he dared not confide even to his closest advisors. And Cossus never gave away a secret, either public or private.

16 So let's get rid of the old commonplaces. "The mind impeded by drink is not under its own control. Just as clay storage jars filled with must tend to burst from the heat of fermentation, and everything inside comes shooting out, so is it when wine flows in intoxicating abundance: whatever lies hidden is cast forth in full view. Just as those who are overloaded with wine cannot keep their food down—for the wine washes it up—so is it with a secret: they spill it out, both their own and other people's." **17** Yes, this does often happen. But it also happens that when there is need, we do consult with people who we know drink freely. This disproves that platitude which is offered in Zeno's defense, that no one shares a secret with a habitual drunkard.

It is much better to attack drunkenness directly, exposing its faults. Even an ordinary decent person will avoid these, and still more the perfectly wise person. The latter is satisfied when thirst is quenched; and although he does sometimes let good cheer urge him to go somewhat further for another's sake, he stops short of drunkenness. **18** We can inquire some other time whether the wise person is mentally affected by an excess of wine and whether he then acts as people usually do when they are drunk. In the meantime, if what you want to establish is that a good man ought not to become inebriated, why do you resort to syllogisms? Just say how disgraceful it is for a person to imbibe more than he can hold, not knowing the size of his own stomach, and how many things people do when they are drunk that would embarrass them when sober. Say that drunkenness is nothing but voluntary insanity. Imagine the drunken state continuing for a number of days; would you hesitate to call that madness? So even as it is, it is not a lesser form of insanity but only a shorter one.

19 Recount the example of Alexander of Macedon, who drove a spear through Clitus, his dearest and most loyal friend, during a dinner party. When he found out what he had done, he wanted to die, and certainly that is what he deserved.* Drunkenness sets every vice aflame, and exposes them too, since it removes the sense of shame that sets constraints on our worst impulses. For more people are inhibited from wrongdoing by the disgrace of it than by their own good intentions. **20** When an excess of wine has possession of the mind, any fault that was hiding comes into the open. Drunkenness does not create faults—it brings out faults that already exist. It is then that the lustful person does not even wait for the bedroom but permits his desires to achieve everything they want without delay; it is then that the shameless person admits his infirmity* and even boasts of it; it is then that the quarrelsome fellow restrains neither his tongue nor his fist. In a rude person, arrogance becomes even more pronounced, as does cruelty in a savage temperament and malice in a spiteful one. Every vice has free rein; every vice is exposed to view.

21 Mention too the loss of self-awareness, the slurred and indistinct speech, the blurred vision, the unsteady walk, the dizziness, the ceiling spinning around as if the entire house were caught in a whirlwind, the pains in the stomach when the wine seethes inwardly and causes bloat through the abdomen. It is endurable, nonetheless, while the effects of the drink still last. But what about afterward, when sleep has soured it and inebriation has turned into indigestion?

22 Think what terrible events drunkenness has caused in human history. There are whole tribes of fierce warriors whom it has betrayed to their enemies; there are long-defended ramparts it has breached; peoples of fiercely independent spirit, who always refused to bear the yoke, have been forced by it to submit to foreign domination. Those who could never be defeated in battle have been vanquished by drink. **23** I spoke earlier about Alexander. He who had passed unharmed through so many campaigns, so many battles, so many winters, who defeated every challenge of climate and terrain, who crossed so many rivers descending from unknown wilds, so many distant seas, was vanquished at last by drinking without moderation from his "Beaker of Hercules"—for him, a beaker of death.*

24 How is holding one's liquor a point of pride? When you have won the drinking bout, when the others are all retching or passing out and refuse your toasts, when you are the only one to survive the party, having defeated everyone by your marvelous prowess, your unmatched capacity for wine, even then you are outdone by a barrel.

25 What was it that destroyed Mark Antony, a man of noble character and exceptional talent? Was it not drunkenness that drove him to foreign habits and the most un-Roman vices? That, and his love of Cleopatra, which was only increased by wine. It was this that made him an enemy to the state, that made him a lesser man than his enemies. It was this that made him cruel, when he used to have the heads of leading statesmen brought to him at dinner—when amid his elaborate feasts and the splendor of kings he would view the hands and faces of the proscribed. Even though he was loaded with wine, he thirsted for blood.* It would have been bad enough if he had been drinking as he did such things; that he did them when already drunk is still more intolerable.

26 A devotion to drink generally does bring cruelty in its train, for one's soundness of mind then becomes flawed and uneven. Just as long illness causes people to become peevish and difficult and prone to take offense at the slightest thing, so continual drunkenness causes the mind to become brutish. For since they are frequently not themselves, the habit of insanity becomes ingrained, and faults acquired under the influence of wine thrive even without it.

27 In your speech, then, tell us why the wise person ought not to become intoxicated. Show us by examples, not words, how ugly a thing it is, how unreasonable its demands. The easiest course is to prove that when our so-called pleasures get out of bounds, they become punishments instead. For if you attempt to argue that the wise man is not affected by large amounts of wine, that the upright character of his mind persists even through dissipation, then you might as well conclude that he would not be killed by drinking poison, would not be put to sleep by a sleeping draft, and would not vomit or expel the contents of his bowels after taking a dose of hellebore. But if his gait is unsteady and his speech is slurred, why should you consider him to be drunk in one part of himself and sober in another?

Farewell.

LETTER 84

The writer's craft

From Seneca to Lucilius
Greetings

---

1 Those trips are shaking the laziness out of me. They have been beneficial, I believe, both to my health and to my studies.* Why they should improve my health is plain to you: since my love of literature makes me lazy and neglectful of my body, I get some exercise through the labor of others. Why they should aid my study I will explain: I have° withdrawn from readings. To be sure, reading is necessary, first that I may not be wrapped up in myself alone, and second that after finding out about the inquiries of others, I may judge concerning their discoveries and ponder what remains to be discovered. Reading nourishes one's talent and refreshes it when it is worn out with study, even though reading itself requires study. **2** We ought neither to write exclusively nor read exclusively: the first—writing, that is—will deaden and exhaust our powers; the second will weaken and dilute them. One must do both by turns, tempering one with the other, so that whatever is collected through reading may be assimilated into the body by writing.

3 We should be like bees, as the saying goes: first they fly about and choose the flowers best suited for making honey, then distribute what they have collected throughout the hive, and as our poet Virgil says,

> let the sweet nectar fill the swelling cells
> and lucent honey flow.*

4 Opinion is divided about bees. Do they merely extract liquid from flowers, which immediately becomes honey, or do they transform what they have collected into that sweet liquid by some intermingling of their own distinctive spirit?* For some hold that their expertise is not in making the honey but only in collecting it. They say that on the leaves of a certain reed in the land of India, one can find a honey that is produced either by the dew of that atmosphere or by the exceptionally thick and sweet juice of the reed itself. Their view is that the same capacity resides in our own plants, though less noticeably, and is found and harvested by the creature that is born to this task. Others think that what the bees gather from flowers and tender grasses changes its character when stored away in the hive, by a process that includes some sort of fermentation, if I may use that term, during which the different flavors combine into one.

5 But I digress from the matter at hand. We also must imitate these bees, and taking the things we have gathered from our diverse reading, first separate them (for things are better preserved when they are kept distinct), then, applying the care and ability of our own talent, conjoin those various samples into one savor, so that even if it is apparent where a thing has been taken from, it may yet appear to be different from that from which it was taken. **6** It is what we see nature do in our bodies through no effort of our own. The nutriments we have taken are burdensome for just so long as they retain their own character and swim as solids in the stomach; but when they have been changed from what they were, then at last they are added to our strength, passing into our bloodstream. Let us accomplish the same with these things that nourish the talent, not permitting the things we have consumed to remain whole but making them part of ourselves. **7** Let us digest them; otherwise they will pass into the memory, not into the talent. Let us faithfully adjust our thinking to theirs and make them our own, so that from the many there may come to be some sort of unity. It is like when a single problem in arithmetic involves various smaller sums: the many individual numbers become one total. Our minds should do the same: they should hide everything that has contributed and show forth only the results. **8** Even if you exhibit a resemblance to some admired author who has left a deep impression on you, I want you to resemble him as a son does, not as a statue does. A statue is a dead thing.

"What do you mean? Won't readers realize whose style, whose argumentation, whose well-turned remarks you are imitating?" It is possible they will not, I think, if a greatly talented man stamps his own form upon all the elements that he draws from his chosen model so that they all fit together into a unity.

9 Do you not see how many voices combine to form a choir? Yet there is unity in the sound they produce. One is a high voice, another low, and another in the middle; women join the men, and flutes accompany them; yet one cannot make out the voices of individuals but only the one voice of them all. **10** The kind of chorus I mean is that known to the old philosophers, for in the shows we have now there are more people singing than there used to be in the audience. When the line of singers fills the aisles and the seating area is ringed with trumpeters and every kind of flute and water organ sounds together from the stage, then from the different sounds is produced a unison. This is what I want our mind to be like: in it are many skills, many precepts, examples from many ages, but all harmonized into one.

11 "How is this to be done?" you ask. By constant concentration: if we do nothing except at the prompting of reason and avoid nothing except at the prompting of reason. If only you will listen, reason will speak to you, saying,

> "Give up those things that everyone always chases after. Give up on wealth: those who have it find it either a danger or a burden. Give up on bodily pleasures, and mental pleasures too: they make a person soft and flabby. Give up on ambition: it is a conceited thing, empty and inflated; it has no ending and is concerned only to get ahead and keep others from catching up. It suffers from envy—envy on both sides, in fact. And you see how unhappy it makes a person to be both the object and the subject of envy. 12 You see before you the homes of powerful men, the doorways thronged with well-wishers all pushing and shoving one another. Many an affront must you endure to get in; more, once you are inside. Pass them by, those staircases of the wealthy, those vestibules built up over our heads. To stand in them is to stand not just on a high ledge but on a slippery one too. Turn your steps, rather, toward wisdom. Seek out the largesse wisdom has to give: great serenity and also great abundance."

13 What seems most eminent in human affairs, even though in reality it is puny and stands out only by comparison with

what is the lowest, is reached nonetheless by steep and difficult paths. It is a rugged road that leads to the summit of prestige. But if you choose to scale *this* mountain, the one that rises above the things of fortune, you will see spread out beneath you everything that most people regard as heights. Yet the path to this summit lies on level ground.*

Farewell.

LETTER 86

The rustic villa of Scipio Africanus

From Seneca to Lucilius
Greetings

1 I write this to you from lodgings right inside the villa of Scipio Africanus, having already paid my respects to the great man's shade and to the altar, which I suspect is also his tomb. His spirit has surely returned to heaven, from which it came. I believe that, not because he led great armies (for even Cambyses had those, and he was insane and took advantage of his insanity), but because of his exceptional self-control and his patriotism, which in my view was even more admirable after he left his homeland than while he was defending it.*

It had to be one or the other: Scipio at Rome, or Rome at liberty. 2 "I want nothing," he said, "that will detract from our laws and customs. Let all our citizens be equal under the law. O my homeland, make use of the service I have done you, but do so in my absence. I am the reason that you are free; I will also be the proof of it: I will depart, if I have grown greater than is in your interests." **3** How can I not admire the greatness of spirit with which he withdrew into voluntary exile and so removed the burden from the state? Things had reached a point where either freedom had to do Scipio a wrong, or Scipio had to do freedom a wrong. Neither would have been permissible; so he gave way to the laws and betook himself to Liternum, making the state his debtor not only for Hannibal's exile but for his own.*

4 I have seen the villa built of squared masonry, the wall enclosing the grove, also the turrets rising in front, guarding the entrance on either side; the cistern below buildings and lawns, capacious enough even for the needs of an army; and the cramped bathing quarters. These last were dimly lit, as the old ones generally were, for our ancestors thought a bathhouse couldn't be hot unless it was dark. **5** So I took great pleasure in pondering the habits of Scipio—and our habits. In this little nook, the famous "terror of Carthage,"* the man who saved Rome from a second capture, would wash his body, worn out from working in the fields. For he took his exercise in the form of hard labor, tilling the soil himself as they did in olden times. This shabby roof was over his head; this cheap tile floor was under his feet.

But nowadays who could stand to bathe in such a style? **6** A man now thinks himself a shoddy pauper unless his walls gleam with large and costly mirrors, unless his Alexandrian marble has a contrasting inlay of Numidian and a mosaic border all around of many colors laid out like a painting, unless the chamber has a glass ceiling, unless Thasian dolomite—once a rare sight even in temples—rims the pools where we plunge our limbs drained by their heavy sweating, unless the water pours from spigots made of silver. **7** And those are just the plebeian fixtures! What shall I say of the bathhouses of freedmen? How many statues there are; how many columns that don't support anything but are put there only for decoration and for the sake of the expense! How many fountains babbling from tier to tier! We have reached such a pitch of luxury that we don't even want to walk unless we tread upon precious stones!

8 In Scipio's bathhouse the windows are tiny, mere slits cut into the stone wall so as to admit light without making the building less defensible. But nowadays they refer to bath buildings as "moth holes" if they are not designed to take in the sunshine at all hours of the day through large windows, if one cannot get a suntan there along with one's bath, if one does not have a view from one's tub of the countryside and of the sea. For that reason, baths that drew admiring crowds at the time of their dedication are despised as outmoded the moment self-indulgence devises some new means of outdoing itself. **9** In the old days, there were only a few bathhouses, and they had no kind of décor: why decorate a building when the admission is only a farthing and the purpose is utility, not amusement? There were no water jets below the surface, no constant supply of fresh water as if from a hot spring, and no one cared whether the water that washed away dirt and grime was crystal clear. **10** And yet, in all truth, how delightful it is to enter those dark bathhouses with their plain stucco, when you know that the aedile who felt the water temperature with his own hand and adjusted it for you was Cato, or Fabius Maximus, or one of the Cornelii!* For aediles from the noblest families used to make it their business to enter the public establishments and ensure cleanliness and a serviceable and healthy temperature—not the temperature you find now, which is more like a furnace. It's so hot that a slave convicted of some crime should be sentenced to be *bathed* alive! As far as I can tell, there's no difference these days between going for a hot bath and entering a burning building!

11 "How uncouth of Scipio," some people now say, "not to have broad panes of mica to let light into his steam room, not to brown in the sun before simmering in the tub! What a hopeless case! He didn't know how to live! His bathwater had not been filtered; it was often murky, and if there had been a lot of rain, it was almost like mud!" Nor did he mind that sort of bath, for he came there to wash off sweat from his body, not perfumed oil.

12 What do you suppose some people will say about that? "I don't envy Scipio: he really did live in exile if he had that sort of bath!" As a matter of fact, he didn't even have that sort every day: accounts of life in old Rome indicate that they washed their arms and legs daily—the parts soiled by work, naturally—but their whole bodies only on market day.* At that someone will say, "Obviously they must have been very dirty! What do you suppose they smelled like?" Like military service; like work; like men. Now that fancy bathhouses have been invented, people are much filthier.

13 When Horace set out to describe a notorious dandy, what did he say? "Bucillus smells of lozenges."* Nowadays you would speak of Bucillus as if he smelled of the goat—he'd take the place of Gargonius, whom Horace contrasted with Bucillus. It's not enough to put on perfume: you are supposed to reapply it two or three times a day so that it won't evaporate from your skin. And they actually take pride in that smell as if it were their own!

14 If all this seems excessively severe, blame it on the villa. There I learned a lesson from Aegialus,* the hardworking head of household (for he now owns the farm): that even the most ancient tree can be transplanted. This is something we need to learn in our old age, for every one of us plants his olive grove for those who come after. For that matter, I've seen such a grove produce acceptable fruit in abundance in its third or fourth season.° **15** You too will enjoy the covering of the tree that

grows later to make shade for your descendants,*

as our poet Virgil says—although Virgil was aiming to produce not an accurate description but an attractive one. What he wanted was not to teach farmers but to delight his readers. **16** To give just one example, here's something I couldn't help noticing today:

In spring the beans are planted, and you too
go in the crumbling furrows, rich lucerne,
and at that time of year is millet tended.*

Should these crops be sown at the same time and both of them in spring? You be the judge: I'm writing to you in June, already getting toward July, and I've just seen them harvesting beans and sowing millet on the same day.

17 Let me get back to that olive grove. I have seen it done by two methods. With the large trees, Aegialus cut back the limbs to one foot and transplanted the trunks with the taproot, trimming the roots and leaving just the central portion to which they were all attached. He coated this with manure, lowered it into the hole, and then instead of just filling it in with dirt he trampled and compressed it. **18** He says nothing else works as well as this—"compaction," he calls it. Presumably it keeps out the cold and wind; also, the tree doesn't move as much, and because of that, new roots are able to get started and to grasp the soil. For while they are still slender and not yet established, even a slight movement would surely dislodge them. He also scrapes the taproot before replanting, for he says that new roots emerge from all the exposed wood. The trunk should not stand more than three or four feet above the ground. In this way, it will sprout new foliage from near the ground, and there will not be a large portion of it that is dry and withered, as there is on old trees. **19** The other method of planting is like this: he took strong branches whose bark was still tender (such as you find on younger trees) and set them in the soil in the same manner. These are a bit slower in growing; but since they have come up as if from a scion, they have nothing gnarly or ill-favored about them.

20 Still another thing I have observed is a grapevine being moved away from its elm at an advanced age.* In this case, one should gather up even the root hairs if possible, and then entrench a generous amount of the vine so that roots will sprout right from the stock. I have seen some that were planted not only in February but even at the end of March, and they are now gripping and embracing elms that were not originally their own. **21** Aegialus adds that all those trees that are large-boled, if I may use that expression, should be nurtured with water from the cistern. If that is beneficial to them, we are not dependent on the rain.

I don't intend to teach you anything more, for fear that I might turn you into a competitor, just as Aegialus did with me.

Farewell.

The beginnings of civilization

From Seneca to Lucilius
Greetings

---

1 Who can doubt, dear Lucilius, that our life is the gift of the immortal gods, but our living well is philosophy's gift? It would surely follow, then, that we owe more to philosophy than to the gods (since a good life is a greater benefit than mere life), were it not for the fact that philosophy itself has been bestowed on us by the gods. They have not granted knowledge of philosophy to anyone, but they have given everyone the capacity to acquire it.* **2** If they had made this knowledge common property, letting everyone be born with good sense, wisdom would have forfeited its greatest excellence—that it is not one of the things acquired by chance. Rather, its special value and splendor consist in the fact that it doesn't just happen, that we have ourselves to thank for it, that it is not to be solicited from anyone else. What would you have to admire in philosophy if it were simply a present?

3 The sole task of philosophy is to discover the truth about matters human and divine. Philosophy is never unaccompanied by piety, reverence, and justice, and all the other assemblage of interrelated and connected virtues.* It teaches us to worship things divine and to love things human; it shows that power rests with the gods while sociability links human beings to one another. This last remained unsullied for a long time, until companionship was pulled apart by greed, which impoverished even those whom it had made wealthiest; for once people opted for private ownership, they ceased to hold everything in common.

4 The first human beings, however, and those of their descendants who followed nature without straying,* took an exceptional individual as both their leader and their law, and entrusted themselves to his authority; for it is natural that the inferior should submit to the superior. Among groups of animals, the dominant ones are either the biggest or the fiercest. The bull that leads the herd is not a poor specimen; he is one that surpasses the other males in size and strength. The tallest elephant leads the herd. Among human beings, though, what matters is not size but excellence, and thus it was once the custom to choose leaders for their qualities of mind. For that reason the most fortunate peoples have been those that awarded power solely on the basis of merit. There is no need to restrict the power of someone who does not believe he has power to do more than he should.

5 Accordingly, Posidonius holds that in the so-called Golden Age, government was in the hands of the wise.* They restrained aggression, protected the weaker from the stronger, dispensed policy, and indicated what was advantageous and what was not. Their good sense saw to it that their people did not run short of anything, their bravery warded off dangers, and their beneficence enhanced the prosperity of their subjects. They gave commands not to rule others but to serve them. They never used to test their strength against those who were the initial source of their power. They had neither the intent nor any reason to act unjustly; because their orders were properly given, they were properly obeyed. A king could utter no greater threat to his recalcitrant subjects than his own abdication.

6 Yet once kingdoms were transformed into tyrannies with

the infiltration of vices, there began to be a need for laws, and these too were first introduced by the wise. Solon, who founded Athens on the principle of equity, was one of the seven men made famous by their wisdom. If Lycurgus had lived at the same period, he would have added an eighth name to that blessed company.* We still revere the laws of Zaleucus and Charondas.* It was not in the Forum or in lawyers' offices that these men acquired knowledge of the judicial principles they established in Sicily (still flourishing at that time), and throughout the Greek communities of Italy, but in the silent and holy retreat of Pythagoras.

7 Thus far I agree with Posidonius. But I will not concede to him that philosophy invented the technologies we use in daily life; I will not claim for philosophy the renown that belongs to craftsmanship. According to him,

> When humans were scattered about, sheltering in huts or caves or hollow trees, philosophy taught them how to build houses.

In my opinion, it was not philosophy that devised the modern engineering of multistoried buildings and sprawling cities, any more than it was philosophy that invented cages for fish so that the gourmand would not have to risk a storm but could continue to fatten up all kinds of fish in the safety of the harbor, however wild the weather. 8 Are you going to say that philosophy taught human beings to keep things under lock and key? Wasn't that what gave the go-ahead to greed? Was it philosophy that piled up our towering buildings that are such a danger to their inhabitants? As if it were not enough for people to house themselves with whatever came to hand, discovering a natural shelter for themselves without artifice and difficulty.

9 Take my word for it, the era that preceded architects and

builders was truly happy. All those artifacts came along with self-indulgence: the squared timbers, the saw slicing through neat markings, the precise carpentry.

For the first humans split soft wood with wedges.*

As well they might, for they were not preparing the roof of a future banquet hall. There were none of these long lines of wagons that make the streets shake, transporting pines or firs to support paneled ceilings laden with gold. **10** Their huts were propped up by forked poles positioned at each end. Bundles of branches and sloping piles of leaves allowed the heaviest rains to run off. Beneath these roofs they lived in security: their thatch let them be free. What dwells under marble and gold is servitude.

11 I have a further disagreement with Posidonius over his claim that iron tools were the invention of wise men. He could just as well say that it was the wise who

learned then to snare wild beasts, to trap the birds,
and to set dogs all round the woodland glens.*

All that was discovered not by wisdom but by human ingenuity. **12** I also disagree with his claim that it was the wise who discovered iron and copper deposits at times when forest fires scorched the ground, melting it and releasing a flow of metal from veins lying near the surface. Such things are discovered by the kind of people who care about them. **13** Again, unlike Posidonius, I don't consider it an interesting question whether hammers came into use before tongs. Both of these implements were invented by someone whose intelligence was keen and active but not great or inspired; and the same applies to everything else that can only be discovered by one whose back is bent, whose mind is focused on the ground.

The sage lived simply; he must have, for even in our modern age he wants to be as unencumbered as possible.* **14** How, I ask, can you consistently admire both Diogenes and Daedalus?* Which of these is wise in your view? Is it the one who invented the saw, or the one who, upon seeing a boy drinking water from his rounded hand, immediately removed the cup from his knapsack and broke it, criticizing himself in the following words: "What a fool I am to have kept unnecessary baggage all this time!" Then he curled himself up in his barrel and went to sleep! **15** Likewise, who do you think is wiser today: the one who discovers how to make saffron perfume spurt to a huge height from hidden pipes, who fills or empties channels with a sudden gush of water, who constructs movable panels for dining-room ceilings in such a way that the décor can be changed as quickly as the courses; or, alternatively, the one who shows himself and other people how nature has given us no commands that are harsh or difficult, that we can shelter ourselves without the marble worker and the engineer, that we can clothe ourselves without the silk trade, that we can have everything we need if we will just be content with what the surface of the earth has provided. Once the human race becomes willing to give this man a hearing, it will realize that cooks are as unnecessary as soldiers.

16 It was the wise, or at least people resembling the wise, who regarded the body's security as something uncomplicated. The essential things are available with little effort; it is pampering that demands work. Follow nature, and you will not miss the artificer. Nature did not want us to be overtaxed in this regard, and has equipped us with the means to comply with all its requirements. "A naked body cannot bear to be cold." What, then? Aren't the skins of wild beasts and other animals quite capable of giving full protection against the cold? Are there not many peoples who use bark to cover their bodies, or make clothing out of feathers? Is it not the case even today that most of the Scythians clothe themselves in the pelts of foxes and martens, materials that are soft to the touch and impenetrable to winds? What, then? Who is there who can't weave a wicker frame, daub it with ordinary mud, cover it with straw or brush, and spend the winter safely with the rain running off down the sides? **17** "But we need denser shade to keep out the heat of the summer sun." What, then? Do there not remain from ancient times many hidden caves hollowed out by the passage of time or some other chance cause? What, then? Is it not a fact that the peoples of North Africa and others who live in excessively sunny climates take shelter in dugouts, finding protection from the heat in the baked earth itself, when nothing else would have been adequate?

18 Nature was not so unfair as to make life easy for all other creatures but impossible for human beings to live without numerous technical skills. No harsh demands have been made of us; nothing needed for our survival has been made difficult to find. We were born into a world where things were already prepared. We were the ones that made things difficult for ourselves by despising what was easy. Housing, clothing, the means of warming our bodies, food, and in fact everything that has now become a huge business was simply there, free for the taking and obtainable with little effort; for no one took more of anything than was needed. It is we who have made these things costly, strange, and only to be acquired by numerous and considerable technical skills.

19 Nature provides what nature requires. Self-indulgence has abandoned nature, spurring itself on every day, growing through the centuries, and abetting vices by its own ingenuity. It lusted first for nonessentials, then for things that were harmful; now, finally, it has surrendered the mind to the body, bidding it serve the body's every whim. All the noisy occupations that hawk their wares to the community are in business for the body's sake. There was a time when all that the body got was rations, like a slave; but now, like a master, it has everything provided to it. This is why you find textile businesses here, craft workshops there; here the aromas produced by chefs, there the sensuous movements of dance teachers and sensuous and effeminate singing. The natural limit we once observed, restricting our wants to what is essential and within our resources, has vanished. Nowadays one is considered unrefined and poverty-stricken if one wants just what is enough.

20 It's unbelievable, dear Lucilius, how easily even great men are diverted from the truth by the enjoyment of their own rhetoric. Take Posidonius, one of those, in my opinion, who have contributed the most to philosophy: wanting to describe, first, how some threads are twisted and others drawn out from loose bunches of wool, then how the hanging weights of the loom hold the warp straight up and down, and how, to soften the coarse warp threads that support the fabric, the weft is pressed tightly together by means of the batten, he has claimed that even the art of weaving was invented by the wise. He forgets that it was only later that this quite intricate procedure was discovered, whereby

> The warp is fixed upon the beam, the threads
> are separated by the cane, the weft
> slides through upon the shuttle, then is pressed
> by the broad comb's indented teeth.*

How would he have reacted if he had seen our modern looms, which produce clothing that is virtually transparent and gives no aid to the body or even to decency?

21 He then moves on to farmers. He gives an equally eloquent account of how the ground is first turned by the plow and then given a second plowing to loosen the earth and facilitate the development of the roots, then how seeds are sown and weeds pulled by hand to prevent stray wild plants from growing up to damage the crops. This too, he says, was the work of the wise, as though agriculturalists were not making numerous discoveries even now for enhancing productivity. 22 Not content with these techniques, he proceeds to lower the sage into the flour mill, saying that it was he who first began to manufacture bread, in imitation of nature:

When grain is taken into the mouth, it is crushed by the hardness of the teeth as they grind together, and anything that escapes is brought back to the teeth by the tongue, then mixed with saliva so that it will be moist and easy to swallow. Once it reaches the stomach, it is digested by the steady cooking action of that organ, and finally it is assimilated to the body. 23 Following this model, someone took two rough-textured stones and placed one on top of the other, to resemble the teeth: one part is fixed in place to let the other grind against it; then, by the friction of the two, the granules are crushed, then reground several times until they are reduced to very fine particles. He then sprinkled the flour with water, kneaded it, and shaped it into bread. At first it was baked in hot coals or in a clay pot; later came the gradual invention of ovens and other types of cookers whose heat can be controlled.

If he had gone just a little further, he would have claimed that it was the wise who invented shoemaking!

24 It was certainly reason that figured out all these things, but not perfected reason. They are the inventions of humanity, not of a sage. And, in fact, the same is true of the boats we use to cross rivers and seas, with their sails equipped to catch the force of the winds and their rudders placed at the rear for steering the vessel this way and that. The idea was derived from fish, which regulate their movements by flicking their tails to one side or the other. **25** He says,

> It was actually a sage who invented all these things; but, because they were too trivial for him to tackle himself, he assigned them to menial assistants.

In reality, they were thought up by exactly the same people who make them their business today. We know for sure that certain products have only appeared in our own time; for instance, the use of windows that let in clear light by means of translucent glass, or bathhouses with vaulted floors and pipes set in the walls for spreading the heat and keeping the upper and lower parts of the room at an even temperature. What need for me to mention the marble that makes our temples and houses gleam, or the columns of rounded and polished stones that support porticoes and buildings large enough for crowds of people, or the shorthand signs that enable the most rapid talk to be taken down and the hand to keep up with the speed of the tongue? All these things have been produced by the lowliest slaves.

26 Wisdom occupies a loftier seat. It does not train the hand; rather, it educates the mind. Do you want to know what it has unearthed and achieved? The answer is not graceful dance movements, nor is it the musical scales produced by trumpets and flutes, which release the air blown into them in one way or another and so transform it into sound. Wisdom does not labor over weapons or fortifications or implements of war. It fosters peace and summons the human race to live in harmony. **27** And it is not, I insist, a maker of tools for everyday needs. Why do you attribute such trivial things to wisdom? What you have before your eye is the technician of life itself. Indeed, it keeps the other crafts under its authority; for inasmuch as wisdom is master of life, it is master also of life's equipment. Wisdom, moreover, has happiness as its goal; it leads the way and opens the doors to that condition. **28** It indicates the things that are really bad and those that merely seem so. It purges our minds of illusion, giving them a substantive dignity while curtailing the sort of dignity that is all empty show, and insisting that we understand the difference between greatness and pomposity. It imparts to us a conception of nature as a whole and a conception of itself. It reveals the identity and attributes of the gods, including the spirits of the underworld, the household deities, and the tutelary spirits, and also those long-lasting° souls that have come to join the second rank of deities, together with their location, activities, powers, and intentions. When we become devotees of wisdom, we are given access not to some local shrine but to the mighty temple of all the gods, the vault of heaven itself, whose phenomena are brought before the mind's eye as they really are; for ordinary vision is inadequate to register so vast a spectacle.

29 Next, wisdom takes us back to the world's origin, the everlasting rationality infused throughout the whole, and the power of all the generative principles to fashion individual things according to their kind.* After this, it starts to investigate the mind, where it comes from, where it is located, how long it endures, how many parts it has.* Then, turning from the corporeal to the incorporeal, it scrutinizes truth and its criteria, and after that, the way to sort out ambiguities both in life and in utterance, for both involve confusions between truth and falsehood.*

30 It is not the case, I maintain, that the sage detached himself, as Posidonius supposes, from technology; he never went near it at all. He would not have considered it worthwhile to invent something that he would not think worthy of continued use. He would not take up anything that had to be subsequently laid aside. **31** According to Posidonius, "Anacharsis invented the potter's wheel that fashions vases by its rotation." Then, because the potter's wheel is mentioned in Homer, he wants us to take this passage to be spurious rather than dismiss his own story.* For my part, I refuse to accept that Anacharsis invented this thing; or, if he did, then a sage did indeed invent it, but not by virtue of his being wise; for the wise do many things simply by virtue of being human. Suppose a sage is a superb runner: he will win a race by his speed and not by his wisdom.

I would like to show Posidonius a glassblower, whose breath forms the glass into many shapes that a careful hand could scarcely fashion. Here we have things that were discovered at a time when the sage himself was no longer to be found. **32** Posidonius tells us that Democritus is reputed to have invented the arch, a device that uses the keystone to secure the curve made by a set of gradually tilted stones. I must insist that this is untrue. Before Democritus there had to be bridges and doorways, the top of which is generally rounded.* **33** You are also forgetting that the very same Democritus discovered the means of softening ivory and of turning a pebble into an emerald by baking it, a procedure by which even today we color stones found to respond to it.* The sage may well have discovered these things, but not by virtue of his wisdom. In fact, he does many things that we observe quite unwise people doing just as well or even with greater skill and ease.

34 Do you want to know what discoveries the philosopher has really brought to light? In the first place, the truths of nature, which he has pursued quite differently from other creatures, whose eyes are dim in relation to the divine. Second, the law of life, which he has brought into line with the universal order of things, teaching us not just to know the gods but to follow them and accept all that happens as their commands. He has told us not to give heed to false opinions and has weighed the value of everything by an authentic standard. He has condemned pleasures that are mixed with regret and praised the goods that will always give satisfaction. He has made known that the most fortunate person is the one who has no need of fortune, and the most powerful person is the one who has power over himself.

35 The philosophy I am describing is not the one that situates the citizen outside his community and the gods outside the world, making virtue the instrument of pleasure, but the philosophy that thinks nothing is good that is not honorable; the one that cannot be captivated by gifts from humans or from fortune; the one whose reward is this: that its followers cannot be swayed by rewards.*

I do not believe that this philosophy existed in that primitive era when technology was absent and the uses of things were still being learned by trial and error. 36 It came after° that happy epoch when nature's blessings were readily available for everyone's use, when greed and self-indulgence had not yet divided human beings against one another and they had not yet learned to abandon sociability for the sake of gain. The men living then were not wise, even if they were acting as the wise should act.

37 One could not imagine a better condition for the human race, not even if God were to grant one the opportunity to fashion earthly things and dispense rules of conduct to peoples. Nor could one prefer another way of life to that which existed among those of whom it is said,

> No plowmen tilled the fields; even to mark
> the land with boundaries was not allowed.
> Their work, their effort, served the common good,
> and earth itself, when no demands were made,
> gave all its gifts more gladly.*

38 What human race could have been more fortunate? Everyone had a share in the fruits of nature. Like a parent, nature provided for the maintenance of everyone: they were free of anxiety, for they used, but did not own, the resources of the community. Surely I may call that people supremely wealthy, for among them you could find no one who was poor.

This optimal state of things was disrupted by greed. In its passion to be acquisitive and turn things into private property, it succeeded in making everything belong to different people, and reduced itself to a mere fraction of its formerly huge stock. Greed introduced poverty, and by desiring much, it lost everything. **39** Nowadays it strives to recover its losses, piles one estate onto another by buying out or forcing out its neighbors, expands its lands into the area of whole provinces, takes a long journey through its own property and calls it ownership. Yet in spite of all this, no extension of boundaries will bring us back to our original condition. When we have completed this project, we shall possess a great deal—but we used to own the whole world.

40 The earth itself was more productive when it was untilled; it was abundant for the needs of peoples who were not plunderers. It was as great a pleasure to share with another what one had found amid nature's bounty as it was to find it in the first place. No one could possibly have either more or less than was needed. Things were shared in mutual harmony. The time had not yet come when the stronger began to lay hands on the weaker, the time when the greedy would conceal things as a supply for their own use and thereby remove the necessities of life from other people. Their concern for others was as great as for themselves. **41** Weapons were not constantly in use; hands unstained with human blood turned all their hostility against wild beasts. The people of that era found protection from the sun in some thick wood. Kept safe from the fierceness of rain and storms by a humble shelter of leaves, they passed their days quite safely, and at night they slept calmly without a sigh. We toss and turn with anxiety on our purple bedclothes, kept awake by the sting of our cares. How softly those people slept on the hard ground! **42** Rather than being overhung by coffered ceilings, they lay out of doors with the stars gliding above them, while the magnificent nightly spectacle of the celestial made its round, silently performing that mighty operation. By day as well as by night, views of this resplendent dwelling opened before them. They enjoyed the sight of constellations setting past the zenith and others rising again into visibility. **43** Must it not have been a delight to roam amid such a vast expanse of wonders?

You moderns, on the other hand, tremble at every sound

your houses make. If something creaks, you flee in terror amid your frescoed walls. Those people did not dwell in homes resembling towns. The free-flowing breath of the open air, the light shade given by rock or tree, crystalline springs, freely running streams unspoiled by industry, pipes, or any artificial watercourse, and meadows with a natural beauty—these were the settings of their rural dwellings embellished only by the handicrafts of country folk. This was a home in agreement with nature. It was a pleasure to live there, made anxious neither by it nor for it. But houses nowadays make up a large part of our fears.

44 Splendid and innocent though their life was, they were not the wise, for this word is only applicable to the greatest of undertakings. Yet I would not deny that they were men of lofty spirit and, if I may say so, but recently descended from the gods. Before the world was exhausted, it certainly gave birth to superior beings. Their natural disposition was in every case hardier and better suited to manual labor, but it correspondingly fell short in perfection. Nature does not bestow virtue: becoming good is a skill. **45** To be sure, those people did not prospect for gold or silver or for gleaming gems to be found in the dregs of the earth. At that time, far from having one human being kill another merely for the pleasure of the spectacle, without even the motive of anger or fear, they were merciful even to the speechless animals. They were not yet wearing embroidered clothes, or clothes interwoven with gold, for gold was still unmined.

46 What is our conclusion, then? These people were innocent out of ignorance. There is a great difference between refusing to do wrong and not knowing how to do it. They lacked the virtues of justice, good sense, moderation, and courage.

Their unsophisticated life did possess certain qualities resembling all these, but real virtue belongs only to a mind that has been trained, thoroughly instructed, and brought to the highest condition by constant practice. We are indeed born for this, but not born with it. Until you provide some education, even the best natures have only the raw material for virtue, not virtue itself.

Farewell.

LETTER 91

A terrible fire at Lyon

From Seneca to Lucilius
Greetings

---

1 Our friend Liberalis is quite upset at news of the fire that has completely consumed the municipality of Lyon.* This catastrophe could have shaken anyone, let alone a person deeply devoted to his native land. It has left him searching for the mental toughness with which he had undoubtedly armed himself against what he thought were possible objects of fear.* I'm not surprised, though, that he had no advance fears of this disaster, so unforeseen and virtually unimaginable, because it was unprecedented. Fire has troubled many cities, but not to the point of completely annihilating them. Even when buildings have been set alight by enemy action, many places escape destruction; and it is rare for fires, even ones that are restarted several times, to consume everything to the point of leaving nothing for the tools of demolition. Even earthquakes have

hardly ever been severe and deadly enough to flatten entire towns. In a word, this has never happened before: a fire of such determined ferocity that afterward there was nothing left to burn.

2 Such a range of splendid structures, any one of them capable of embellishing a city all by itself—and a single night has leveled them all! During such an extensive period of peace, we have suffered a greater loss than anything we might have feared from war. How is this credible? With military operations in abeyance everywhere, with security now extended throughout the civilized world, Lyon, which was the jewel of Gaul, is lost to view. In the past, people afflicted by a general disaster have at least had opportunity to fear such an eventuality before the fact; nothing of great importance has been wrecked in a mere instant. But here, a single night marked the difference between a mighty city and none at all. Its end took less time than I have taken in telling you of it.

3 Although our friend Liberalis is no weakling in facing his own troubles, he is quite depressed by all of this. It's no wonder he is downcast. When one is unprepared for a disaster, it has a greater effect: shock intensifies the blow. No mortal can fail to grieve more deeply when amazement is added to the loss. 4 Accordingly, we should let nothing catch us unprepared. We should try to anticipate everything and reflect on what's possible rather than what usually happens.

Absolutely anything can be overthrown in its finest hour by the caprice of fortune. The brighter it shines, the more it is liable to be attacked and shaken: for fortune, nothing is arduous, nothing difficult. 5 Not always does it come by a single road, not always by paths that are well worn. Sometimes it turns our hands against each other; at other times, relying on its own resources, it finds dangers for us that need no agent. No moment is exempt. In the midst of pleasure, things arise that cause us pain. In a time of peace, war breaks out, and all that one had relied on for security becomes an object of fear: friends turn into foes, allies into enemies. The calm of a summer day is suddenly transformed into storms greater than those of winter. Even without an enemy at hand, we suffer war's effects. If there are no other reasons for calamity, excessive prosperity finds its own reasons. The most careful people are attacked by illness; the sturdiest by physical decline; punishments affect those who are completely guiltless; riots those who live in total seclusion. People who have almost forgotten the power of chance find themselves picked out to experience some novel misfortune. **6** The achievements of a lifetime, put together with great effort and many answered prayers, are cast to ruin in a single day. But to speak of a day is to make our hastening calamities slower than they really are. An hour, a mere moment is enough to overturn an empire. It would be some relief to our frailty and our concerns if everything came to an end as slowly as it comes into existence. The reality is that it takes time for things to grow but little or no time for them to be lost.

7 Whether public or private, nothing stands still. People and cities alike are caught up in destiny's momentum. When all is quite calm, terror emerges; and with no disturbing factors on the horizon, trouble bursts out from where it is least expected. Regimes that have remained standing through civil and foreign wars collapse without anyone's intervention. How rare it is for a city to experience prosperity for long! Therefore we must think of everything and fortify our minds to face every possible contingency.

8 Exile, torture, war, shipwreck—keep rehearsing them in your mind. You could be snatched away from your country, or your country from you; you could be driven out into the desert, or the place where you are now jostled by crowds of people could itself become a desert. We should set before our eyes the entire range of human fortunes, and calibrate our thoughts about the future not by the usual scale of events but by the magnitude of what could happen. If we wish not to be overwhelmed, stunned by rare occurrences as if they were unparalleled, we must take a comprehensive view of fortune. **9** How often have cities of Asia and Greece been leveled by a single earthquake! How many towns in Syria and Macedonia have been swallowed up! How often has this disaster devastated Cyprus! How often has Paphos collapsed onto itself! We have frequently had news that entire cities have been destroyed, and we are only a tiny fraction of the people who frequently hear about them.

So we should stand up to the hazards of fortune, knowing that rumor always exaggerates the importance of what has happened. **10** A wealthy city has burned, one that was in the provinces and yet not of them but rather an ornament to them; still, it was located on a single hill, and that not a very large one. But all those cities that enjoy a splendid and glorious reputation today will have even their traces removed by time. Do you not see how the most famous cities in Greece have now been demolished? Not even the foundations are left standing to show that they once existed. **11** Nor is it only the work of our hands that falls away, only human constructions that are overturned by the passage of time. Mountaintops crumble, entire regions have subsided, lands that were situated far from sight of the sea have been covered by the waves. Powerful volcanic fires have eroded the hills through which they used to glow, radically reducing the once lofty peaks that were a comforting landmark to sailors. Since nature's own works are not unassailed, we should not complain about the destruction of cities. **12** They stand only to fall: this end is waiting for every one of them. Either subterranean wind pressure bursts its barriers and topples them, or floodwaters build up underground and burst out against them with shattering force,* or a volcanic eruption breaks the earth's crust, or age, from which nothing is safe, gradually overwhelms them, or an epidemic wipes out the population and the abandoned buildings crumble from neglect. It would take too long to count up all the ways by which misfortune may come. But I know one thing: whatever we mortals construct is condemned to be mortal. We live amid things that will die.

13 These, then, are the kinds of consolations I send to our friend Liberalis, burning as he is with an incredible love for his native land. Perhaps it has been consumed so that it may be rebuilt better than it was before. Damage has often made room for greater prosperity. Many things have fallen only to rise to greater heights. Timagenes, an opponent of our city's success, used to say that the only reason he was grieved by the fires at Rome was that he knew the rebuilt structures would be superior to those that had burned down.* **14** In the case of Lyon too, everyone will probably strive to rebuild even finer and taller buildings than those they have lost. Let us wish that their work may be more enduring and founded with happier prospects for a longer future. This municipality only dates back a hundred years, not even as old as the longest human life. Founded by Plancus, it grew into the densely populated center that we know, thanks to its favorable location.* Yet consider how many grievous disasters it has suffered within the life span of one elderly person!

15 Let us, therefore, shape our minds to be such as will understand and endure our lot, knowing that fortune shrinks from nothing, but exerts the same rights over empire and emperor alike, and the same powers over cities as over persons. We have no grounds to resent these things. We have come into a world where life is lived on such terms: accept them and comply, or reject them and leave by whatever route you like. You may resent any unfairness that is directed against you personally. But if it is a necessity that binds all social classes in its compass, make your peace with destiny, which brings everything to an end. **16** There is no reason for you to measure us by our tombs and by the monuments along the road, all of different heights. Once reduced to ashes, we are all the same size. Born unequal, we die equal. My point is the same for cities as for their inhabitants: Rome was captured just as Ardea was.* The one who established humanity's rights drew no distinction among us on the basis of birth or celebrity except for the duration of our lives. Once we arrive at the end of our mortal term, he says, "Away with ambition; let one law apply to everything that walks the earth." We are equal in that each of us is liable to every suffering: no one is more vulnerable than another; no one is more assured of surviving till tomorrow.

17 Alexander the Great had begun to study geometry—a study that would make him wretched, when he learned how puny the earth is and how little of it he had captured.* I say it again: he was wretched, for he should have realized that his title was unjustified: who can be "great" in an area that is miniscule? The subjects he was studying were complicated and only to be learned with close attention—nothing that could be easily understood by a crazy person whose thoughts were flying far across the ocean. "Teach me the easy bits," he said; to which his teacher replied: "They are the same for everyone, and equally difficult." **18** Imagine the nature of things to be saying the same to you: "What you are complaining about is the same for everyone. I can't give anyone anything easier, but anyone who wants to can make them easier for himself." How so? By keeping himself serene.

You are obliged to feel pain and thirst and hunger and, if you happen to be granted a longer duration among human-kind, old age; you are obliged to grow sick, experience loss, and finally die. Still, there's no reason for you to accept the views dinned into your ears by those around you. **19** There's nothing really harmful in these matters, nothing intolerable or harsh. Those people's fear has no basis except that they are all in agreement about it. It puts you in the position of treating death like the fear of a rumor, whereas nothing is more absurd than a person afraid of words. Our friend Demetrius has a witticism by which he indicates that the sayings of ignorant people mean no more to him than the rumblings of the digestive tract: "What is it to me," he says, "whether they make their sound from above or from below?"* **20** It's the height of madness to worry about being despised by the despicable. You had no good reason to fear what people say, and it's just the same with those things you would never fear if it were not for what people say. Could unfair gossip do any harm to a good man? Surely not, and neither should we listen to unfair gossip about death, for it too has a bad reputation. No one who brings charges against death has ever experienced it. Until that happens, it is rash to condemn what you don't know. But this much you do know—how many there are for whom it is a blessing, how many it liberates from torture, want, illness, suffering, and weariness. We are in no one's power when death is in our power.

Farewell.

LETTER 97

A trial in the time of Cicero

From Seneca to Lucilius
Greetings

---

1 You are mistaken, dear Lucilius, if you think that our era is particularly culpable for self-indulgence and for neglect of high moral standards. One likes to blame such deficiencies on one's own times, but in reality it is not the times that are at fault but the people. No era has ever been free of blame. Indeed, if you begin to assess the iniquity of every age, I am ashamed to tell you that misconduct has never been more in evidence than it was in the time of Cato and in his very presence.* **2** It's hard to believe, but money changed hands when Publius Clodius was tried for secret adultery with Caesar's wife. Clodius had committed sacrilege against the ceremonial sacrifice which is said to be performed "for the people" and which is supposed to involve such an extreme exclusion of every male from the precinct that even pictures of male animals are covered up. And yet the jurors were bribed and—still more shocking—to sweeten the deal, married women and youths of noble birth were made to have sex with them. **3** The charge was less heinous than the acquittal. The one who had been accused of adultery instigated multiple adulteries, and only secured his own safety by making the jury as guilty as himself. This all took place at the proceedings where Cato gave evidence, though that was all he did. I will quote Cicero's words, because the facts would otherwise be incredible:

> **4** He invited the jurors over, made promises to them, pleaded with them, and bribed them. But by god! there was still worse to come: as the ultimate reward, some of the jury were offered nights with specific women and assignations with youths of noble birth.*

5 The bribe was bad enough, but the extras were still more shocking. "That straitlaced fellow—would you like to have his wife? I will give her to you. That rich man, how about his? I'll see to it that she sleeps with you. If you don't get somebody's wife, then vote to convict me! That beauty you desire—she'll come to you. I promise you a night with her, and I'll be quick about it. My promise will be fulfilled within the two-day court recess." Arranging adulteries is more immoral than committing them, since it involves putting pressure on respectable married women. **6** Clodius's jury had sought protection from the Senate—which was necessary only if they were going to convict—and their request was granted. That's why, after the defendant was acquitted, Catulus amusingly told the jury: "Why did you ask us for protection? Was it so that your bribes would not be confiscated?"* Amid these jokes, a man got off who before his trial was an adulterer and during it a pimp. What he did to escape conviction was worse than what he did to deserve it.

7 Do you believe that anything has ever been more depraved than the moral standards of people impervious to restraint by religion or by courts of law, people who, in the special senatorial proceedings, committed a greater crime than the one being investigated? The question at stake was whether someone guilty of adultery could remain at liberty. What came out was the fact that such a person could not be acquitted without recourse to adultery. 8 This was negotiated in the presence of Pompey and Caesar, in the presence of Cicero and Cato. Mind you, this is the same Cato in whose presence the populace is said to have stopped asking for performances from the strippers at the festival of Flora.* If you can believe it, the audiences of that time had stricter standards than the juries!

Such things will be as they have been before; but while civic decadence will sometimes subside under pressure and fear, it will never do so of its own accord. 9 You should not suppose, then, that our time has yielded more to lust than any other, or less to the laws. The youth of today is much more disciplined than it was then, when an accused person denied an adultery charge before his jury, while the jury confessed to the same before him; when orgies were held to settle the case; when a Clodius, benefiting from the same vices that he was guilty of, arranged liaisons during the actual conduct of the case. Would anyone believe this—that a man undergoing trial for a single adultery could be acquitted by means of many adulteries?

10 The likes of Clodius are to be found in every age; the likes of Cato are not. We tend toward the worse, because there's always someone to lead the way and someone to follow. And even without them, the act goes on apace. We don't just incline toward wrongdoing, we dive right in. In other skills, mistakes are an embarrassment to the craftsman, who is upset by his errors; in life, wrongdoing is a source of positive delight. It's this

that makes most people impossible to correct. **11** A helmsman doesn't get pleasure from an upturned vessel, or a physician from his patient's funeral, or an attorney if he loses the case for his defendant, but everyone enjoys his own immorality. One man takes delight in an adulterous affair, excited by the very difficulty of it; another gets a thrill out of forgery and theft and only reproaches himself when his luck fails. We have become accustomed to behaving badly, and this is the result.

12 On the other hand, all people do conceal their misdeeds. However well those things turn out, they hide the facts while they enjoy the profits. That tells you that even people who have gone utterly astray still have some sense of what's right; they are not ignorant of what's wrong, they just disregard it. But a good conscience wants to come into the open and be seen; wickedness fears even the dark. **13** That is why I think Epicurus put it well when he said: "A wrongdoer may happen to remain concealed, but he cannot be confident of concealment." A better way to express this thought would be "Wrongdoers gain nothing from concealment, because even if they have the good fortune to be concealed, they don't have the confidence of remaining so."* In other words, crimes cannot be safe. **14** This view is not inconsistent with our Stoic school, in my opinion, if we elucidate it in this way. How so? Because the first and greatest punishment for wrongdoers is the fact of having done wrong. No crime, even one embellished with the gifts of fortune or protected and safeguarded thereby, is free from punishment, since the penalty for crime lies in the crime. But even so, these secondary penalties—constant fear, dread, and distrust of security—follow right on the heels of that primary one. Why should I free wickedness from this punishment? Why should I not leave it in perpetual suspense?

15 We should disagree with Epicurus when he says that there is nothing that is just by nature, and that the reason one should refrain from misdeeds is that one cannot avoid the anxiety resulting from them;* we should agree with him, though, that the wrongdoer is tormented by conscience and that his worst penalty is to bear the hounding and the lash of constant worry, because he cannot trust those who guarantee him security. This is proof in itself, Epicurus, that we have a natural horror of misdeeds: every criminal is afraid, even in a place of safety. **16** Fortune exempts many from punishment, but none from anxiety. Why, if not because we have an innate aversion to what nature has condemned? The reason one can never be sure that concealment will be successful is that conscience convicts people and reveals them to themselves. Wrongdoers are characteristically filled with dread. Since many crimes escape the retribution of the law and the designated penalties, we would be in a very bad way if it were not that such offenses are naturally and heavily penalized from our immediate resources, with fear taking the place of punishment.

Farewell.

LETTER 104

Why travel cannot set you free

From Seneca to Lucilius
Greetings

---

1 I have run away to my villa at Nomentum.* Why, do you think? To escape the city? No, I wanted to avoid a fever that was creeping up and had already cast its hold on me. My doctor was saying that it had started with a rapid and irregular pulse. So I gave orders for my carriage to be made ready at once. I insisted on leaving in spite of my dear Paulina's attempts to stop me. All I could say was what my mentor Gallio had said when he was on the point of starting to have a fever in Greece.* He immediately boarded a ship, and kept insisting that his sickness was due to the location and not to his body. **2** I told this to Paulina.* She is very anxious about my health. In fact, realizing that her soul is completely bound up with mine, I am beginning, in my concern for her, to be concerned about myself. Getting on in years has made me more resolute in facing lots of things, but here I am losing the benefit of age. I have come to think that within this old man there's a young person who needs indulgence. Since I can't prevail on her to show more courage in loving me, she prevails on me to love myself more carefully.

3 One has to give in, you see, to honorable feelings. There are times when, for the sake of loved ones, one has to summon back one's dying breath, however painfully, and actually hold it in one's mouth. A good man should live not as long as it pleases him but as long as he ought to. The person who does not think enough of his wife or his friend to prolong his life—who insists on dying—is thoroughly self-indulgent. When the interest of loved ones demands it, the mind should require even this of itself: even if one not only wants to die but has actually begun to do so, one should interrupt the process and give oneself over to their needs. **4** Returning to life for another's sake is the mark of a lofty spirit, as great men have often done. But, in addition, I think it is supremely kind to be especially careful of your old age if you are aware that such behavior is pleasing, useful, and desirable to any of your loved ones, highly enjoyable though it is at that time to be more relaxed about one's survival and more daring in one's manner of living. 5 Besides, such self-care brings with it great joy and rewards, for what can be more delightful than being so dear to your wife that you consequently become dearer to yourself? And so my Paulina succeeds in burdening me not only with her fears but also with my own.

6 I suppose you are curious to know how my travel project has worked out. As soon as I got away from the city's heavy atmosphere and the smell that smoking kitchens make when they discharge their accumulation of noxious fumes and dust, I felt an immediate change in my health. Can you imagine how much my strength increased once I reached my vineyards? Like an animal let out to pasture, I really attacked my food. The result is that I am fully myself again now, without a trace of physical unsteadiness and mental weakness. I'm beginning to concentrate completely on my studies.

7 For that, location is of no avail unless the mind makes time for itself, keeping a place of retreat even amid busy moments. On the contrary, if you're always choosing remote spots in a quest for leisure, you'll find something to distract you everywhere. We are told that Socrates gave the following response to someone who complained that travel had done him no good: "It serves you right—you've been traveling with yourself!"* 8 How well some people would be doing if they could get away from themselves! Their pressures and anxieties and failings and terrors are all due to themselves. What good is it to cross the sea and move to a new city? If you want to escape from your troubles, what you need is not to be in a different place but to be a different person. Imagine you have come to

Athens or Rhodes. Choose any city you like. Does the character of the place make any difference? You'll be taking your own character with you. **9** You'll still regard wealth as a good, and be tortured by what you falsely and most unhappily believe to be your poverty. No matter how much you own, the mere fact that someone has more will make you think that your resources are insufficient by exactly the amount that his are greater. You will go on regarding public office as a good, and be upset when one fellow is elected consul and another even reelected. You will be jealous whenever you read someone's name a number of times in the official records. Your craze for success will still be so great that you think no one is behind you if anyone is ahead of you.

10 You'll go on regarding death as the worst of all things, even though the worst thing about death is what precedes it— the fear. You'll be terrified by mere apprehensions as well as by real dangers, constantly troubled by phantoms. How will it help you

> to have eluded
> so many Argive towns, and steered your flight
> right through the enemy's midst?*

Peace itself will supply you with fears. Once your mind has yielded to alarm, your confidence will not hold even in situations that are safe: having acquired the habit of thoughtless anxiety, it lacks the capacity to secure its own safety. It does not shun danger but rather takes flight, even though we are more exposed to dangers when we don't face them.

11 You'll continue to regard the loss of anyone you love as a most grievous blow, though all the while this will be as silly as weeping because leaves are falling from the lovely trees that adorn your home. Look on everything that pleases you the same way as you look at verdant leaves:° enjoy them while they last. One or another of them will fall as the days pass, but their loss is easy to bear, because leaves grow again. It's no different with the loss of those you love and think of as your life's delight. They can be replaced, even though they are not reborn.

12 "But they will not be the same." Even you yourself will not be the same. Every day changes you, and every hour; but when other people are snatched away the change is quite obvious, whereas in your own case this escapes notice, because it is not happening on the outside. Other people are taken from us, but at the same time *we* are being stolen imperceptibly from ourselves. You will not be conscious of these changes, nor will you be able to remedy the afflictions, but you will nonetheless make trouble for yourself by hoping for some things and despairing of others. Wisdom lies in combining the two: you should neither hope without doubting nor doubt without hoping.

13 What has travel as such been able to do for anyone? It doesn't control pleasures, curb desires, check outbursts of temper, or mitigate love's wild assaults: in a word, it removes no troubles from the mind. It does not bestow judgment or shake off error; all it does is provide a change of scene to hold our attention for a moment, as some new trinket might entertain a child. 14 Apart from that, travel exacerbates the instability of a mind that is already unhealthy. Indeed, the very movement of the carriage makes us more restless and irritable. The result is that people who had been passionate to visit some spot are even more eager to leave it, just like birds that fly from one perch to another and are gone more swiftly than they arrived. 15 Travel will acquaint you with other races, it will show you

mountains of strange shape, unfamiliar plains, and valleys watered by inexhaustible streams. It will enable you to observe the peculiarities of certain rivers—how the Nile rises in its summer flood, how the Tigris vanishes and then reappears in full force after traveling some distance underground, or how the Meander repeatedly winds around (a theme that poets love to embellish) and often loops back nearly into its own channel before flowing on—yet it will not improve you, either in body or in mind.

16 We need to spend our time on study and on the authorities of wisdom in order to learn what has already been investigated and to investigate what has not yet been discovered. This is the way for the mind to be emancipated from its miserable enslavement and claimed for freedom. But as long as you are ignorant of what to avoid and what to pursue, and remain ignorant of the just, the unjust, the honorable, and the dishonorable, you will not really be traveling but only wandering. **17** Your rushing around will bring you no benefit, since you are traveling in company with your emotions, and your troubles follow along. Indeed, I wish they *were* following you, because then they would be further away! As it is, you are not staying ahead of them but carrying them on your back: wherever you go, you are burdened with the same burning discomforts.

A sick person does not need a place; he needs medical treatment. **18** If someone has broken a leg or dislocated a joint, he doesn't get on a carriage or a ship; he calls a doctor to set the fracture or relocate the limb. Do you get the point? When the mind has been broken and sprained in so many places, do you think it can be restored by changing places? Your trouble is too grave to be cured by moving around. **19** Travel does not make one a doctor or an orator. One does not learn a skill from one's location. Do you suppose that wisdom, the greatest of all skills, can be assembled on a journey? Believe me, there is no journey that could deposit you beyond desires, beyond outbursts of temper, beyond your fears. If that were so, the human race would have headed there in droves. So long as you carry around the reasons for your troubles, wandering all over the world, those troubles will continue to harass and torment you. 20 Are you puzzled that running away is not helping you? What you are running from is with you. You need to correct your flaws, unload your burdens, and keep your desires within a healthy limit. Expel all iniquity from your mind.

If you want to have pleasant travels, look to the company you keep. Greed will cling to you as long as the people you spend time with are greedy or mean. Conceit will stick to you as long as you spend your time with arrogant types. You will not rid yourself of cruelty if you make a torturer a close friend, and the company of adulterers will only inflame your lusts. 21 If you really want to be rid of your vices, you must stay away from the patterns of those vices. If a miser, or seducer, or sadist, or cheat were close to you, they would do you a lot of harm— but in fact, these are already inside you! Make a conversion to better models. Live with either of the Catos, or with Laelius, or Tubero; or, if you prefer to cohabit with Greeks, spend your time with Socrates or Zeno.* The former will teach you, if it is necessary, how to die; the latter, how to die before it is necessary. 22 Live with Chrysippus or Posidonius. They will educate you in the knowledge of things human and divine; they will tell you to work not so much at speaking charmingly and captivating an audience with your words but at toughening your mind and hardening it in the face of challenges.

There is only one haven for this stormy and turbulent life of ours: to rise above future events, to stand firm, ready to receive the blows of fortune head-on, out in the open and unflinching. **23** Nature brought us forth to be resolute. It made some creatures fierce, others cunning, and others timid, but its gift to us was a proud and lofty spirit that seeks where it may live most honorably rather than most safely; a spirit that closely resembles that of the universe, which it follows and strives to match, as far as that is permissible to the steps of mortal beings.* This spirit advances itself, it is confident of being praised and highly regarded. **24** It is master of everything and superior to everything. Consequently, it should not submit to anything or find anything heavy enough to weigh a man down:

Death and distress: shapes fearsome in appearance.*

Not in the least fearsome, if one can fully face them and break through the darkness. Many things that seem terrifying at night turn out to be amusing in the daylight. "Death and distress: shapes fearsome in appearance": our poet Virgil put it very well when he called them terrible not in fact but "in appearance," meaning that they seem terrible, but are not. **25** I repeat: what is as dreadful about these things as is commonly attributed to them? I beg you, Lucilius, to tell me: Why fear hard work, when one is a man? Why fear death, when one is a human being? I frequently encounter people who think that what they themselves cannot do is impossible, and who say that our Stoic theories are beyond the capacities of human nature. **26** I myself have a much higher opinion of human beings: they are actually capable of doing these things, but they are unwilling. Has anyone who really made the effort ever found the task beyond him? Hasn't it always been found easier in the doing? It is not the difficulty of things that saps our confidence, but our lack of confidence that creates the difficulty.

27 If you need a model, take Socrates, a very patient old man.* He suffered all kinds of hardships, but he was overwhelmed neither by poverty (which his domestic troubles made more onerous) nor by the physical work he had to endure, including military service. He was hard-pressed at home, whether we think of his ill-mannered wife with her shrewish tongue or his ineducable children, resembling their mother rather than their father. Outside the home,° he lived either in war or under tyranny or in a freedom that was more cruel than war and tyrants.* **28** The war lasted for twenty-seven years. After it ended, the state was subjected to the harm caused by the Thirty Tyrants, many of whom were personally hostile to Socrates. Finally, he was charged with the most serious offenses. He was accused of undermining religion and corrupting the youth by inciting them against the gods, their fathers, and the state. After this came prison and the hemlock. All this had so little effect on Socrates's mind that it did not even alter his facial expression.* How admirable that was, and how extraordinary! Right up to the end, no one ever saw Socrates any more or less cheerful than usual. Amid the extreme changes of fortune, he was always unchanged.

29 Would you like a second model? Take the younger Cato, against whom fortune's assaults were more violent and more persistent.* At every juncture, and finally at his death, Cato showed that a brave man can both live and die in defiance of fortune. He spent his entire life either as a soldier in the civil wars or in the peace° that was already breeding civil war. You may say that he, just like Socrates, pledged himself to liberty in the midst of slaves°—unless you happen to think that Pompey, Caesar, and Crassus were the allies of freedom. **30** No matter how often the political world changed, no one ever observed any change in Cato. He maintained the same character in every circumstance, whether elected to office or defeated, as a prosecutor or in the province;* in his political speeches, in the army, in death. In sum, at the moment of national crisis, with Caesar on one side equipped with ten legions in peak condition and the support of entire foreign nations, and with Pompey on the other, Cato was ready to stand alone against them all. When one faction was leaning to Caesar, and the other to Pompey, Cato was the only one who took the part of the Republic. **31** If you would like to form a mental image of that time, picture, on one side, the general populace—the common people, all keyed up for revolution; on the other side, the highest nobility and equestrians, all that were of the highest rank in the state; and in between two remnants, the Republic, and Cato. You will be amazed, I tell you, when you catch sight of

> Atreus's son and Priam, and the scourge of both, Achilles.*

32 Both sides meet with reproof, and both are stripped of their weapons, when Cato states his view of both; namely, "If Caesar wins, I will choose death; but if Pompey wins, I will go into exile." What did Cato have to fear? He had appointed for himself, whether in defeat or in victory, outcomes as stern as his enemies could have appointed at their most hostile. He died, then, by his own decree.

33 You see that human beings are able to endure toil: Cato led an army on foot through the middle of the African deserts. You see that they can put up with thirst: Cato dragging the remains of his ill-equipped and defeated force over arid hills did not moisten his lips while dressed in full armor, and whenever water was available he was the last to drink.* You see that one can rise above status and distinction: Cato played ball on the same day that he lost his election.* You see that it is possible not to fear those with superior power: Cato challenged Pompey and Caesar at the same time, though no one else dared to offend the one without gaining the favor of the other. You see that one can rise above death as well as exile: Cato condemned himself both to exile and to death, and in between to war.

34 Once we remove our necks from the yoke, we are capable of facing these troubles with the same degree of fortitude. We must begin by spurning pleasures; they weaken and emasculate us with their many demands, and they make us demand much of fortune. Next, we must spurn wealth: it is the recompense of slavery. We should give up gold and silver and everything else that weighs down prosperous houses. Liberty does not come for free. If you value it highly, you must devalue everything else.

Farewell.

LETTER 108

Vegetarianism and the use of literature

From Seneca to Lucilius
Greetings

---

1 Your inquiry is on a matter there is no point knowing about except just to know; and still, with no other point than that,

you are in a hurry to find out and aren't willing to wait for the books I'm now putting together covering the entire domain of ethics.* I'll get to it right away, but first I'll write about how you ought to hold off on your desire for learning—a burning desire, I see—so that it doesn't become counterproductive. 2 You ought not to take up every subject you encounter, nor should you delve greedily into every topic in its entirety: pieces of it will give you a sense of the whole. We should adjust the burden to our strength, not taking on more than we can handle. Don't drink as much as you want, but as much as you can hold. Just keep the right attitude, though, and the time will come when you can hold as much as you want. The more the mind takes in, the larger it becomes.

3 I remember how Attalus used to teach us when we were constantly in attendance at his lectures, being the first to come and last to leave, and asking him to expound on various topics even when he was out walking—for he did not just receive pupils; he went out and found them. "Teacher and learner should have the same purpose," he used to say, "the one to enable progress, the other to make progress."* 4 One who studies with a philosopher should have some benefit to take home with him every day, either better health or a mind more open to healing. But he will, for the power of philosophy is so great that it aids not only students but even casual bystanders. People who are out in the sun get a tan, even if they didn't go out for that purpose; people who sit around for a while in a perfume shop carry the aroma of the place away with them; and those who have been around a philosopher necessarily take away something beneficial, even if they don't make any effort. Observe: I say "even if they don't make any effort," not "even if they resist."

5 "What do you mean? Don't we know people who have

studied with a philosopher for many years and have not gained even a tinge of color?" Of course I do, and very persistent people too, but I would describe them as hangers-on rather than as students of philosophy. 6 Some people come not to learn but only to listen. It is like when we are enticed into the theater to delight our ears with speech or song or story. You can see that the majority of this audience regards a philosophical lecture as a mere diversion. They are not seeking to lay aside any of their faults or to adopt any rule of life by which to regulate their habits, but only to find enjoyment in the pleasures of the ear. Some even come with notebooks, not to record the content but to take down phrases that they can then repeat, with no more benefit to others than they have derived themselves. 7 Some are stirred by fine-sounding speeches and take on the emotion of the speakers. Their expressions are eager; their spirits are aroused; they are as excited as Phrygian eunuchs,° half-men raving on command at the sound of the flute.* Others are swept away by the beauty of the subject matter, not the sound of empty words. Whenever someone speaks fiercely against the fear of death, or boldly against the vagaries of fortune, they are ready to act immediately on what they have heard. They are very responsive; they are just what they are told to be—if the mood stays with them, if their fine resolve is not assailed by the people, that great discourager of honorable conduct. Few are able to take home with them the intention they have formed.

8 It is easy to rouse a listener and make him desire what is right, for nature has given everyone the foundations and seeds of the virtues.* We are all born for such things; and when someone provides a stimulus, the good awakens in our minds as if from sleep. Have you not observed how applause echoes in

the theater when certain lines are spoken which we, the public, recognize and affirm as true?

> 9 Penury is deprived of much, but avarice of all.
> The greedy man is good to none, but worst to his
> own self.*

The vilest criminal applauds these lines, rejoicing to hear an attack on his own vices. Just imagine the effect when the lines are spoken by a philosopher, when healthful precepts are imbued with poetic rhythms to drive them deeper into the minds of the uneducated. 10 For, as Cleanthes used to say,

> Just as the sound of our breath is amplified when driven
> through a trumpet with its narrow windings, flared at the
> end, so our thoughts are amplified by the stringent require-
> ments of verse.*

The same points are attended to less carefully and make less of an impact when expressed in plain speech. When meter with its specified pattern of long and short syllables is added to an excellent idea, that same sentiment is hurled, as it were, by a stronger arm. 11 Much is said about not caring for money; long speeches advise people that riches are found in the mind, not in the bank account, and that the wealthy person is the one who adjusts to his poverty and makes himself rich with little. But our minds are struck much more when we hear verses like these:

> That mortal man needs least whose wants are least.
> He who can want what is enough, has what he wants.*

12 When we hear such things, we feel compelled to admit that they are true, for even people who are never satisfied with what

they have admire them and cheer for them and cry aloud how they hate money. When you see this reaction, press your advantage: load everything onto them, and leave behind all those subtleties, those syllogisms and sophisms and other clever but pointless tricks. Speak against avarice; speak against self-indulgence; and when you see that you are making progress and having an effect on your audience, press harder still: you will be amazed how beneficial such a speech can be when it is intent on the cure and entirely devoted to the good of its audience. It is easy to turn the hearts of young people toward the love of what is honorable and right. When people can still be taught—that is, when they are only lightly corrupted—truth lays its hand upon them if only it finds a suitable advocate.*

13 In my own case, when I used to hear Attalus at the climax of a speech against faults, against errors, against everything bad in life, I often felt pity for the human race and thought that Attalus was an exalted being, above the pinnacle of human affairs. He said himself that he was a king; but I thought he was more than that, for here was a man who could censure kings. **14** And when he started recommending poverty, arguing that any possessions in excess of our basic needs are only a burden to weigh us down, I often wanted to walk out of the lecture a poor man. When he began to castigate our pleasures, praising a chaste body, an abstemious diet, and a pure mind—pure not only of illicit pleasures but even of unnecessary ones—then I wanted to put a check on my gluttonous belly.

15 Some of the resolutions I made at that time are still with me, Lucilius. For I went at it all with great enthusiasm; and even after I resumed a more urbane manner of living, I kept a few of those good habits. All my life since then, I have refrained from eating oysters and mushrooms. These are not food; they are only tidbits meant to entice those who are full to eat some more (which is what the glutton wants, to stuff himself beyond capacity), for they go down easily, and come back up easily too. **16** All my life since then, I have abstained from perfumed oil: the best smell for the body is no smell at all. Since then I have kept my stomach free of wine, and all my life I have avoided the baths. Boiling one's body and then draining it by sweating seems to me both pointless and decadent. Other practices I had given up have since returned; but though I have ceased to abstain from them, I observe very strict limits. Such restrictions are near to abstinence and in fact may even be more difficult, because some habits are easier to break than to reduce.

17 Since I have started telling you how much more eagerly I went after philosophy as a young man than I hurry after it now that I am old, I won't be embarrassed to admit how smitten I was with love for Pythagoras. Sotion explained to me why Pythagoras abstained from animal foods, and why Sextius later did the same.* Their reasons were different, but impressive in both cases. **18** Sextius held that a person could get enough to eat without resorting to butchery; and that when bloodshed is adapted to the purposes of pleasure, one develops a habit of cruelty.* He also used to say that one should pare away the resources of self-indulgence, and he offered reasoning to show that variety in food is alien to our bodies and detrimental to health. **19** Pythagoras, for his part, spoke of a relationship among all things and of an interchange of minds passing from one form to another. If you believe him, no soul ever dies, or even ceases its activity except for the brief instant when it transfers to another body. Eventually, we will find out how many ages must pass, how many times it must travel from one lodging to the next before it returns into a human being. In the meantime, Pythagoras instilled in humankind a fear of wrongdoing—more specifically, of parricide. For if some spirit related to them happened to be dwelling in a given body, they might, without realizing it, assault the soul of their parent with the knife or with their teeth. **20** After Sotion had explained all this, filling it out with his own arguments, he added,

> Do you not believe that souls are allotted to one body after another, and that what we call death is really transmigration? Do you not believe that in these cattle, these wild animals or sea creatures, there lives a mind that was once that of a human? Do you not believe that things in this world do not perish, but only change their location—that not only do the heavenly bodies revolve in definite orbits, but animate creatures also cycle through the ages, their minds coming round to where they started? Great men have believed these things. **21** Therefore refrain from judgment, if you will, but be open-minded about it. If these things are true, then abstaining from animal foods means not harming anyone; if they are false, it is a matter of economy. How much of a loss is it for you to refrain from savagery?° I am only depriving you of the food of lions and of vultures.

22 Inspired by these words, I began to abstain from animal foods, and a year later the habit was both easy and pleasant for me. I thought my mind was livelier, and even today I suspect it might have been. Would you like to know why I gave it up? The time when I was a young man was in the early years of Tiberius's principate. Religions of foreign origin were then being eliminated, and abstinence from animal foods was considered proof of adherence. So at the request of my father (who did not fear opprobrium but had a hatred of philosophy), I returned to my former habits; he had no trouble, really, in persuading me to dine in better style. **23** Attalus used to recommend a mattress that would not yield to the body. I use such a mattress even in my old age, the kind that does not hold an imprint.

My purpose in telling you all this has been to show how excited brand-new recruits can become about every form of good behavior when they have someone to exhort and encourage them. But there is also some wrongdoing, both on the part of instructors, when they teach us how to argue a point and not how to live, and on the part of students, when their purpose in attending is not to improve their minds but to develop their rhetorical talent. Hence what used to be philosophy has now become mere philology.

24 It matters a great deal what one's purpose is in approaching any field of study. When the prospective literary scholar examines his copy of Virgil, and reads that exceptional line,

time flies on irretrievable,*

his thought is not "We must take care—if we do not make haste, we will be left behind—the fleeting moment hurries on, and hurries us—heedlessly are we swept along—we are always procrastinating—opportunity hurtles by and still we make delays." No, he reads it just so that he can observe that every time Virgil speaks about the rapid movement of time, he uses the word "flies" (*fugit*), as follows:

The best times of our lives, poor mortal creatures,
fly first away, and in their place come illness
and sad old age and suffering and pain,
until hard pitiless death takes us away.*

25 The person who looks to philosophy takes these same lines and applies them as he ought. "The reason Virgil never says that time 'passes,' but always that it 'flies,' is that flying is the quickest kind of movement, and his point is that the best people are the first to be taken away. Why not quicken our own steps to match the pace of that swiftest of all runners?" Our better days are hastening on; worse days will follow. **26** Our life is like a storage jar: the purest of its contents are decanted first; all the sediment and turbid matter sink to the bottom. Are we going to let the best of our lives be siphoned off for others, and keep only the dregs for ourselves? Keep these lines always in mind; let them be to you as an oracular response:

> The best times of our lives, poor mortal creatures,
> fly first away.

27 Why the best? Because what remains is uncertain. Why the best? Because when we are young, we are able to learn, since our minds are still flexible and can be turned toward better things; because this is the time of life that is suited to strenuous effort, to exercising the mind with study and the body with work. What remains is slower, wearier, nearer to the end. Let us therefore forget all our diversions and aim for this one thing with all our mind, lest we come too late to understand the rapidity of fleeting time, which we cannot detain. Let us be pleased with each new day as the best that life will give us, and so add it to our store. Life is flying away; we must catch it."

28 The one who reads with the eye of a literary scholar does not consider why the best times of our lives come first—that in their place comes illness, that old age looms over us even while we are still intent on our youth. Instead, he says that Virgil always uses the words "illness" and "old age" together. So he does, and with good reason! For old age is an illness that has no cure. **29** "Moreover," he says, "Virgil employs a fixed epithet for old age: he calls it 'sad':

> and in their place come illness
and sad old age . . .

Elsewhere he says,

> where wan diseases dwell and grim old age."*

Each person finds in the same material reflections suited to his own pursuits. And no wonder: in one and the same meadow the ox looks for grass, the dog for a hare, and the stork for a lizard. **30** When three people, one an antiquarian, one a literary scholar, and one a philosopher, pick up Cicero's treatise *On the Republic*, each directs his attention to something different. The philosopher is amazed that so many points could have been made against justice.* The antiquarian, reading the same passage, takes note of the fact that there were two Roman kings, one of whom had no father and the other no mother. For there are no clear reports about Servius's mother, and Ancus is not said to have had a father but only to have been the grandson of Numa.* **31** He remarks also that the official whom we call a "dictator" was in ancient times called "master of the populace." That information can be found today in the augurs' record book, and there is further evidence in the fact that the dictator's appointee is called "master of horse." He points out, furthermore, that Romulus died during an eclipse of the sun, and that there was such a thing as the appeal to the people even during the monarchy. This is also in the pontifical record, and Fenestella and a few others° share this view.* **32** When the literary scholar expounds these same scrolls, the first thing he puts into his commentary is the fact that Cicero uses the word *reapse* for *re ipsa* ("in reality"), and likewise *sepse* for *se ipse* ("himself"). Then he moves on to changes in linguistic usage over time. For instance, Cicero writes, "Since his interruption has called us back from the very lime line," that is, the finish line. What we now call the chalk line (*creta*) at the races, the old writers called a lime line (*calx*). **33** Then he collects various lines of Ennius, especially the ones about Scipio Africanus,

> whom neither citizen nor foe
> could ever repay the price of his assistance.*

From these lines, he concludes that in the old writers the word "assistance" (*ops*) meant not just "aid" but also "endeavor." For Ennius's point is that no one, neither citizen nor foe, could ever repay Scipio the price of his endeavor. **34** Next, he congratulates himself for finding out the source of Virgil's line,

> Above whom heaven's massive portal thunders.*

He says that Ennius stole the line from Homer, and Virgil took it from Ennius; for Cicero, in the same work *On the Republic*, quotes this couplet of Ennius:

> If it be right for anyone to mount the skies,
> for me alone does heaven's great portal open.

35 But I don't mean to turn into an antiquarian or literary scholar on my own account. My business is elsewhere. I am only advising that when we read and listen to the philosophers, we should direct our attention toward our goal, which is happiness. We should not be trying to track down archaic words, neologisms, peculiar metaphors, and figures of speech, but to seek out beneficial precepts and courageous and inspiring utterances that will soon find application in our lives. Let us learn them so thoroughly that words turn into actions.

36 But of all those who have done humankind a bad turn, the worst are those who teach philosophy for money, as if it were some tradesman's craft, and then live their lives in a manner very different from their precepts. For, being prime examples of the very faults they criticize in others, they provide a fine demonstration of how useless their teaching is. 37 Such instruction cannot do me any good, any more than a helmsman who is prone to seasickness during a storm. When the waves are coming fast and a hand is needed to grip the tiller, to wrestle with the sea itself, to take down the sail in a high wind, what is the use of a helmsman who is panicking and throwing up? And life is beset by worse storms than any ship. I don't need someone to talk at me; I need someone to steer!

38 Everything they say, all their fine speeches before crowds of listeners, are taken over from someone else. The words are those of Plato, or of Zeno, or of Chrysippus or Posidonius or one of the many other great names in philosophy. How can they prove that those ideas are their own? I'll tell you: they must practice what they preach.

39 Since I have finished saying what I wanted to convey to you, I shall now comply with your request. I'll put your inquiry into a fresh letter so that you won't be fatigued when taking up a thorny subject that needs a thoughtful and attentive hearing.

Farewell.

A difficult pupil

From Seneca to Lucilius
Greetings

---

1 I really do want your friend to be fashioned according to your desire, and I have made a start, but he proves to be a hard case.* No, it's worse than that: he is a very soft case, a man depraved by a bad habit that has been long established.

2 Let me give you an analogy drawn from a hobby of mine.* It is not every vine that takes a graft: if it is old and gnarled, or weak and spindly, it either will not accept the scion or will not nourish it; it won't be joined with it and take on its quality and nature. For that reason, we usually make the initial cut above the soil so that if the vine doesn't respond, we can try again, grafting a second time below the soil.

3 This fellow you are writing to me about with all these instructions has no strength in him; he has indulged his faults. He is at one and the same time both enervated and hardened: he can neither accept reasoning nor provide it with nourishment. "But he himself wants this." Don't believe it. I don't mean that he is lying to you: he thinks that he wants it. He is fed up with self-indulgence; soon he will be reconciled to it again.

4 "But he says he is tired of his way of life." No denying that; who isn't? People love their faults and hate them at the same time. So let's reserve judgment about him until he supplies us with proof that he and self-indulgence have become enemies. Right now, it is just that they are not getting along.

Farewell.

Is virtue an animate creature?

From Seneca to Lucilius
Greetings

---

1 You want me to send you my opinion on the question our school has bandied about, as to whether justice, courage, prudence, and the other virtues are animate creatures.* Minutiae of this kind, dearest Lucilius, have made people think that we train our minds on trivialities and waste our free time on discussions that will do us no good. I will comply with your request and expound our school's doctrine, but I warn you that I am of a different opinion. My view is that some topics are only right for people who go in for Greek shoes and cloaks.

So I will tell you what arguments moved our predecessors, or rather, what arguments they themselves set in motion:

2 The mind is an animate creature; that is uncontroversial, since the mind makes us animate creatures and the expression "animate creatures" (*animalia*) is derived from it.*

But virtue is just the mind disposed in a certain way.*

Therefore virtue is an animate creature.

Again:

Virtue does something.

But nothing can be done without an impulse.

So, since it has an impulse, and only an animate creature has an impulse, virtue is an animate creature.

3 One might say, "If virtue is an animate creature, virtue itself possesses virtue." Why shouldn't it possess itself? In the way that the wise person does everything by means of virtue, so virtue acts by means of itself.

"In that case, all crafts are animate creatures, and likewise everything we consider and have in our minds. It follows that many thousands of animate creatures are dwelling in the narrow confines of our breast, and that each of us individuals is a multitude of animate creatures or possesses such a multitude." Do you wonder how to respond to this challenge? Although each one of these will be an animate creature, they will not be a multitude of animate creatures. How so? I will tell you, if you give me your close and undivided attention.

4 Individual animate creatures must have individual substances. The animate creatures you are speaking of have only one mind each; therefore it is only possible for each of them to be one animate creature, not multiple animate creatures. I myself am both an animate creature and a human being, yet you will not say that there are two of us. **5** Why not? Because the two would have to be separate. I mean that the one would have to be disjoined from the other, to constitute two. Anything that is multiple in a single entity falls under a single nature. Hence it is single. My mind is an animate creature, and so am I, but we are not two. Why not? Because my mind is a part of me. Something will only be counted by itself when it stands on its own. As long as it is a component of something else, it cannot be regarded as a different thing. Why not? Because that which is a different thing must be a thing in its own right, having its own distinctive property and being complete in itself.*

6 I warned you that I myself have a different opinion. If this doctrine is accepted, not only the virtues will be animate creatures but their opposing vices will be too, and also the emotions like anger, fear, grief, and mistrust. The matter will go on and on. All opinions and all thoughts will be animate creatures. That is completely unacceptable. Not everything done by a human being is itself a human being. **7** "What is justice?" one asks. The mind disposed in a certain way. "So if the mind is an animate creature, justice is as well?" Not at all. Justice is a condition of the mind, a particular capacity. One and the same mind undergoes a variety of configurations, but it is not a different animate creature every time it does something different. Neither is everything done by the mind an animate creature.

8 If justice is an animate creature, and likewise courage and the other virtues, do they cease to be animate creatures from time to time and begin again, or are they always so? Virtues cannot come to an end. In that case many, or rather innumerable, animate creatures are circulating in this one mind.

9 One might say, "They are not many, because they are connected to a single thing, by virtue of being the parts and the components of a single thing." So we are giving our mind a shape like that of the hydra, any one of whose heads fights just by itself and causes harm just by itself. Yet not one of those heads is an animate creature; it is the head of an animate creature, while the hydra itself is a single animate creature. No one has said that the lion or the dragon in a Chimaera is an animate creature. These are its parts, and parts are not animate creatures.

10 Why do you deduce that justice is an animate creature? "It does something; that is, it benefits; anything that acts and benefits has an impulse; and what has an impulse is an animate creature." This is true if it has its own impulse, but in the case of justice the impulse belongs to the mind.

11 Every animate creature retains its original identity until it dies. A human being is a human being until he dies, a horse is a horse, and a dog is a dog. They cannot turn into something else. Suppose that justice—that is, the mind disposed in a certain way—is an animate creature. If we believe that, then courage is an animate creature because it is the mind disposed in a certain way. What mind? The mind that just now was justice? That mind is housed in the earlier animate creature; it cannot cross over into a different one. It must persist in the animate creature where it began its existence.

12 Besides, a single mind cannot belong to two animate creatures, much less a larger number. If justice, courage, self-control, and the other virtues are animate creatures, how will they have a single mind? They must each have minds of their own; otherwise they are not animate creatures. **13** A plurality of animate creatures cannot have a single body. This our opponents themselves admit. What is the body of justice? "The mind." And what is the body of courage? "The same mind." Yet two animate creatures cannot have a single body. **14** "But that same mind clothes itself in the garb of justice, of courage, of self-control." That's how it would work if the mind were not courage at the time it is justice, and were not self-control at the time it is courage. But in fact all the virtues are present at the same time. How, then, will the individual virtues be animate creatures, seeing that a mind is single and cannot make more than a single animate creature?*

15 Finally, no animate creature is a part of another animate creature; but justice is a part of the mind; therefore it is not an animate creature.

I think I am wasting effort on something obvious, something to be annoyed about rather than to debate. No animate creature is a part of something else. Look around at the bodies of everything. Not one of them is without its characteristic color, shape, and size. **16** There are many reasons for marveling at the divine creator's intellect, and they include, in my opinion, the fact that in the vast supply of things nothing ever turns out to be just the same. Even things that seem alike are different when you compare them. The creator has made numerous kinds of leaves, each one with its own distinctive property—numerous animate creatures, yet not one of them is exactly the same size as another, or without at least some difference. The creator imposed a requirement on himself that things that were different should be dissimilar and unequal. The virtues, as you Stoics say, are equal. Therefore they are not animate creatures.

17 No animate creature fails to do things by itself; yet virtue does nothing by itself but acts only in conjunction with a human being. All animate creatures are either rational, like human beings, or nonrational, like beasts and cattle; virtues are certainly rational, but they are neither human nor divine; therefore they are not animate creatures.

18 No animate creature endowed with reason does anything unless, first, it has been prompted by the impression of some particular thing; next, it has entertained an impulse; and finally, assent has confirmed this impulse. Let me tell you what assent is. "It is fitting for me to walk": I walk only after I have told myself this and have approved my judgment. "It is fitting for me to sit": then only do I sit.* This assent is not found in virtue. **19** Imagine that it is prudence: how will prudence assent to the judgment "It is fitting for me to walk"? This is not within its nature. Prudence looks to the interests of the thing it belongs to, not to itself, since it is incapable of walking or sitting. Therefore prudence does not possess assent, and what does not possess assent is not an animate creature endowed with reason.

If virtue is an animate creature, it is something rational; but it is not something rational; therefore it is not an animate creature. **20** If virtue is an animate creature and every good is virtue, every good is an animate creature. Our school grants this. Saving one's father is a good, prudently stating one's opinion in the Senate is a good, and so too is justly rendering judgment. Therefore saving one's father is an animate creature, and likewise prudently stating one's opinion. The point will go° so far that you cannot stop laughing. Prudently holding your tongue is a good, <and so too is dining well>°; therefore holding your tongue and dining are animate creatures. **21** Indeed, I will not stop playing around and amusing myself with these pedantic absurdities. If justice and courage are animate creatures, they are certainly earthly. Every earthly animate creature gets sick, and hungry, and thirsty. Therefore justice gets sick, courage gets hungry, and mercy gets thirsty.

22 What next? Won't I ask them what shape these animate creatures have? Is it a human being's or a horse's or a wild beast's? If they give them a round shape like that of a god, I will ask whether greed, luxury, and madness are equally round. For they too are animate creatures.* If they make them round too, I will even ask whether prudent walking is an animate creature. They have to grant that, and go on to say that walking is an animate creature—and in fact a round one.

23 You shouldn't think that I am the first member of our school to extemporize and have my own opinion. Cleanthes and Chrysippus did not agree about what walking is. Cleanthes says that it is the vital breath stretching from the directive faculty all the way to the feet, whereas Chrysippus says that it is the directive faculty itself.* Why, then, following the example of Chrysippus, shouldn't each man assert his own freedom and make fun of these animate creatures that are so numerous that the world itself cannot contain them?

24 The opponent says, "The virtues are not a multitude of animate creatures, and yet they are animate creatures. Just as someone can be both a poet and an orator while remaining a single person, so these virtues are animate creatures but not a multitude of animate creatures. One and the same mind is also a just mind, and a sensible mind, a brave mind, being disposed in a certain way relative to each of the virtues." **25** <The controversy is>° settled; we are in agreement. For I too grant for the moment that the mind is an animate creature, deferring my final judgment on the matter to a later date. However, I deny that the mind's actions are animate creatures. Otherwise all words will be animate creatures, and so will all lines of verse. For if prudent speech is a good, and every good is an animate creature, speech is an animate creature. A prudent line of verse is a good, and every good is an animate creature, therefore a line of verse is an animate creature. In that case, "Arms and the man I sing" is an animate creature—but they cannot call it a round one, since it has six feet!*

26 "For heaven's sake!" you say. "What a web you are weaving at this point!" I burst out laughing when I envision that solecisms, barbarisms, and syllogisms are animate creatures, and like a painter, I give them suitable faces. Is this what we are discussing with bent brow and knotted forehead? Can I not quote Caecilius* and say, "What solemn idiocy!" It's simply ludicrous. So let's instead turn to something that is useful and salutary for us, and ask how we can arrive at the virtues and what route will bring us to them.

27 Don't teach me whether courage is an animate creature but that no animate creature is happy without courage, that is, unless it has acquired the strength to resist chance occurrences, and by pondering every contingency has mastered them before they happen. What is courage? It is the impregnable fortification for human weakness. By encircling himself with it, a person can calmly endure throughout this life's siege, because he uses his own strength and his own weapons. **28** At this point, I want to tell you the view of our Stoic philosopher Posidonius:

> You should never think that the weapons of fortune will make you safe: fight with your own! Fortune does not arm us against fortune itself. Hence men who are equipped to resist the enemy are unarmed to resist fortune.*

29 Alexander, it's true, destroyed and routed the Persians, the Hyrcanians, the Indians, and all the nations stretching from east to west; but he himself lay in darkness after killing one friend and again after losing another, alternately grieving over his crime and his loss. The conqueror of so many kings and peoples was felled by anger and gloom. He endeavored to control everything except his passions.*

30 How terribly those people go astray who long to extend their imperial authority beyond the seas and deem themselves supremely fortunate if they hold many provinces with their armies and add new ones to the old, ignorant of that realm which is of equal greatness to the divine—self-mastery, the greatest command of all. **31** Teach° me the sanctity of the justice that looks to another's good, seeking nothing for itself except opportunities to be active. May it have nothing in common with self-seeking and reputation, but be content with itself!

Above all else, each person should convince himself of the following principle: "I should be just without reward." No, that is too little: he should persuade himself to enjoy spending unstintingly on this most lovely virtue. All his thoughts should be as distant as possible from personal advantages. You should not look around for the reward from a just action: there is a greater reward in simply doing the just thing.

32 Keep concentrating on what I told you a while ago, that the number of people who are familiar with your fair-mindedness is completely irrelevant. People who want their virtue to be advertised are working for renown rather than virtue. Aren't you willing to be just without renown? In fact, of course, you will often have to combine being just with being disgraced. And then if you are wise, you should take delight in the bad reputation you have won by your good behavior.

Farewell.

LETTER 116

The Stoic view of emotion

From Seneca to Lucilius
Greetings

1 The question has often been raised whether it is better to have moderate emotions or none at all. Philosophers of our school exclude them altogether, whereas the Peripatetics restrain them. I myself don't see how it can be healthy or useful to have even a moderate amount of an illness.*

Don't be afraid, I am not going to rob you of anything that you don't want to be refused. I will be accommodating and compliant to your own tendencies and to the things you regard as life's necessities, utilities, and joys; I will merely remove what's faulty. After I have banned desire, I will allow for wanting,* so that you will do the same things without anxiety and with firmer resolve, and will experience even your pleasures with greater intensity. Why shouldn't pleasures come your way even more easily if you are their master rather than their slave?

2 You respond, "It's natural for me to suffer torment at the loss of a friend. Allow my justified tears the right to fall! It's natural to be affected by people's opinions and to be saddened when they are negative. Why won't you let me have such an honorable fear of being badly thought of?" No fault lacks its advocate. At the start they are all bashful and persuadable, but then they grow and grow. You won't succeed in stopping them once you allow them to begin. 3 All emotions are feeble at first; then they arouse themselves and gather strength as they advance. It's easier to refuse them entry than to drive them out.

No one is denying that all emotions stem from a source that is, in a sense, natural. Nature has endowed us with a concern for ourselves; but once we indulge this concern excessively, it becomes a fault. Nature infused the necessities of life with pleasure, not so that we would pursue pleasure, but so that the supervening pleasure would make what is indispensable more welcome to us.* If the pleasure is pursued for its own sake, it becomes self-indulgence. Let us, then, resist emotions as soon as they start to come in, since, as I said, it's easier to refuse them admission than to get them to leave.

4 I hear you say, "Let me grieve to some extent, and feel apprehension to some extent." But this "some extent" of yours goes on and on, and it refuses to stop when you want it to. The wise person can safely restrain himself without getting upset, and can put a halt to his tears and pleasures when he wants to. We others have difficulty in withdrawing, and so it's best for us

not to go on at all. **5** I think Panaetius gave a neat response to the youth who asked whether the wise man would fall in love. "As regards the wise man," he said, "we shall see; but as for you and me, who are a long way from achieving wisdom, we had better refrain so as to avoid a condition that is frantic, out of control, enslaved to another, and lacking in self-worth. If our advances are accepted, we are excited by the other person's favor; if not, we are set on fire by the disdain. An easy love affair is as harmful as one fraught with difficulty; we are drawn in by ease, and we struggle against difficulty. Knowing our weakness, then, we do better to stay calm. Let us not entrust our feeble disposition to wine or beauty or flattery or any other temptation."*

6 My point is that Panaetius's response to the question about love applies to all emotions. Let's stay off the slippery ground as far as possible, since it's hard for us to stand firm even on dry land. **7** You will confront me on this issue with the standard objection to the Stoics: "Your promises are too great; your demands are too exacting. We are merely little folk; we can't deny ourselves everything. We are going to feel sorrow, but just a bit; we are going to long for things, but in moderation; we shall get angry, but not implacably so." **8** Do you know why we aren't capable of such things? We don't believe that we have that capability.

In fact, though, there's something else involved: our love for our own faults. We defend them and we would rather make excuses for them than shake them off. Human nature has been endowed with sufficient strength if only we use it. We have only to assemble our resources and get them all to fight on our behalf rather than against us. Inability is just an excuse; the real reason is unwillingness.

Farewell.

Self-awareness in animate creatures

From Seneca to Lucilius
Greetings

---

1 You will sue me, I'm sure, when I set today's little problem before you, the one we have been stuck on for long enough already. You're going to shout out again: "What's this got to do with ethics?"* Start shouting; but meanwhile, let me first find you some other opponents to sue, namely, Posidonius and Archedemus: it's these men who will go to court.* Next, let me say that what pertains to ethics does not necessarily make for ethical conduct. **2** One study pertains to the nutrition of human beings, others to our physical training, our clothing, our learning, or our entertainment: all of them are concerned with human beings, even if not all of them make people better. As for our moral character, there are different ways of influencing it. Some studies correct and regulate it, while others investigate its nature and origin. **3** When I ask why nature produced human beings and why it made them superior to other animals, do you conclude that I have abandoned the field of ethics? That would be incorrect. I mean, how will you know what conduct should be adopted unless you have discovered what is best for a human being and have studied human nature? You will not understand what you should do and what you should avoid until you have learned what you owe to your own nature.

4 "I want," you say, "to learn how to reduce my desires and my fears. Shake me out of my superstition. Teach me that so-called happiness is a trivial and empty thing, which very easily takes on the additional syllable and becomes *un*happiness." I will satisfy your desire: I will encourage your virtues and flog your vices. Even if someone finds me excessive and intemperate in this role, I will not cease to persecute wickedness, to curb the fiercest passions, to check the advance of pleasures that turn into pain, and to protest against our prayers. I mean it; for our prayers are for the very things that are worst for us, and when they are gratified we get everything for which we need consolation.*

5 Meanwhile, allow me to thrash out topics that seem a bit more distant from our present concern. We were discussing whether all animals have a perception of their own constitution. The principal evidence that they do is how suitably and adroitly they move their limbs, just as though they were trained to do so. No creature lacks agility in managing its own parts. A skilled craftsman handles his tools with ease; a navigator knows how to steer his ship; a portrait painter is very quick in selecting from his copious supply of colors and moves with ready eye and hand between his palette and his work of art. An animal is equally agile in all the use it makes of itself. 6 We often admire skillful pantomime dancers, because their hands are ready to convey all the meaning of the subject matter and its emotions, and their gestures keep up with the rapidity of the spoken word.* What art gives to artists, nature gives to animals. Not one of them has difficulty in handling its limbs; not one falters in making use of itself. They do this from the moment they come into the world—the knowledge is with them from the beginning. They are born trained.

7 One might say, "The reason why animals are adept at moving their limbs is that they would feel pain if they moved

them in any other way. Thus it is under compulsion that they do as people of your school say; and what causes them to move in the right way is fear, not volition." This is wrong. Things that are driven by necessity are slow; agility is the mark of spontaneous movement. Indeed, instead of being compelled to move by fear of pain, they actually strive for their natural movement even when pain hinders them. **8** Consider a baby that would like to stand up and is just getting used to supporting itself: as soon as it begins to test its strength, it falls down; but it keeps getting up again, crying all the time, until it has painfully trained itself to do what its nature demands. When certain animals with hard shells are turned upside down, they keep twisting and digging with their feet and moving sideways until they get back into their proper position. An inverted tortoise feels no pain, but it is disturbed by missing its natural condition and keeps rocking itself until it stands on its feet. **9** Thus all animals have a perception of their own constitution, and this explains why they are so dexterous in managing their limbs. Indeed, this is our best evidence that they are born with this awareness: no animal is unskilled in making use of itself.

10 "According to the members of your school," says the opponent, "constitution is 'the mind's directive faculty disposed in a certain way relative to the body.'* How could a baby understand something so intricate and refined, which even you yourselves are scarcely capable of describing? All animals would have to be born logicians in order to understand a definition that is obscure to the majority of Romans." **11** That objection would be valid if I said that animals understood the definition of constitution, as distinct from their constitution as such. It is easier to understand nature than it is to describe it. So the baby does not know what constitution is, but it does know its own constitution. It does not know what an animal is, but it perceives that it is an animal.

12 Furthermore, its understanding of its own constitution is vague, rudimentary, and unclear. We, likewise, know that we have a mind and yet do not know what the mind is, where it is located, what it is like, or where it comes from. We are aware of our mind, even though we do not know its nature and location. Such is the case with all animals' awareness of their own constitution. Animals necessarily have a perception of that through which they also perceive other things; they necessarily perceive that which they obey, that by which they are governed. 13 Every one of us understands that there is something that activates one's impulses, but we do not know what it is. One knows that one has a motivating principle, but one does not know what it is or where it comes from. In the same way, even babies and animals have a perception of their directive part, but that perception is not properly clear and distinct.

14 "You say that every animal from the outset is attached to its own constitution, but also that the human constitution is a rational one. Therefore the human being is attached to itself not as an animate creature but as a rational creature, for the human being is dear to itself by virtue of that part that makes it human. How, then, can a baby be attached to a rational constitution when it is not yet rational?"

15 Each stage of life has its own constitution: one for the baby, another for the child, another for the young person, and another for the mature. Each is attached to the constitution it is in. A baby has no teeth; it is attached to this, its present constitution. The teeth emerge; it is attached to this constitution. For even a blade of wheat, which will eventually yield a crop, has one constitution when it is young and scarcely taller than

the furrow, another when it has gained strength and stands on a stalk which, though soft, can bear its weight, and yet another when it grows golden and the grain hardens in the ear, forecasting harvest time. Whatever constitution the plant arrives at, it retains and adapts to. **16** The stages of life are different—infancy, childhood, youth, and maturity. Yet I, who have been a baby, a boy, and a youth, remain the same person. So, although each thing's constitution changes, it is attached to its constitution in the same way. My natural attachment is not to the boy or the youth or the mature man but to myself. Therefore a baby is attached to its own constitution, the one it has as a baby, and not to the one it will have as a youth. Even though it will later mature into a greater condition, that does not imply that the condition in which it is born is not also in accordance with nature.

17 An animal is attached first to its very self; for there must be something to which everything else may be referred. I seek pleasure. For whom? For myself. So I am looking after myself. I try to avoid pain. For whom? For myself. So I am looking after myself. If I do everything for the sake of looking after myself, my concern for myself is prior to everything else. This concern is present in all animals; it is not grafted onto them but innate. **18** Nature raises its own offspring and does not reject them. And because the most reliable guardian is the closest, each individual has been entrusted to itself. Hence, as I have said in earlier letters,* even young animals, when just born or hatched, know at once by themselves what is harmful and avoid things that could cause their death. They even display fearful reactions at the shadow of things flying overhead, vulnerable as they are to birds of prey. No animal enters life without fear of death.

19 "How can an animal at birth have understanding of what either promotes its safety or could cause its death?" First of all, our question is whether it can understand these things, not how it does so. That animals have this understanding is evident from the fact that if they were now to gain such understanding, they would not do anything beyond what they do already. Why is it that a hen does not shun a peacock or a goose, but flees a hawk, which is much smaller than those birds and not even something it is acquainted with? Why are chickens afraid of a weasel but not of a dog? It is evident that they have within them a knowledge, not derived from experience, of what will injure them; for they avoid something before they can have experience of it. **20** Secondly, to prevent you from thinking that this happens by chance, they do not fear things other than those that they should, and they never forget this precaution and attentiveness. They are consistent in their avoidance of danger. In addition, they do not become more timorous in the course of their lives. This shows that they arrive at this condition not by experience but as a result of a natural instinct toward self-preservation. What experience teaches is late in coming and unevenly distributed; everything that nature transmits is immediate and consistent in all cases.

21 If, however, you press me, I will tell you how every animal cannot help but understand what is dangerous. It is aware that it consists of flesh; and so it is aware of what can cut flesh or burn or crush flesh, and of which animals are equipped with the means of doing it harm. It acquires an impression of these as dangerous and inimical. These tendencies are interconnected: at the same time as each animal is attached to its own preservation, it both seeks out what will be beneficial and avoids what will be harmful. Impulses toward useful things are natural, aversions to their opposites are also natural.

Whatever nature prescribes takes place without any reflection to prompt it, without any premeditation. **22** Don't you see how clever bees are in constructing their cells, how harmonious in performing their respective tasks? Don't you see how a spider's web is beyond human capacity to imitate, and what a task it is to arrange the threads, some of them in straight lines as support, with others running in a circle at increasing intervals, so that the smaller creatures the web is made to catch may be entangled and held as in a net? **23** This art is innate, not learned. That is why no animal has more learning than another. You will see that spiders' webs are all the same, and that in a hive all the angles of a honeycomb are equal. Whatever training imparts is variable and uneven; capacities that come from nature are distributed equally.

Nature has conferred nothing beyond the instinct to preserve oneself and a facility in doing so, which is why animals begin to learn at the moment they begin to live. **24** And it is not surprising that they are born with exactly the abilities without which their birth would be fruitless. This is the first equipment nature conferred on them for their continuing existence—attachment to self and love of self. They would not have the power to survive unless they desired to do so. This desire just by itself was not enough to help them, but without it nothing else would have done so. In no animal will you find a low regard for self, or even a neglect of self. Mute creatures, though dull-witted in other respects, are clever at living. You will see that creatures which are useless to others are not deficient when it comes to themselves.

Farewell.

Resisting external influences

From Seneca to Lucilius
Greetings

---

1 Late at night I have reached my Alban villa,* exhausted from a journey that was uncomfortable rather than long. I find nothing in readiness except myself. So I have settled my weary self down now in my study, and get this much good from the fact that my cook and baker are delayed. In fact, this is the very thing I am discussing with myself, how nothing is serious if one takes it lightly, nothing needs to be annoying, provided that one doesn't add one's own annoyance to it. **2** My baker has no bread, but my manager has some, and so do my head slave and my tenants. "Bad bread," you say. But wait! It will become good. Hunger will soon make it into a soft loaf of the finest flour. That is why one ought not to eat before hunger gives the command. I will delay my meal, then, until I have good bread again or else until I don't mind having bread that is bad.

3 It is essential to get accustomed to lean fare. Difficulties of time and place confront even those who are wealthy and well equipped for pleasure,° thwarting their intentions. No one can have everything he wants. What a person can do is give up wanting what he doesn't have and use cheerfully the things that are available. A big part of independence is a well-disciplined stomach, one that can put up with rough treatment. **4** It's beyond all estimates how much pleasure I get from the fact that my weariness is at peace with itself. I am not looking for a massage or a bath, just the healing effects of time. Rest removes the accretions of toil. The coming dinner, whatever it is, will be more delightful than an inaugural feast.* **5** In short,° I have instantly put my mind to a sort of test, and a particularly straightforward and accurate test at that. For when the mind has prepared itself and made a resolution to be patient, we have no clear indication of its true resolve. The most reliable proofs are those that come on the spur of the moment, if the mind views troubles not only dispassionately but serenely, without resentment and without complaint, and if it makes up for whatever is missing by not wishing for it, and reflects that while something may be lacking in its routine, in itself it lacks nothing.

6 With many things, we only realize how superfluous they are when they begin to run short. We were using them not because we had to but because they were available. How many things we acquire only because other people have bought them or because they are in other people's homes! Many of our problems stem from the fact that we live by conforming to other people's standards, following fashion instead of taking reason as our guide. If only a few people did something, we would refuse to copy them; yet as soon as more people take up the practice, we adopt it as well, as if mere frequency somehow made it more honorable. Once a misconception becomes widespread, we let it stand in for rectitude.

7 Nowadays everyone travels with an escort of Numidian horse and a troop of runners leading the way. It is a disgrace to have no attendants to push oncoming travelers off the road, to indicate the coming of a dignitary by a great cloud of dust. Everyone nowadays has a mule train to carry their collection of crystal and agate cups and fine-wrought silver vessels. It is a disgrace to give the impression that the sum total of your baggage is stuff that could be jostled along without breaking.

Everyone has a retinue of pages who slather their faces with lotion when they travel so that the sun or the cold won't harm their tender skin. It is a disgrace to have youthful attendants with healthy skin who need no pharmaceutical products!

8 We should avoid conversation with all these people. They are the sort who pass on their faults and trade them with one another. We used to think it was terrible when people would show off in words; today, though, there are people who make a show of their faults. Conversation with them does a lot of harm. For even if it has no immediate effect, it leaves seeds in the mind; it stays with us even after we have left their company, a bad effect that will rise up again later on. **9** After listening to a concert, people's ears are still full of the melody and of the sweet singing that restricts their ability to think and makes them unable to focus on serious matters. In the same way, the talk of flatterers and those who encourage vice lingers long after it is heard. It is not easy to shake the mind free from a sweet sound. It keeps on; it persists; it comes back at intervals. For this reason, our ears need to be closed to harmful voices from the outset. Once those voices have made a start and gained admission, they are all the more audacious.

10 Next, we come among such sayings as the following:*

"Virtue, philosophy, and justice are just the noise of meaningless words! The only happiness is to do well in life. Eating, drinking, spending one's fortune: this is living, this is remembering that one is mortal. The days flow by; life moves on irretrievable. What are we waiting for? What's the good of cultivating philosophy? We can't have pleasure when we are old, so why impose austerity on our life now, when we are still capable and still want things? So° get ahead of death, and let everything that it will steal from you be spent now on yourself.° You don't have a girlfriend, and neither do you have a catamite to make your girlfriend jealous. You never get drunk, and your dinners give the impression that you are waiting for your father to approve your daily expenses. This is not living, it's attending to someone else's life! **11** It is totally crazy to deny yourself everything, devoting your attention to property that will just go to your heir. That way, the size of your estate will turn your friend into an enemy: the greater his inheritance, the more he will rejoice at your death. As for those prigs, those stern critics of other people's lives and enemies of their own, who like to lecture the public—don't give them a second thought; don't hesitate to prefer a good life to a good name."

12 Voices like these are as much to be shunned as those that Ulysses refused to pass until he was tied to the mast.* They have the same power: they alienate you from your country, your parents, your friends, and your virtues, and lure you into a life of shame with promises that make you unhappy, even if they were not shameful.° How much better it is to follow a straight path and let it finally guide you to the point where only what is honorable gives you pleasure!

13 We shall be able to reach that point if we understand that there are two kinds of things that can either entice or repel us. The enticing ones are wealth, pleasures, beauty, ambition, and everything else that is seductive and pleasing. We are repelled by hard physical work, death, pain, public disapproval, and an austere diet. Hence we should train ourselves neither to fear the latter things nor to desire the former. We should contend against our inclinations, resisting the attractive things and advancing against those that assail us.*

14 Don't you notice how much people's posture differs when they are climbing a hill from when they are descending? While going down they lean their bodies back, but when climbing they lean forward. It is a deliberate error, when descending, to let your weight go forward, and similarly, to let it go backward when ascending. We descend into pleasures, Lucilius, but to face difficulties and hardships we have to climb. In the latter case, we should push our bodies forward, but in the former case we should hold them back.

15 Do you suppose that my point right now is that the only people who are dangerous to our ears are those who praise pleasure and who alarm us with the thought of pain, a thing that is fearsome enough on its own? No, I think we are also harmed by those who, under the guise of the Stoic school, urge us into vices. For instance, they insist that only a person who is wise and highly educated is a lover.*

> "The wise man is the only one with expertise in this area. Likewise, he has the greatest skill at engaging in symposia and dinner parties. Let us investigate the following question: up to what age should young men be objects of love?"

16 Consigning these points to Greek custom, we should lend our ears rather to the following:

> "No one is good by accident; virtue has to be learned. Pleasure is a poor and pathetic thing, of no value. Even speechless animals have a share in pleasure; the smallest and most trivial species of animal fly after it. Glory is an empty thing, more fleeting and volatile than air. Poverty is only a prob-

lem for those who don't accept it. Death is no evil. What is it, then, you ask? It is the one right that belongs in equal measure to all humankind. Superstition is a crazy mistake. It fears those who should be loved and trespasses against those it worships. If you are going to malign the gods, you might as well deny that they exist."

17 These are the lessons you need to learn or, rather, take to heart. Philosophy should not supply excuses for vice. The sick have no hope of healing when their doctor recommends intemperance.

Farewell.

LETTER 124

The criterion for the human good

From Seneca to Lucilius
Greetings

---

1 I can convey the wisdom of the ancients
to you unless you balk at it, unless
you find it hard to learn their subtle thinking.*

But you do not balk; you are not put off by any technicality. Your mind is of high quality and is not concerned only with big issues. Yet I also applaud how you relate everything to some self-improvement: the only time you lose patience is when the highest degree of technicality achieves nothing. I will try to ensure that that does not happen now.

The question here is about whether the good is grasped by

the sensory faculty or by the intellect. This inquiry is related to the thesis that the good is not present in animals devoid of speech and in infants.* **2** All those who put pleasure in the highest position judge the good to be an object of the senses. We, on the other hand, who assign the good to the mind, take it to be an object of the understanding.

If the senses were what ascertain the good, we would not reject any pleasure, since there is no pleasure that does not entice and please us.* Conversely, we would never willingly undergo any pain, because there is no pain that is not an unwelcome sensation. **3** Moreover, people who are too fond of pleasure and who have an extreme fear of pain would not deserve criticism. Yet we disapprove of gluttons and people addicted to sex, and we despise those who are dissuaded from every manly undertaking by fear of pain. If the senses were the criteria of good and bad, how would these people do wrong by obeying them? For you have ceded to the senses the authority to decide what to pursue and what to avoid. **4** But obviously it is reason that has charge of that. Reason settles questions about the happy life, virtue, and the honorable, and likewise about the good and the bad. By letting the senses make pronouncements about the good, our opponents allow the least valuable part to pass judgment on the superior; for sense perception is dull and imprecise, and is less acute in human beings than in other creatures. **5** Suppose someone wanted to distinguish tiny things by touch instead of by sight! We have no further sense, more precise and focused than vision, that would enable us to distinguish the good and the bad. So you can see that someone for whom touch constitutes the criterion of the ultimate good and bad is wallowing in the depths of ignorance and has thrown the sublime and the divine down to the ground.*

6 The opponent says, "Every branch of knowledge and every skill must have some basis in what is evident and available to the senses, and grow and develop from there. In the same way, the happy life has its foundation and point of origin in what is evident and what is available to the senses. Surely it is your view as well that the happy life has its origin in things that are evident."

7 Our view is that to be happy is to be in accordance with nature, and that whether something is in accordance with nature is just as obviously and directly apparent as whether something is intact and whole. Even a newborn has a share in what is in accordance with nature, but this I call not the good but only the beginning of the good. You accord the ultimate good, pleasure, to the stage of infancy, with the consequence that one who is just being born starts out at the place to which the perfected person arrives. You are placing the top of the tree where the root belongs! **8** It would be patently wrong to say that a fetus, a frail, incomplete, and still unformed thing, with even its gender undetermined, is already in a state that is good. Yet how much difference is there, really, between a newborn infant and one that is still a heavy weight hidden in the mother's womb? Both are equally immature as concerns the understanding of good and bad. An infant is not yet capable of grasping the good, any more than a tree is, or some animal devoid of speech. So why is the good not present in a tree or an animal? Because reason is not there either. In the same way, the good is not present in the infant: the infant too lacks reason. Only when it gets to reason will it get to the good.

9 Some animals are devoid of reason, some are not yet rational, and some are rational but only imperfectly. The good is not present in any of these creatures; only with the advent of reason does it come. What, then, is the difference between the animals I just mentioned? In the one that is devoid of reason, the good will never be present. In the one not yet rational, it is not possible for the good to be present at this time. In the one that is rational but only imperfectly, it is possible for the good to be present, but it is not in fact present. **10** This is what I mean, Lucilius: the good is not found in just any body nor at just any stage of life; it is as distant from infancy as the last is from the first or as the complete is from what is just beginning. Hence the good is not in a little body that is soft and just beginning its development. Not at all—no more than in a seed.

11 You could state the matter thus. We do acknowledge a kind of good for trees and plants. This is not present in the first shoots at the moment when they break through the ground. There is a kind of good for wheat. It is not present in the tender stalk or when the soft ear detaches itself from the husk but only when the wheat has been ripened by summer heat and proper maturity. No nature brings forth its own good unless it has achieved fulfillment. Thus the good of human beings is only to be found in one in whom reason has been perfected.* **12** What is this good? Let me tell you: it is a mind that is free and upright, puts other things beneath itself but itself beneath none. This good is so far beyond the grasp of infancy that it is not to be expected in a child, or even properly in a young adult. Old age is doing well if it arrives there after long and concentrated study. If this is the good, it is also an object of the understanding.

13 "You have said that there is a kind of good for trees and for plants. So infants too can have a good." The truly good does not exist in trees or in animals devoid of speech; what is good in these beings is called good by indulgence. "What is it, then?"

you say. It is what accords with the nature of each. To be sure, the good cannot possibly befall a speechless animal; rather, it belongs to a more fortunate and superior nature. There is no good where there is no place for reason. **14** There are four natures to be considered here, those of trees, animals, humans, and gods. The latter two are of the same nature insofar° as they are rational, but they also differ in that one of them is mortal and the other one immortal. The good of one of them—that would be the god, of course—is perfected just by nature; in the other, namely, the human, it is perfected by effort. The rest, which lack reason, are only perfect in their own nature, not truly perfect. This is because unqualified perfection means perfection in accordance with universal nature, and universal nature is rational. Other things can be perfect in their own kind. **15** A creature that lacks the capacity for happiness also lacks the capacity for that which produces happiness; but it is goods that produce happiness. A speechless animal has neither the capacity for happiness nor the capacity for what produces happiness; hence a speechless animal does not have a good.

16 An animal grasps the present by means of its sensory faculty. It recalls the past only when this faculty is prompted by some event. For example, a horse recalls a road when it is brought to where the road starts; in the stable, however, it has no memory of the road, no matter how often it has passed that way. The third division of time, the future, has no significance for animals. **17** How, then, can we suppose that a perfect nature is possible for creatures whose experience of time is imperfect? Time consists of three parts, past, present, and future. Animals are granted only the part that is most fleeting and transitory, the present. Their memory of the past is only occasional and never brought back except by contact with something in the present.* **18** Therefore the good of a perfect nature cannot exist in a nature that is imperfect; if that were the case, even plants would have it. I am not denying that speechless animals are endowed with very strong impulses to pursue things that appear to accord with their nature, but such impulses are unorganized and sporadic. The good, on the other hand, is never unorganized and sporadic.*

19 "How is this?" you are saying. "Do animals move in a sporadic and unsystematic manner?" I would describe their movements in this way if their nature were capable of order, but the truth is that they move in accordance with their own nature. Something is disorganized if and only if it is capable of being organized, just as the anxious is what could be free of anxiety. There is no vice in anyone who lacks the possibility of virtue. The movements of animals result from their nature. **20** Not to belabor the point, there will be a kind of good in an animal, a kind of virtue, a kind of perfection, but it will not be unconditionally a good or a virtue or perfect. All these are found only in rational beings who have the privilege of understanding the cause, the extent, and the procedure.

21 Are you wondering where this discussion is heading and how it will be of benefit to your mind? I respond: by training and sharpening the mind, and by keeping it on the right track in all its future activities. It is even beneficial in that it delays us from running off into some course of depravity. I have this too to say. There is no greater benefit I can do you than by showing you your own good, by distinguishing you from the speechless animals and situating you with the divine.

22 Why, may I say, do you nurture and train your bodily strength? Nature has granted greater power to domestic and wild animals. Why do you cultivate your appearance? When you have done everything you can, you will still not be as beautiful as animals are. Why do you spend huge efforts on your hair? Whether you let it down in the Parthian fashion or tie it up as the Germans do or let it go wild in the Scythian way, any horse will have a thicker mane to toss; the mane that bristles on any lion's neck will be more handsome. After practicing for speed, you will still be no match for a hare. **23** Why not abandon all the points on which you are bound to be surpassed, cease to strive after what is foreign to your nature, and return to the good that is your own?

What is this good? Just this: a mind made flawless, a mind that rivals the divine, that elevates itself above the human sphere and places nothing beyond itself.* You are a reasoning animal. What, then, is the good in you? It is perfect reason. Take your reason from where it is now to its own ultimate achievement, let it grow to its fullest possible extent. **24** Do not judge yourself to be happy until all your joys arise from yourself, until, after viewing the objects of human competition, covetousness, and possessiveness, you find—I will not say nothing to prefer, but nothing to set your heart on. I will give you a brief rule by which to measure yourself, to gauge when you have achieved perfection: you will possess your own good when you understand that the truly fortunate are those least blessed by fortune.*

Farewell.

Notes

Abbreviations

GL   Graver, M., and A. A. Long. 2015. *Seneca: Letters on Ethics to Lucilius.* Chicago: University of Chicago Press.

LS   Long, A. A., and D. N. Sedley, eds., *The Hellenistic Philosophers*, 2 vols. Cambridge: Cambridge University Press, 1987.

SVF *Stoicorum Veterum Fragmenta*, ed. H. von Arnim, 4 vols. Leipzig: Teubner, 1903–24.

1.1.   Seneca begins his published work with the words "Do that" (*ita fac*), as if referring to a previous letter by Lucilius. This stylized device is similar to the openings of many of the subsequent letters, in which Seneca frames the topic he wants to write about as a response to some question or remark made by his correspondent. We can easily imagine Lucilius's letters, whether or not they ever existed in fact.

The expression "assert your own freedom" refers to the most common legal procedure for manumission, in which a third party had to make a formal assertion of the enslaved person's freedom. For Lucilius, and for the general reader, dedicating themselves to philosophical study will be a form of liberation from other demands on their time. Compare 8.7 in this volume and Seneca, *On the Shortness of Life* 4.2; and, for the expression, compare 33.4 and 113.23 in this volume.

1.2.   In letter 24, Seneca writes, "We die every day, for every day some part of life is taken from us. Even when we are still growing, our life is shrinking. We lost our infancy, then childhood, then youth. All our time was lost in the moment of passage, right up to yesterday, and even today is divided with death as it goes by. As the water clock does not empty out its last drop only but also whatever dripped through it before, so our last hour of existence is not the only time we die but just the only time we finish dying. That is when we arrive at death, but we have been a long time coming there" (24.20, in GL, 89).

1.5.   A Greek version of the proverb appears in Hesiod, *Wors and Days* 369. For the thought, compare 108.26 in this volume.

2.5.   Epicurus was the founder in Athens of the Garden, a school of philosophy based on natural science and on hedonism in ethics. For Epicurus, pleasure (or the avoidance of pain) is the only rational motivation for human action; but the most pleasurable existence overall for a human being consists in mental tranquility, and an unambitious life of frugality is the best way to achieve this. Seneca, like Cicero, sees Epicureanism as the direct rival to Stoicism, and his remarks about it are often sharply polemical. (Examples in this volume include 9.8–10 and 90.35, and see also Seneca, *On Leisure* 7.1, *On Benefits* 4.2–3, and *On the Happy Life* 7.1–3, 12.5.) Nonetheless, he is quite knowledgeable about Epicurean principles and major figures in the school, and he expresses warm appreciation for some aspects of Epicurus's character and writings. Here, as often in the early letters, he quotes from a work of Epicurus that has not otherwise survived, perhaps the letter collection implied in 9.1 or a collection of maxims. See further Graver 2020.

3.2.   Theophrastus was an associate of Aristotle and succeeded him as head of the Lyceum in 322 BCE. The saying alluded to here must have been "Judge first, then love."

3.6.   Either L. Pomponius, a writer of *fabula togata* (comedy) and farce in the early first century BCE; or P. Pomponius Secundus, a contemporary of Seneca, mentioned in Tacitus and Quintilian as a talented tragedian who resisted oppression under Tiberius. Seneca's quotation is not in verse.

6.1.   Philosophical study is presented both as a means of self-cultivation and as the basis for a deeper form of friendship. In speaking of a "transformation," Seneca may be referring to the Stoic concept of perfected wisdom as an ideal existence to which anyone may aspire. Here and elsewhere he represents himself as a person with many faults but one who is making progress toward wisdom.

6.3.   Both companionship (*societas*) and commonality (Gk. *koinōnia*) were important elements in the Stoic conception of friendship. Seneca will say more on Stoic friendship in 9.3–18.

6.6.   Zeno founded the Stoic school in Athens around 300 BCE; Cleanthes succeeded him as its head in 262.

Metrodorus, Hermarchus, and Polyaenus were close friends and colleagues of Epicurus.

6.7.   Hecaton was a Stoic philosopher of the early first century BCE, a pupil of Panaetius (see the note on 116.5) and an associate of the Quintus Aelius Tubero mentioned in 104.21. He was the author of several treatises on ethics.

7.5.   Cruelty is injurious to oneself because it teaches others to be cruel in return. The thought seems to be proverbial, as in letter 81, where Seneca writes, "Bad examples too revert to those who set them: no one wins any pity when the wrongs they suffer are just what they taught others how to do" (81.18, in GL, 268; a similar idea is found in Plato, *Apology* 25e). In this case, though, the gladiator at whom the people are shouting can hardly become any worse.

7.6.   All three are mentioned repeatedly by Seneca as examples of moral rectitude, and often together; for instance in 11.10 and 104.21. Seneca probably has the elder Cato in mind here (cf. 11.10), but he sometimes mentions the younger Cato as well in such lists. Laelius, the friend of Scipio Aemilianus, was associated with Stoicism. For Seneca's view of Socrates, see 104.27–28.

7.10.   The inclusion of a philosophical maxim at the end of every letter is becoming a bit of a joke. Playfully, Seneca speaks in financial metaphors, as if the maxim were a bit of money that he owes to Lucilius each time he reads a letter. That payment is, as it were, borrowed from the author of the maxim. Compare "the daily dole" in 6.6 and 14.17; "your account" in 8.10; "another's property" in 12.11, and so on.

Democritus, a contemporary of Socrates, was as much renowned for moral philosophy as for his views on atoms and void.

7.11.   The statement is not otherwise recorded; see the note on 2.5.

8.1.   The opening of the letter is in the voice of a pupil, perhaps Lucilius, who sees a contradiction between Seneca's Stoic allegiance and his advice to retreat into solitude. Stoic ethics favored active service to society throughout life, unless prevented by adverse circumstances. Seneca explores the Stoic position further in letter 68 (see GL, 204–6) and in his brief treatise *On Leisure*, arguing that retirement is permissible if circumstances prevent one from being effective—for instance, if one is in poor health or lacks sufficient power and influence, or if the state is hopelessly corrupt. Further, he holds that philosophical study and writing can itself be a legitimate form of public service.

8.3.   The speech that follows gives an initial statement of the core message of Stoic ethics, that what is truly valuable in human life is to be found not in the fortuitous advantages most people think of as good but in the human mind; i.e., in one's own character and conduct. The same idea will be expressed later on in terms more characteristic of Stoicism; see the note on 31.6.

8.7.   The saying is not otherwise recorded; see the note on 2.5.

Part of the manumission ceremony required the former master to turn the freed slave around in a circle.

8.8.   The *fabulae togatae* were comic (or seriocomic) plays not based on Greek models.

8.9.   Publilius Syrus produced scripts for a popular form of drama known as "mime"—i.e., light comedy or farce. Publilius was especially known for his aphorisms, a collection of which was still being read in schools in the time of Jerome (Jerome, *Letter* 107.8). The line Seneca quotes here appears at the beginning of the surviving collection as edited by Friedrich ([1880] 1964).

8.10.   Both quotations are in verse, in the same meter as the preceding quotation from Publilius Syrus. Seneca refers to Lucilius's talents as a writer a number of times in the collection; e.g., in letter 46 and in 79.4–7.

9.1.   Seneca critiques the Epicurean position on friendship and explains why he prefers the Stoic position. As was common in the Hellenistic period, he presents the ethical issue as a question about the character and experience of the sage; i.e., the person who is entirely wise. Since both sides agree that the wise person must be self-sufficient, the point at issue is *why* friendship is valuable: is it for the sake of utility, or is it a matter of affection independent of one's own interests? For more on Epicurus, see the note on 2.5. This one of his letters is known only from what Seneca says about it here and later in this letter (9.8, 9.18).

Stilpo practiced philosophy in Megara during the late fourth and early third centuries BCE. He was an associate of Crates the Cynic, with whom he shared an emphasis on personal virtue and self-reliance, and a teacher of Zeno of Citium. See Diogenes Laertius 2.113–20.

9.2. *Impatientia* (nonsufferance) is the closest Latin equivalent for the Greek *apatheia* (impassivity) in terms of derivation, but it does not have the required meaning.

9.3. Seneca is fully in agreement with the usual Stoic position on ordinary emotions such as grief, fear, and desire—namely, that they are causally dependent on false notions of value and should be eliminated altogether (see especially letter 116). At the same time, he is quick to point out that the Stoics do not aim for an unnatural lack of feeling: they agree with everyone else that the emotions have a basis in human nature, and they hold that even a morally perfect person would experience certain kinds of feelings: blushing and similar bodily reactions (letter 11), joy in genuine goods (23), pangs of grief or fear (57). The more extreme position that eliminates all feelings from the wise person is associated in his mind with the Cynic philosophers; compare Seneca, *On the Shortness of Life* 14.2 ("to conquer human nature with the Stoics; to abandon it with the Cynics").

Like Aristotle in *Nicomachean Ethics* 1.7, the Stoics posited that one who seeks to live the best possible life must be self-sufficient; i.e., not dependent on anyone else for happiness. Nonetheless, they held that because we are social beings by nature, a person of good character will want to have friends. They explained this position by appealing to the notion of a shared existence (companionship and commonality, as in 6.3) and by pointing out that friendship provides opportunities for virtuous activity. For more on the Stoic background, see Cicero, *On Ends* 3.65–70; Diogenes Laertius 7.123–24; Stobaeus 2.7.5l (73W = *SVF* 3.112) and 2.7.11i, 101–2W (*SVF* 3.626); Seneca, letter 109.3–6 (see GL, 434–35).

9.4. The analogy between a deceased friend and a missing part of one's own body may owe something to Stilpo: compare the report in Stobaeus 4.44.83, where Stilpo argues that the correct response when a friend or relative dies is to care more tenderly for one's other connections, just as a farmer would take better care of other branches of a tree that lost one branch, or a person would take better care of other parts of his own body after losing one.

9.5. The thought belongs to the consolatory tradition; compare 63.10–11. The Athenian sculptor Phidias, a contemporary and friend of Pericles, was especially known for his works in ivory and bronze.

9.6. On Hecaton, see the note on 6.7.

9.7. Attalus is mentioned by Seneca the Elder (*Suasoriae* 2.12) as a Stoic philosopher, "the subtlest and most eloquent of our age," who lost his property under Sejanus. Seneca was deeply impressed by him as a young man (108.13–16) and quotes several of his sayings.

9.8. For the doctrine, compare Epicurus, *Principal Doctrines* 28 and the first of the three Epicurean positions reported by Cicero in *On Ends* 1.66–70: friendship provides the intelligent hedonist with security against future misfortune, a necessary element in happiness (Epicurus, *Vatican Sayings* 33; Cicero, *Tusculan Disputations* 3.38; Plutarch, *That a Follower of Epicurus Cannot Live Pleasantly* 1089d [frag. 68 Usener]).

9.11. The argument is a fortiori. Even though romantic love is a base emotion, it arises from disinterested motives: no one falls in love merely to make a profit or for the sake of ambition. But the basis of friendship can hardly be *less* honorable than that of a base emotion, and so friendship must arise from disinterested motives as well.

9.14. Chrysippus of Soli was the most widely influential of the early Stoic philosophers and the leader of the school from 232 BCE until his death ca. 206 BCE. Seneca knew at least some of his writings and greatly admired his intellect (see Seneca, *On Benefits* 1.3.8). The remark quoted here was known also to Plutarch, who quoted it in Greek (*On Common Conceptions* 1068a = *SVF* 3.674). In his Latin rendering of it, Seneca plays on two senses of the expression *opus esse*, either "have need of" or "have a use for."

9.16. Seneca writes in letter 74 that virtue "is equally great even if it withdraws into itself, closed off on every side. For its spirit is no less great, no less upright, no less precise in intelligence, no less inflexible in justice" (74.29, in GL, 234). In Stoic cosmology, the entire universe is at intervals dissolved into fire and then regenerated by Zeus, the supreme and providential divinity who is equated with the designing fire that structures all things. During the periods of conflagration, Zeus is alone with his own thoughts and does not mind the absence of other gods (Epictetus, *Discourses* 3.13.4–8; cf. Plutarch, *On Common Conceptions* 1077d = *SVF* 2.396).

9.17. In Stoic thought, "attachment" (*conciliatio*; Gk. *oikeiōsis*) is the instinctual process by which human beings come to recognize some objects as akin to themselves and therefore to prefer them over their opposites: physical preservation over destruction, understanding over ignorance, human contact over solitude. This last preference supplies the basis for friendship and familial love. See 121.14, and compare Cicero, *On Ends* 3.16–21, 3.62.

9.18. Demetrius Poliorcetes's sack of Megara occurred in 307 BCE. The anecdote recounted here is told also in Diogenes Laertius 2.115 (where Stilpo goes on to explain that he retains his eloquence and his knowledge); see also Stobaeus 3.40.8 (738–39W).

9.20. The statement (frag. 474 Usener) is not otherwise recorded; see the note on 2.5.

9.21. The source of the line is unknown.

11.1. The Stoics held that a person who possessed a full understanding of the world would not experience such ordinary emotions as shame or fear; see the note on 9.3. However, such a person would still be subject to such involuntary reactions as blushing and stage fright, which are not dependent on false beliefs about value and in no way morally culpable. Compare 57.3–6; Seneca, *On Anger* 2.3–4.

11.4. Lucius Cornelius Sulla held absolute power in Rome from 82 to 80 BCE, during which time he ordered several thousand executions. Gnaeus Pompey "the Great," though not an accomplished speaker, achieved extensive military victories and a political career rivaling Julius Caesar's.

Papirius Fabianus was one of Seneca's personal models in rhetoric and philosophy. Described by the elder Seneca as a *philosophus*, he is admired by both Senecas especially for his probity of life and his elegant oratory. See 40.12 and 58.6 in this volume; see also Seneca, *On the Shortness of Life* 10.1; Seneca the Elder, *Controversiae* 2 pref.; Seneca, letter 100 (in GL, 397–400).

11.8. The statement (frag. 210 Usener) is not otherwise recorded; see the note on 2.5.

11.10. It was the elder Cato who was known for his severity: Seneca comments elsewhere (e.g., in 87.9–10; see GL, 301–2) on his austere habits. Laelius, the friend of Scipio Aemilianus, was associated with Stoicism.

12.1. This estate must be the one mentioned in Tacitus, *Annals* 15.60.4, as the scene of Seneca's death. Seneca also mentions two other villas, one in Nomentum (104.1) and one in the Alban Hills (123.1).

12.3. Gifts of clay figurines (*sigillaria*) were made especially at the festival of Saturnalia, which masters celebrated jointly with their slaves. (See further on 18.1.) But children might have played with such things at any time.

12.6. That is, according to our year of birth. The Roman censors kept a register of citizens according to age.

12.7. Heraclitus of Ephesus (ca. 535–475 BCE), called "the Obscure" for his riddling aphorisms (Cicero, *On Ends* 2.15).

12.8. This Pacuvius governed Syria during the 20s CE as proxy for Aelius Lamia, who was detained in Rome by the emperor Tiberius. "By possession" is humorous exaggeration: in Roman law one could acquire title to a tract of land by possessing it for two years, but governors did not own their provinces.

12.9. Virgil, *Aeneid* 4.653. The same verse is quoted in Seneca, *On the Happy Life* 19.1, by an Epicurean as he dies by suicide.

12.10. The statement (frag. 487 Usener) is attributed below to Epicurus. It is not otherwise recorded (see the note on 2.5), but compare Epicurus, *Letter to Menoeceus* 127.

14.1. Seneca consistently maintains that we have an innate inclination to preserve our physical selves and under normal circumstances a responsibility to do so. (The point is explored further in 121.17–18.) That being said, however, there are times when our natural concern for the body has to be subordinated to our larger aims as identified by reason. All this is in keeping with the standard Stoic position concerning preferred and dispreferred indifferents, on which see further the note on 31.6.

14.2. If circumstances require it, we should be prepared to accept death willingly, or even to take our own life. The topic of suicide is explored further in letter 70.

14.8. An oblique reference to Lucilius's position within the imperial administration as procurator (civil governor) of Sicily. Seneca alludes to his addressee's position chiefly as an opportunity for sightseeing (e.g., in 31.9 and 79.1–4). In the preface to Seneca, *Natural Questions* 4A, the post is called a "leisurely" one, such as would afford plenty of time for study and writing.

   The treacherous currents of the Straits of Messina, between the Italian peninsula and the island of Sicily, were thought by Romans to have been the originals of Scylla and Charybdis in Homer's *Odyssey*, book 12.

14.9. For this uncommon type of cruelty, see the note on 83.25.

14.10. The proverb is not otherwise known.

14.11. These "stoles" were long strips of carded wool called *infulae*, worn by priests in token of purity during a sacrifice.

14.12. Marcus Porcius Cato Uticensis (Cato the Younger) was a major political figure of the Late Republic. Championing the interests of the optimate class, he resisted the increasing power of Caesar and Pompey during the 50s BCE but in the civil war of the 40s gave his support to Pompey, who commanded the legions of the Senate. After Pompey's defeat at the battle of Pharsalus in 48 BCE, Cato assisted Caecilius Metellus Scipio in leading the resistance to Caesar in North Africa and eventually took his own life. Seneca regards Cato as an especially prominent example of Roman virtue and mentions him frequently; including especially in 70.19 and 104.29–33.

14.13. The paragraph that follows provides a sample of the kind of arguments that were sometimes made in the course of rhetorical training, where Cato was a stock figure: compare Seneca, *On Tranquility of Mind* 19; Persius, *Satires* 3.45–48; Seneca the Elder, *Controversiae* 9.6.7 (cf. 10.1.8), 6.8, and *Suasoriae* 6.2, 4, 10. The attitude expressed toward Cato's decision is quite different from what Seneca says elsewhere; see Griffin 1968.

The first event mentioned in this paragraph occurred during the consulship of Julius Caesar in 59 BCE. Cato made a speech opposing legislation that would have made grants of public lands to Pompey's returning soldiers; Caesar, who had proposed the legislation, stopped the speech by having Cato dragged from the Forum. In a later incident, Cato spoke so insistently against a measure assigning powerful military commands to Pompey and Crassus that he was jailed by the presiding tribune (Plutarch, *Cato the Younger* 43).

14.14. "Laws for humankind" are moral principles as opposed to political laws.

14.15. Seneca uses this odd expression also in *Natural Questions* 4a pref. 5, where the point seems again to be that even the most careful and skilled efforts may not always suffice to defend oneself.

14.16. The robber represents chance misfortune. There is no shame in losing one's life to random events.

14.17. Metrodorus belonged to the school ("shop") of Epicurus; compare 6.6. Seneca is familiar with some of his writings, which include personal letters like those of Epicurus. For the thought here, compare Epicurus, *Letter to Menoeceus* 130.

15.1. The formula is only five words in Latin (*si vales, bene est, valeo*) and was standard enough to be abbreviated to *SVBEV*. A play on words introduces the topic of the letter: to "be well" (*valere*) is also to be physically sound (*validus*) and in good health (*valetudo*).

15.3. In Stoic philosophy, the mind or spirit is a fine-textured material substance called "breath" (*pneuma*). See the note on 90.29.

Oil was used to massage the muscles before exercise.

15.4. The fuller performed the distasteful work of laundering woolens by trampling or jumping on them in a vat of water mixed with urine.

15.7. Members of the upper classes sometimes engaged specialists in dietetics to monitor and improve their eating habits and exercise routines.

"Quirites" is an elevated expression for "Roman citizens."

15.9. The author is Epicurean, as in 14.17, but the statement (frag. 491 Usener) is not otherwise recorded; see the note on 2.5. Compare Epicurus, *Letter to Menoeceus* 127, "the future is neither wholly ours nor wholly not ours."

Baba and Ision appear to be names (or stage names) of jesters; compare *Pumpkinification* 11, where the names Augurinus and Baba are mockingly associated with that of the emperor Claudius.

16.1. Seneca lays great stress on the difference between learning a philosophical doctrine and being able to apply it. For the latter, one has to internalize what has been learned through repeated study and reflection in a process he usually calls "rehearsal" (*meditatio*), analogous to practicing an instrument or for giving a speech. See also the note on 91.1, for "prerehearsal of future ills" as a way to prepare oneself for various calamities.

16.5. Of the three views listed, only the second would be accepted by a Stoic; see the note on 76.23.

16.7. The saying (frag. 201 Usener) is not otherwise recorded, but compare Epicurus, *Principal Doctrines* 15 and 21.

18.1. The Saturnalia during the third week of December was Rome's carnival season, celebrated with parties and gift exchange and with a playful exchange of roles between masters and slaves.

18.2. The toga was the attire of business and government, too formal as well as too heavy for a convivial occasion. Looser and more colorful garments would be made of silk or cotton.

18.3. During the Saturnalia, slave owners might for fun put on the *pilleus*, a tall felt hat usually worn by freedmen.

18.7.   Seneca speaks of some fashionable practices of mock asceticism. The name of Timon, of the fifth century BCE in Athens, was associated with misanthropy and suggests simple meals without guests; "paupers' cells" must be small unfurnished rooms used by the wealthy for periods of retreat or perhaps only for show.

18.9.   Epicureans (unlike modern epicures) practiced abstemious living even on ordinary days: see 21.10, and compare Diogenes Laertius 10.11; Epicurus, *Letter to Menoeceus* 130–31.

Polyaenus was one of Epicurus's principal colleagues; compare 6.6. The archonship of Charinus is datable to 308/7 BCE.

Epicurus probably wrote in terms of the *obol*, the small silver penny of Athens; Seneca translates it to the *as*, the bronze coin of Rome. For Metrodorus, see the note on 14.17. In letter 52, Seneca quotes Epicurus as saying that Metrodorus is a good follower but that his intellect is "of the second tier" (52.3, in GL, 150).

18.12.   Virgil, *Aeneid* 8.364–65. In the *Aeneid*, these words are spoken by Evander as Aeneas enters his cottage, reminding the hero that Hercules, later to be deified, had also stayed in that house.

18.14.   The management of anger was an important topic for Epicureans as well as Stoics. The connection with insanity was a commonplace; it may be understood either metaphorically or literally; compare Seneca, *On Anger* 1.1, 2.5. The statement quoted here (frag. 484 Usener) is not otherwise recorded for Epicurus.

Anger at slaves features in a number of the anecdotes in Seneca's treatise *On Anger* (e.g., at 1.15.3).

20.1.   Seneca writes in letter 74 that "virtue is made up of consistency: all its actions harmonize and agree with one another" (74.30, in GL, 234). People act in accordance with their beliefs and intentions, and beliefs that are true will be consistent with one another, since truth itself is consistent. See also 31.8. The emphasis is in accordance with earlier Stoic thought, where it is consistency that distinguishes the fully virtuous person from the one who is drawing near to virtue (Stobaeus 4.39, 906W [LS 59I], quoting Chrysippus; also Cicero, *On Ends* 3.20).

20.9. This saying of Epicurus (frag. 206 Usener) is not otherwise recorded; for the asceticism, compare 18.9, 21.10.

Demetrius, a personal acquaintance of Seneca, practiced philosophy in the manner of the Cynics, renouncing not only material possessions but even the desire of possessions (Seneca, *On the Happy Life* 18.3). Seneca mentions another of his earthy sayings in 91.19.

20.13. Compare 18.5–7.

21.1. Lucilius is represented as hesitating, on the verge of giving up his pursuit of fame and influence but reluctant to follow through on his convictions. At the moment he is merely *sympathetic* to Stoicism, whose fundamental axiom is that honorable conduct (*honestum*, Gk. *to kalon*) is the sole human good and thus the only source of happiness. Seneca will have more to say on that point in letter 76 and elsewhere.

21.3. Idomeneus was a close associate of Epicurus and a writer of history, biography, and philosophy, in addition to the political achievements mentioned here. Epicurus wrote a letter urging him to retire from politics (frag. 132 Usener). Compare Plutarch, *Against Colotes* 1127d (frag. 134 Usener).

21.4. Titus Pomponius Atticus was Cicero's closest friend and the recipient of most of his extant correspondence. Though interested in historical research, he did not seek fame on his own account (Cicero, *Letters to Atticus* 17.17.5). Marcus Vipsanius Agrippa, Octavian's friend and most important military commander, married Atticus's daughter Caecilia. Their daughter Vipsania was Tiberius's first wife and the mother of Drusus the Younger.

Seneca's verb *adplicuisset* refers specifically to Cicero's writing Atticus's name after his own in the salutations of his letters.

21.5. The survival of which Seneca speaks here is the survival of one's reputation through literature; compare Ennius's epitaph: "Living I roll / through mouths of men," and Horace, *Odes* 3.31; Ovid, *Metamorphoses* 15, 875–79.

Virgil, *Aeneid* 9.446–49. The two people addressed are Nisus and Euryalus, young soldiers, adventurous but not especially intelligent, who lose their lives on a nighttime spying mission. Virgil's apostrophe to them implies a strong claim for the efficacy of his own poetic narrative.

21.7. Pythocles was another colleague of Epicurus and the recipient of one of his three extant letters. The fragment is preserved in Greek in Stobaeus 3.17.23, 495W (frag. 135 Usener).

21.9. The procedures of the Roman Senate allowed senators to reject one portion of a proposed piece of legislation but endorse another. Seneca is in general strongly opposed to Epicurean hedonism; see the note on 2.5.

Epicurus held that virtuous behavior as conventionally understood is an essential means to a tranquil and therefore pleasurable existence (*Principal Doctrine* 5, *Letter to Menoeceus* 10.131–32). An Epicurean allegiance thus did not provide an excuse for dissolute living. For the thought here, compare Seneca, *On the Happy Life* 13.3; for Epicurean asceticism, compare 18.9, 20.9.

23.1. To "rejoice" (*gaudere*) is to experience joy (*gaudium*). In normal Latin usage, "joy" might refer to any form of delight, regardless of what occasioned it. Seneca now restricts joy to the feeling of gladness that, according to Stoicism, accompanies a virtuous disposition.

23.3. Unlike the ordinary flawed person who delights wrongly in empty things, the wise person who is the Stoic ideal (see the note on 9.1) would experience joy in his own character and good deeds or those of virtuous friends. This joy is a strong feeling; it is called "exhilaration" and, in Stoic terminology, an "elevation of mind" (Seneca, *On the Happy Life* 4.4, letter 59.2, in GL, 172). To experience it, Lucilius must perfect his character, since only a fully virtuous and wise person possesses the genuine goods that are the proper object of joy. For the Stoic background, see Cicero, *Tusculan Disputations* 4.13; Diogenes Laertius 7.116; Graver 2007.

23.4. Seneca's expression *hilariculo vultu* conveys more than the literal equivalent "with a cheerful countenance." From what he says here, it appears to be a fashionable phrase connoting deliberate good cheer. We give the French equivalent to capture something of the resonance.

23.6. Seneca regularly belittles the body, with its pleasures and pains, in contrast to the grandeur of the mind. Compare 41.4, 58.29, and 65.22 in this volume; Seneca, *On the Happy Life* 4.4, *Consolation to Helvia* 11.7.

23.9. Epicurus is "your dear Epicurus" in that Lucilius is represented as having a proprietary interest in the maxim enclosed at the end of each letter, most of which have been drawn from the writings of Epicurus. See the note on 7.10. There is no implication that Lucilius is attracted to Epicurean philosophy.

The saying (frag. 493 Usener) is not otherwise recorded; see the note on 2.5.

30.1. Aufidius Bassus is mentioned in Quintilian 10.1.103 as a writer of histories, including a history of the wars in Germany. Seneca does not say directly that Bassus is an Epicurean, but the arguments Bassus makes in this conversation about the fear of death are all strongly associated with Epicurean thought. The connection is made explicit in 30.14.

30.6. For the Epicurean, the fear of death is irrational, because once death has occurred, there is no longer any self that would experience it. The reasoning is spelled out in Epicurus, *Letter to Menoeceus* 125, and in Lucretius 3.830–42.

30.12. This paragraph recalls the address of Nature in Lucretius, especially in the claim that death disassembles materials that will be reassembled to make a new life (3.964–71) and in the analogy to satisfaction with an ample meal (3.960).

30.14. Bassus's remarks on pain (frag. 503 Usener) suggest familiarity with Epicurus, *Principal Doctrine* 4 [LS 21C], which states that severe pain lasts only a short time, while chronic illnesses involve a preponderance of pleasure over pain.

31.2. In book 12 of the Odyssey, Odysseus (called by the Romans Ulysses) seals the ears of his crew with wax to prevent them from hearing the dangerous song of the Sirens, who enticed men to their death.

In Stoic thought, the human being is designed by nature for development toward the human good, which is perfected reason. In nearly all cases, however, we are corrupted, sometimes by the intrinsic plausibility of certain kinds of error (e.g., that wealth is a good thing in itself), but most often by the influence of other people (Diogenes Laertius 7.89; Galen, *Precepts of Hippocrates and Plato* 5.5.13–20 [*SVF* 3.229a]; Calcidius, *On the Timaeus of Plato* 165–66 [*SVF* 3.229]). The corrupting influences of the surrounding culture, including even the prayers of our parents on our behalf, are a frequent theme in Seneca, notably in 123.12, which again uses the image of the Sirens' song.

31.5. In Stoic physics, heat and cold are properties imparted to substances by the admixture of elemental fire and elemental air, respectively; see, for instance, Galen, *Precepts of Hippocrates and Plato* 5.3.8 [LS 47H].

31.6. The Stoic doctrine on preferred and dispreferred indifferents supplies the basis for reasonable pursuit of such objects as health, financial security, life, and good repute, and for avoidance of their opposites. But the wise person pursues and avoids the indifferents without either desiring them as genuinely good things or fearing them as genuinely bad. They are only the tools or material with which virtue has to work; and although our preferences in regard to them are grounded in human nature, there will be situations in which it is appropriate to set aside those preferences. For the Stoic background, see Diogenes Laertius 7.102–5 [LS 58A–B]; Sextus Empiricus, *Against the Mathematicians* 11.64–67 [LS 58F]; Epictetus, *Discourses* 2.6.9 [LS 58J]; Plutarch, *On Common Conceptions* 1069e [LS 59A].

31.8. The mind of the wise person is equal to the divine in that its perfected rationality reflects the coherent organization of the cosmos. It is not inferior to God in blessedness, although it lacks immortality. Compare Cicero, *On the Nature of the Gods* 2.153; Plutarch, *On Common Conceptions* 1061f [LS 63I]. Seneca returns to the point often, notably at 53.11–12; also at *On Providence* 1.5, *On the Constancy of the Wise Person* 8.2, *Natural Questions* 1 pref. 11–17). See further the note on 104.23.

31.9. It is unclear why Lucilius's work as governor of the province of Sicily in 63–64 CE would have required him to face the Pennine and the Graian Passes (Alpine passes now known as the Little St. Bernard Pass and Great St. Bernard Pass) or the mountains of Illyria on the Balkan Peninsula. It is more plausible that he would have had to voyage past Scylla and Charybdis (i.e., the Straits of Messina) and the Syrtaean shoals just north of modern Libya.

31.11. Both Seneca and Lucilius belonged to the equestrian order, membership in which required substantial wealth.

The quotation is from Virgil, *Aeneid* 8.364–65; the imagery concerns figurines of the gods in terra-cotta. In *Consolation to Helvia* 10, Seneca more explicitly associates such figurines with the simplicity and probity of earlier generations of Romans, who kept the oaths they swore by them.

33.1. These "flowery bits" (*flosculi*) are aphorisms expressed with some rhetorical flourish; compare 33.7. For the use of philosophical maxims, especially maxims drawn from Epicurus, compare 2.4–5, and see the notes on 7.10 and 23.9.

33.2. Men's garments usually did not have sleeves.

33.4. Zeno, Cleanthes, Chrysippus, Posidonius, and Panaetius were all important Stoic authors; Hermarchus and Metrodorus were associates of Epicurus. As concerns Metrodorus, the statement is an exaggeration, for Seneca sometimes quotes him as a philosopher in his own right; see the note on 14.17.

The quotation is from Ovid, *Metamorphoses* 13.824.

33.7. A *chreia*, or "set piece," was a pithy remark attributed to a named individual. Boys were required to memorize such remarks as an early stage of their training in oratory.

38.1. The shortest letter in the collection is appropriately devoted to a reflection on how useful short pieces of writing can be. Yet the effectiveness of letters in philosophical teaching is not only a matter of length but also of their informal style.

38.2. The image is Platonic; compare *Phaedrus* 276b–277a.

40.2. The philosopher Serapio is unknown except for what Seneca says here.

The younger orator is Odysseus (*Iliad* 3.221–23); the elder is Nestor, as in *Iliad* 1.248–49. Cicero had similarly contrasted the two in *Brutus* 40; see also Plato, *Phaedrus* 261b.

40.9. These anecdotes belong to the Augustan period. Publius Vinicius (consul in 2 CE) is mentioned by Seneca the Elder as a talented speaker who did not put up with foolishness (*Controversiae* 7.5.11). "Asellius" is identified with Arellius Fuscus, a well-known orator (Seneca the Elder, *Controversiae* 10, pref. 13) and the teacher of Fabianus (see 40.12, 11.4 in this volume). Quintus Varius Geminius held important magistracies under Augustus (*Prosopographia Imperii Romani pars III* 385.187); he had a reputation for turning a phrase (e.g., Seneca the Elder, *Controversiae* 6.8).

40.10. Quintus Haterius (consul in 5 BCE) had a political career under Augustus and Tiberius; his public speaking is described by Seneca the Elder as rapid to a fault (*Controversiae* 4.7), and by Tacitus (*Annals* 4.61) as dependent more on excited delivery than on content.

40.11. The few samples we have of Roman handwriting suggest that punctuation consisted primarily of dots separating the words.

40.12. On Fabianus, see the note on 11.4.

41.1. Seneca reminds Lucilius of the dignity of the rational mind and urges him to cultivate and perfect it. For the divinity of the wise person's mind within Stoicism, see the note on 31.8.

41.2. Virgil, *Aeneid* 8.352.

41.5. The imagery throughout this passage recalls the Platonic image of the body as an earthly prison for a mind or soul that is of divine origin. See also the note on 58.27, and compare Plato, *Phaedo* 82d–83b; Cicero, *Tusculan Disputations* 1.74–75.

41.8. A fuller version of the same argument is given in 76.7–12.

46.1. Seneca compliments Lucilius on his newest composition, remarking on its length and praising its style.

As Livy and Epicurus were both voluminous writers, it is implied that Lucilius's literary production to date (his *corpus*, or body of work) was of modest proportions—and that the same is true of Seneca's own. Concerning Livy, Seneca writes in letter 100 that "his writings include dialogues (works that are as historical as they are philosophical) and books that deal specifically with philosophy" (100.9, in GL, 399). Livy was highly regarded as a stylist; see Seneca, *On Anger* 1.20.6; Quintilian 8.1.3.

47.1. Both Seneca and Lucilius owned slaves, as did other Romans of their status. While Seneca does not seek to eliminate the institution of slavery, he urges Lucilius to treat enslaved persons decently, interacting with them as human beings and eliminating cruel and humiliating punishments.

47.4. This would include giving evidence against him in court.

47.9. The freedman Gaius Julius Callistus was one of Caligula's most powerful advisors and was later implicated in his death. Universally feared, Callistus kept his power intact through the change of regime and amassed great wealth under Claudius. From what Seneca says here, it appears that Callistus was originally purchased by Caligula at open auction and subsequently freed. The name of the former master is unknown.

47.10. Three legions under the command of Publius Quinctilius Varus were defeated by German tribes in 9 CE; nearly all were killed, but some military personnel in the area were instead captured and enslaved.

47.12. Three examples from mythology and history are followed by two from the biographies of philosophers. Hecuba, the elderly queen of Troy, was enslaved after the city fell; Croesus, king of Lydia, was defeated by the Persians and became the slave of Cyrus; the aged mother of the Persian king Darius III was captured by Alexander in 333 BCE. The story that Plato was once sold as a slave in Sicily is told in Diogenes Laertius 3.19–21; that of Diogenes of Sinope, in Diogenes Laertius 6.29–30.

47.17. Pantomime dancers, both male and female, used singing and movement to enact episodes from mythology. Highly popular as entertainers, they were either slaves or freed persons.

47.18. Seneca anticipates the shocked response of those who will read his letter as a radical call for universal emancipation. The verb *colere*, "to respect," also meant "to pay one's respects," as in the customary morning call that freedmen paid to their former owners.

49.1. The initial reflection on the passage of time provides Seneca with an opening for an invective against contemporary dialecticians, who devote their time to logic puzzles rather than to the improvement of character.

Campania is the coastal region around the Bay of Naples, where Pompeii and a number of other towns were situated. For Lucilius's association with Pompeii, compare 70.1, but also "your town of Parthenope" (i.e., Naples) in 53.1.

49.2. Sotion was an associate or pupil of Quintus Sextius (see the note on 108.17), but nothing is known of Sotion's own teaching beyond the sample Seneca provides in 108.17–21.

49.5. The remark of Cicero is not found in his extant works; it is sometimes assigned to the lost *Hortensius*, which was devoted to the value of philosophy.

49.6. The study of logic, including semantics, syntax, and forms of argumentation, was a major concern of the Stoic founders, especially Chrysippus; see LS chaps. 31, 36, 37. Seneca has no objection to the study of ethical arguments in the form of syllogisms, but he complains of those who make logic an end in itself. In particular, he is concerned that the logical puzzles called *sophismata* may displace serious work in ethics. See Barnes 1997, 12–23.

49.7. Virgil, *Aeneid* 8.385–86.

49.12. Euripides, *Phoenician Women* 469.

53.1. This poor decision illustrates the need for self-knowledge, which is the principal theme of the letter.

Parthenope was an ancient name for the city of Naples; Puteoli is now Pozzuoli, about ten miles west along the coast. The isle of Nesis, now called Nisida, lies along the sea route from one to the other.

53.3. Virgil, *Aeneid* 6.3 and 3.277.

53.7. In using the term "infirmities," Seneca alludes to the Stoic theory of negative traits of character, typical examples of which include greed, irascibility, and ambition. Such traits are essentially erroneous judgments of value that have become ingrained through repetition in the absence of rational reflection. The acquisition of virtue thus depends on continuous self-scrutiny and training. Compare 75.10–12; also Cicero, *Tusculan Disputations* 4.24–25; Stobaeus 2.7.10e, 93W (*SVF* 3.421); Epictetus, *Discourses* 2.8–10.

53.10. Seneca is interested in Alexander the Great chiefly as an example of unrestrained and insatiable passions, especially pride and lust for conquest (compare 91.17), but also excessive drinking, anger, and grief (83.19, 83.23, 113.29). This particular anecdote is not paralleled in our other sources for Alexander.

53.11. On the wise person's godlike potential, see the note on 31.8.

54.1. The Greek word Seneca has in mind is presumably *asthma* (gasping). Remarks in other letters suggest that Seneca had a history of respiratory difficulties including shortness of breath, sinus infections, and fainting spells. See further Griffin 1992, 42–43.

54.4. This Epicurean argument against the fear of death appears also in Lucretius 3.832–43 and 972–77. Seneca alludes to it even more pointedly in letter 77, where he writes, "Suppose someone were to burst into tears because he was not born a thousand years earlier; would you not think that ridiculously foolish? It is just as foolish for someone to weep that he will not be alive a thousand years in the future. The two are equal: your future nonexistence and your past" (77.11, in GL, 249).

56.1. Seneca now represents himself as having taken temporary lodgings above one of the numerous bathing establishments at Baiae, a fashionable resort town on the Bay of Naples. Baiae was known for its luxury bathing establishments, which were supplied by mineral springs heated by subterranean magma.

56.3. The translation reflects the reading *Crispum*, an easy correction for *Crisipum* or *Chrysippum* in the MSS. Seneca's friend Passienus Crispus was a wealthy and prominent orator and statesman and a stepfather to Nero; he is mentioned also in *On Benefits* 1.15.5 and *Natural Questions* 4a pref. 6. The supposed death by visitation is not to be taken literally; it must be a bon mot by Crispus, who was noted for his acerbic wit.

56.4. The Meta Sudans was a street fountain, no doubt similar in design to the fountain of that name built in Rome under Augustus.

56.6. The line is by Varro of Atax; it is cited by Seneca the Elder (*Controversiae* 7.1.27), who remarks that it was also known to Ovid.

56.10. For the negative traits of character termed "infirmities," see the note on 53.7.

56.12. Virgil, *Aeneid* 2.726–29.

56.15. He sealed their ears with wax, as in 31.2.

57.1. Baiae is some fifteen miles from Naples overland; the sea route was longer but less time-consuming in fair weather. Having had a bad experience with the sea voyage (as described in letter 53), Seneca opts for land travel, which at one point required passing through a tunnel almost half a mile in length. The entrance to this ancient tunnel can still be seen today in the neighborhood of Piedigrotta near Naples.

A typical athletic regimen involved wrestling, which would take place in an area made soft with mud, or ball playing and other exercises on a packed-earth surface. Athletes might also use dust on their hands for a better grip.

57.3. On these involuntary reactions, see the note on 11.1.

57.6. "Balcony" is our conjectural translation for *vigiliarium*.

57.7. The Stoic claim against which Seneca is arguing is not otherwise recorded; however, it is only a special case for the more general Stoic position, which was that the human mind or spirit, being composed of a light and fiery substance (see the note on 90.29), can survive death for a limited period—in the case of a wise person, until the next world conflagration (see the note on 9.16, with Diogenes Laertius 7.157; Eusebius, *Evangelical Preparation* 15.20.6 [LS 53W]).

57.8. For the ability of lightning to pass through narrow openings, compare Seneca, *Natural Questions* 2.52; Lucretius 6.225–30, 348–49. Seneca assumes that lightning returns to its source after striking; compare *Natural Questions* 2.40.

58.1. Seneca will devote several paragraphs to the issue of terminology before reporting the conversation itself, beginning in 58.8. The poverty of the Latin language (i.e., its lack of resources for rendering the Greek philosophical lexicon) is similarly a complaint of Lucretius (1.136–39).

58.2. Virgil, *Georgics* 3.146–50.

58.3. Virgil, *Aeneid* 12.708–9.

58.4. The verb form *iusso* was archaic; first-century-BCE speakers regularized it to *iussero*. The quotation is from Virgil, *Aeneid* 11.467.

58.5. Ennius (ca. 239–169 BCE) and Accius (ca. 170–86 BCE) were at one time the most respected Latin poets but had been superseded by Virgil and other writers of more recent date. For the activity of literary scholars in Seneca's time, compare 108.24–32.

58.6. The Latin word *essentia* ("is-ness," the noun derived from *esse*, "to be") was not in common usage at this date. Quintilian, who attributes it to one Sergius Plautius, calls it "very harsh" (8.3.33). If, as Seneca asserts, the term was used by Cicero, the work in question does not survive. For Fabianus, see the note on 11.4. Although Seneca requests permission to use the word, he does not in fact make use of it either here or elsewhere.

Seneca's phrase "a necessary item" (*res necessaria*) seems to be a play on words. Not only is it necessary that he find some equivalent for the Greek word *ousia*, but *ousia* (being or substance) is a necessary principle in metaphysics. Our translation assumes that *natura* is in the nominative case, renaming *ousia*.

58.7. Greek for "the existent" or "the thing that is."

58.8. Although the discussion that follows has clear antecedents in the Platonic dialogues themselves (see especially *Sophist* 243d–49d, *Timaeus* 27e–29d), the listing of six "ways" (*modi*) in which Plato speaks of "the existent" is an interpretation by Seneca's friend or perhaps by Seneca himself, or one found in some book he has read. His approach, combining an enumeration of the "ways in which a thing is said" with a division of existent things by species, genera, and then "higher" or more fundamental genera, suggests both Aristotelian and

Stoic influences. The letter has been extensively discussed and divergently interpreted, especially with regard to Seneca's attitude to Platonic metaphysics; see Boys-Stones 2013; Dillon 1996, 135–39; Inwood 2007b; Inwood 2007c, 109–30; Long 2017.

58.11. In Stoic physics, a "body" (or corporeal thing) was anything that could act or be acted upon. Among the things Stoics counted as incorporeals are time, place, void, and "things said"; i.e., the meanings of linguistic expressions (Sextus Empiricus, *Against the Mathematicians* 10.218 [LS 27D]).

58.14. Seneca's word "animate creatures" (*animalia*) refers to all living things that have "mind" (*animus*) or the capacity for self-motion, including not only animals in our sense but also human beings and gods.

58.15. Although centaurs and the like do not exist, they are still *something*, since we have an image of them in our minds and can speak coherently about them. For Stoic thought on this topic, see Alexander of Aphrodisias, *On Aristotle's Topics* 301.19–25 [LS 27B].

58.16. What was said in 58.8 was that Plato has six ways of using the expression *to on*, not that those different ways of speaking neatly divide up everything that exists. Either way, the division is not made by Plato himself.

58.17. In Plato, *Laws* 716a, God is "the beginning, middle, and end of the things that are"; in 716c, "the measure of all things."

58.18. In a Platonic context, the Greek word *idea* does not refer only to a thought or concept, as in modern English, but is closer in meaning to *eidos* (usually translated as "form"); the two words are etymologically related. Plato himself does not always distinguish the terms as clearly as Seneca does here. See also the note on 65.7.

58.19. Compare Plato, *Timaeus* 48e.

58.22. The things that exist "commonly" are usually taken to be everyday objects or individual members of various genera; e.g., Cato, or the particular table one is looking at. On this interpretation, "commonly" means "in the ordinary sense of the word," and "begin to relate to us" (*incipiunt ad nos pertinere*) means "fall within sense experience."

These would then be the very items that Seneca says just below are *not* counted by Plato as things that are. Another possibility is that the things that exist "commonly" are various sorts of collections, the metaphysics of which are treated by Seneca in letter 102 (see GL, 404–10). This reading takes "commonly" to mean "in common" (cf. 58.17) and "begin to relate to us" to mean "begin to resemble Stoic thought."

58.23. Heraclitus of Ephesus (ca. 535–475 BCE) was called "the Obscure" for his riddling aphorisms (Cicero, *On Ends* 2.15). His dictum about the river is quoted by Plato in *Cratylus* 402a.

58.27. Here and in 65.16–18, Seneca is clearly attracted to the thought that the mind is inherently divine, that it is imprisoned within the body as form or cause within matter (cf. also 41.5–6), and that when it contemplates abstract ideas, it finds release and some form of immortality. All this is strongly Platonic in coloring: compare *Phaedo* 82d–83b, and note the emphasis on the resistance of matter and the question whether concrete objects truly exist. But at least some of these notions can also be given a Stoic interpretation, for Stoics likewise spoke of a creator god who acts within the universe and who provides reason to human beings as our means of becoming godlike. See also the note on 31.8.

58.29. In Stoic thought, the universe itself is a living being, with its own impulses and appropriate actions; it is mortal in that it is periodically consumed and regenerated by its own designing fire (see the note on 9.16). The providence or foresight of the universe is analogous to the mind of a human being; compare Cicero, *On the Nature of the Gods* 2.58. For the denigration of the body, see the note on 23.6.

58.30. Ancient tradition associated the name Plato with the Greek word *platus*, meaning "broad" or "flat." For such biographical details, compare Diogenes Laertius 3.1–45.

58.35. A life (*vita*) includes the use of one's mental faculties; merely being alive might include only the basic life functions such as respiration (*anima*). For the position on suicide stated here, see the note on 70.5.

63.1. Educated Greeks and Romans regularly composed letters or treatises of consolation, meant to comfort friends or relatives who had suffered bereavement or some other major affliction. Such works generally sounded familiar themes such as the sweetness of memory, the healing effects of time, and the inevitability of death for all human beings; often too they included examples from literature or history of individuals who rose above similar misfortunes. Compare Cicero, *Ad Familiares* 5.16.2, *Letters to Atticus* 12.11, *Tusculan Disputations* 3.55–64, 4.75–79. In the present letter, Seneca discusses the experience of grief in conjunction with Stoic views on the emotions and on friendship. Nothing further is known about the identity of the deceased man Flaccus.

63.2. In *Iliad* 19.226–29, Odysseus advises Achilles to abandon his grief for Patroclus on grounds that in wartime a single day is all that can be allowed for mourning. Later, in *Iliad* 24.602–17, Achilles reminds the grieving Priam that even Niobe, whose grief for her twelve children was proverbial, stopped on the tenth day to eat a meal.

63.4. "Bite" or "biting" (*morsus*, Gk. *daknos*) is often used in Stoic contexts to refer to the feeling of mental pain, as distinct from grief itself, which depends on false beliefs (Galen, *Precepts of Hippocrates and Plato* 4.2.4–6, 4.3.2; Cicero, *Tusculan Disputations* 3.83, 4.15; Seneca, *Consolation to Marcia* 7.1).

63.5. On Attalus, see the note on 9.7.

63.13. Roman law imposed on widows a one-year period of mourning before remarriage (Cassius Dio 56.43; Ovid, *Fasti* 1.33–36). There was no corresponding law for widowers.

63.14. Seneca's relative Annaeus Serenus had died suddenly of poison after having risen to some prominence in the imperial administration (Pliny the Elder 22.96; Tacitus, *Annals* 13.13; Griffin 1992, 447–48). Three of Seneca's shorter philosophical dialogues are addressed to him.

63.16. Seneca may be thinking especially of Plato, *Apology* 40e-41c, *Phaedo* 67ab. Seneca's personal views on survival after death are optimistic, but he makes no claim to certainty: compare 57.8, 58.27, 79.12.

65.1. While the central portion of the letter is devoted to a series of philosophical analyses of causation, the beginning and ending concentrate on the contrast between body and mind. For Seneca's illness, see the note on 54.1.

65.2. The word Seneca uses for matter (*materia*) is also his regular word for the material from which something is made. In Stoic thought, cause and matter are the two primary components of the universe. Matter (or "material") is featureless and inert, capable of taking on whatever shapes, qualities, and motions are imparted to it by cause, which is also called "reason" and "God." See Diogenes Laertius 7.134 [LS 44B]; Sextus Empiricus, *Against the Mathematicians* 9.75–76 [LS 44C]; and Calcidius 292–93 [LS 44D–E], and compare 58.28–29.

65.4. Seneca provides a summary version of Aristotle's theory of causality laid out in *Physics* 2.3 and *Metaphysics* 5.2. For the term *eidos*, compare 58.20–22, where a similar understanding of it is attributed to Plato.

65.5. The "spear bearer" (*doryphoros*) and "youth tying a headband" (*diadumenos*) were statue types that would have been familiar to Seneca's readers. Both were believed to have been copied from originals by the Greek sculptor Polyclitus (Pliny the Elder 34.55).

65.7. Although Plato obviously does not "add" to Aristotle's later account, his discussion of the patterns (*paradeigmata*) used by the demiurge in *Timaeus* 27d–28d gives "cause" a distinctly different signification from anything in Aristotle. For the term *idea*, compare 58.18. The account of Plato's position that follows resembles teachings by Platonists of Seneca's time and later; see Boys-Stones 2013; Dillon 1996, 135–39; Inwood 2007b; Inwood 2007c, 136–55; Long 2017.

65.10. Compare Plato, *Timaeus* 29d.

65.12. Seneca satisfies his demand for "the primary and generic cause" by specifying the Stoics' active principle, the "designing fire" or God (see the note on 9.16). This cause is "the one that makes," since for Stoics it is the active principle that makes everything what it is by acting upon prime matter, called the "passive principle." In saying that matter and cause are "simple" (unitary and undifferentiated), he is referring not to the bronze of the statue and the human craftsman but to matter and cause as such, taken generically.

65.16. Seneca remarks elsewhere that the study of astronomy and other abstract subjects elevates the mind and reminds it of its divine origin (*On Leisure* 5.5–6, *Natural Questions* 1 pref.).

The imagery of the imprisoned mind is Platonic; see the note on 41.5.

65.18. Either military service or service as a gladiator.

65.22. For the denigration of the body, see the note on 23.6.

70.1. What begins as literal travel soon becomes a metaphor for the journey through life. Lucilius must have grown up in the vicinity of Naples: see the note on 49.1.

70.2. Virgil, *Aeneid* 3.72.

70.5. Life in itself—its mere duration—is of no intrinsic value in Stoic thought: it is one of the preferred indifferents (see the note on 31.6); but there are situations in which suicide is appropriate, when dispreferred circumstances prevail without possibility of improvement. See Cicero, *On Ends* 3.60–61 [LS 66G]; Diogenes Laertius 7.130 [LS 66H]. In his presentation of the doctrine, Seneca stresses that while no hard-and-fast rule can be given, and while the motivating circumstances need not be immediate or extreme, it is important to take into consideration not only one's own comfort but also one's responsibilities to other people. Compare 58.32–36 and 104.3, and see further Griffin 1992, 372–83.

70.6. Telesphorus of Rhodes, held captive by the tyrant Lysimachus. His suffering is described in detail in Seneca, *On Anger* 3.17.

70.9. The situation is as described in Plato's *Crito*.

70.10. Scribonia was Octavian's second wife; Marcus Scribonius Libo Drusus, her great-nephew, was brought to trial in 15 CE on a charge of conspiring against Tiberius (Tacitus, *Annals* 2.27–32).

70.14. This is the position expressed by Socrates in Plato, *Phaedo* 62a–c.

70.19. For Cato (the Younger) see the note on 14.12. In letter 24, recounting (there as well) the story of Cato's suicide, Seneca mentions "how he was reading a book by Plato with his sword right next to his head" (24.6, in GL, 86). The book was Plato's *Phaedo*, which recounts the death of Socrates together with philosophical arguments justifying belief in an immortal soul. The *Phaedo* does not, however, condone suicide, except in exceptional circumstances (when "God sends some necessity," 62c).

70.20. Seneca's description in 7.4 indicates that the morning fights with wild animals were mainly a sadistic way of executing prisoners.

70.22. For Cato and Scipio (i.e., Caecilius Metellus Scipio), see the note on 14.12. Like Cato, Metellus Scipio took his own life after his defeat.

75.1. In writing about the prose style that is appropriate for letters, Seneca speaks primarily of the character of the writer and the potential benefit to the recipient. This leads into a discussion of the levels of moral progress that are recognized in Stoic theory.

75.8. Because Stoic doctrine takes virtue and vice to be absolute and mutually exclusive conditions, anyone who has not attained virtue is necessarily flawed (Cicero, *On Ends* 3.48; Plutarch, *On Common Conceptions* 1063a–b). But one can still make progress toward virtue (Diogenes Laertius 7.91); for while all imperfect conditions are equally imperfect, they are not alike in other respects.

75.9. The reference seems to be to 71.4: "But sometimes people know things without knowing they know them" (GL, 215). However, the point being made in that context is quite different.

75.10. Many negative traits of character were described by Stoics as tendencies to experience certain emotions especially often or for trivial cause. For these "infirmities," see the note on 53.7.

75.12. Seneca (or his source) combines two standard Stoic definitions of "emotion": "a movement of mind contrary to reason" and an "overly vehement impulse"; see, for instance, Diogenes Laertius 7.110; Stobaeus 2.7.10, 88–90W [LS 65A]; Cicero, *Tusculan Disputations* 4.11; Galen, *Precepts of Hippocrates and Plato* 4.2.10–18 [LS 65J]. Like other Stoics, he holds that emotions as defined can and should be eliminated altogether. See further the notes on 9.3 and 116.1.

75.13. In letter 92, Seneca writes, "For the person who takes second rank in that he is not sufficiently consistent to preserve the right in all situations—the one whose judgment is still fallible and weak—even he is near the mark. . . . . But in the imperfect man there remains some tendency toward badness, because his mind is still capable of being motivated toward wrongdoing, although deeply ingrained and active badness is gone from it. He is not yet good, only someone being fashioned in that direction" (92.28–29, in GL, 347).

76.1. Seneca had written extensively about the Stoic claim that the only real good for a human being consists in "the honorable"; that is, in excellence of character as expressed in right actions. (See especially letters 71.4–21 and 74.1–29, in GL, 215–19 and 228–34.) In the present letter he undertakes to explain the reasoning behind this core thesis of Stoic ethics. Somewhat whimsically, the letter begins by representing Seneca as a lifelong learner, who has recently been attending lectures on moral philosophy.

76.2. Squires (*trossuli*) are mentioned elsewhere as fashionable young men given to lavish expenditure on horses (Varro, *Menippean Satires* 480; Persius 1.82, Seneca, *Letters* 87.9, 123.7). Here, it seems rather to be a mocking term for young philosophy students.

76.4. The philosopher Metronax is known only from Seneca's mention of him here and in letter 93.1 (in GL, 349), where he is said to have died recently.

76.7. The proof attempted in the following paragraphs is closely related to arguments given by Plato (*Republic* 1.352d–354a) and Aristotle (*Nicomachean Ethics* 1.7) for believing that happiness (*eudaimonia*) consists essentially in virtuous character and conduct. However, neither of those philosophers deemed perfected reason to be the *only* human good. The Stoic version of the argument is found also in Epictetus, *Discourses* 1.6 [LS 63E].

76.11. That is, if a person's *reasoning* is bad or good, the person will be criticized or praised accordingly.

76.22. If the essence of the honorable and of the virtues is reason, then it would be contradictory to suppose that there could be any nonrational goods.

76.23. The Stoics held that all events depend on antecedent causes, with nothing at all occurring by chance in the sense of occurring randomly and without reason. Considered collectively, antecedent causes constitute fate; i.e., a sequence or web of causes which is also the immutable and providential will of Zeus. Our actions are nonetheless in our power, since it is our own acts of assent that bring them about, even though those acts of assent are themselves part of the fated sequence. The virtuous attitude is to acquiesce in the divine governance of events and to perform willingly whatever one perceives as incumbent on a rational being. For the Stoic background, see Alexander of Aphrodisias, *On Fate* 191–92 [LS 55N]; Cicero, *On Divination* 1.125–26 [LS 55L]; Cicero, *On Fate* 39–43 [LS 62C]; Seneca, *Letters* 107.11 (quoting a hymn of Cleanthes).

76.28. On joy, see the note on 23.3.

76.33. Virgil, *Aeneid* 6.103–5.

76.35. The wise person employs the technique of prerehearsal: see the note on 91.1.

79.1. Lucilius was genuinely interested in the geography of Sicily. In *Natural Questions* 3.1.1, Seneca quotes a hexameter line from a poem of his concerning the fountain of Arethusa, which was said to come from an underground river originating in the Peloponnese ("from springs of Sicily there leaps an Elian stream"). In speaking of Scylla and Charybdis, Seneca has in mind the Straits of Messina, whose rocks and treacherous current were identified by the Romans with the terrifying monster and enormous whirlpool described in book 12 of the *Odyssey*.

79.5. Ovid's description is in *Metamorphoses* 15.340–55; Virgil's, in *Aeneid* 3.571–82. Cornelius Severus was an epic poet, a friend of Ovid (*Letters from Pontus* 4.16.9), whose poem on the Sicilian War is mentioned in Quintilian 10.1.89.

79.10. In Stoic thought, wisdom and virtue are the sort of properties that cannot be scaled up or down, just as a straight line in geometry cannot be either more or less straight than it is. The point is explained in Cicero, *On Ends* 3.48; Simplicius, *On Aristotle's Categories* 237.25–238.20 [LS 47S]. The magnitude of stars is constant as opposed to that of comets and other variable phenomena of the night sky (Seneca, *Natural Questions* 1.1.10).

79.12. The imagery of the imprisoned mind is Platonic; see the note on 41.5.

79.13. Compare Cicero, *Tusculan Disputations* 1.91.

79.14. A popular legend held that the people of Abdera, Democritus's home-town, supposing him to be insane, requested help from the physician Hippocrates, who told them they were mistaken.

For Cato, see the note on 14.12. P. Rutilius Rufus, an associate of the younger Scipio, was exiled on a trumped-up charge in 92 BCE but bore it in a principled manner and subsequently declined to return (Seneca, *On Benefits* 6.37; Cicero, *De Oratore* 1.227–30).

79.16. On Metrodorus, see the note on 14.17.

83.5. The Canal was in the Campus Martius in the middle of Rome. The Maiden was one of the aqueducts that supplied Rome and was known for particularly cold water; compare Ovid, *Ars Amatoria* 3.385.

83.9. In letter 82, Seneca complains of Zeno's habit of propounding syllogisms, calling it perverse to address ethical topics in a way that seems unlikely to motivate deep reflection (82.9, in GL, 272–73). Here, he is more interested in the syllogism itself and in a proposed defense of it by Posidonius.

83.10. The Stoic philosopher Posidonius, a pupil of Panaetius (see the note on 116.5), taught at Rhodes in the first half of the first century BCE. Seneca is well acquainted with a number of his works and regards him as one of the most important names in philosophy. His various remarks about Posidonius are treated in detail in Kidd 1988.

83.12. Lucius Tillius Cimber had held the praetorship under Caesar in 46 BCE; at the time of Caesar's murder, he had just been appointed to an important governorship. It was he who gave the signal for the assassination to begin. See also Seneca, *On Anger* 3.31.5.

83.13. Although he has promised just one example, Seneca provides two. Lucius Calpurnius Piso (consul in 15 BCE) held the office of city prefect from 14 CE to 32 CE; Cossus Cornelius Lentulus (consul in 1 BCE) later assumed the same office. Both are mentioned in Suetonius as drinking companions of Tiberius (*Tiberius* 42).

83.19. On Alexander, see the note on 53.10.

83.20. Shamelessness is called an "infirmity" in the sense of a negative trait of character; see the notes on 53.7 and 75.10. The term would be equally applicable to the other faults listed here.

83.23. Among the conflicting accounts of Alexander's death, one (preserved in Diodorus Siculus 17.117) connects it with his draining a wine goblet of twelve pints' capacity in honor of Heracles, or Hercules.

83.25. The Latin word *crudelitas* (cruelty) is etymologically connected with *crudus* (raw) and is often associated by Seneca with the eating of raw flesh: compare 108.18 in this volume, Seneca, *On Clemency* 1.25; Seneca, *On Anger* 2.5; and see *On Clemency* 2.4, where such bloodthirstiness is distinguished from the ordinary vice of cruelty (i.e., excessive severity). Antony's devotion to wine was part of his public image; compare Pliny the Elder, *Natural History* 14.28.

84.1. These "trips" are excursions in a sedan chair ("through the labor of others"). Seneca had recommended such excursions in 15.6 as a way to relax the mind and limber up the body; in letter 55, he describes his own experience of one (55.1–2, GL, 157). While 15.6 also mentions the possibility of reading or giving dictation while riding in the chair, the point here is rather that these excursions have given Seneca a break from reading, to the benefit of his writing: the two should be done by turns. Toward the end of the letter, the process of writing in alternation with reading becomes a technique for the creation of an integrated self (see Graver 2014).

84.3. Virgil, *Aeneid* 1.432–33.

84.4. In Stoic thought, the abilities characteristic of a species are imparted by the particular kind of "spirit" or "breath" (*pneuma*) present in each. See also the notes on 90.29.

84.13. The thought is made clearer by comparison with Seneca, *On Anger* 2.13. Although progress toward virtue is challenging in itself, it is level ground in comparison to the toil and danger of moneymaking and political ambition.

86.1. P. Cornelius Scipio Africanus, one of Rome's most successful generals and political leaders, fell into legal difficulties in 184 BCE and chose to retire to his estate at Liternum in Campania, where he died a year later. The historian Livy confirms that his tomb was there (Livy 38.53). Cambyses was king of Persia 530–522 BCE; the account of his madness is in Herodotus 3.25, 29.

86.3. Scipio's campaign against Carthage caused Hannibal to withdraw his forces from Italian soil.

86.5. Lucretius 3.1034.

86.10. An aedile was a high-ranking official who held responsibility for the construction and oversight of public buildings, including baths, and for the enforcement of sumptuary laws. Cato the Elder held the office in 199 BCE; Scipio Africanus in 193. Quintus Fabius Maximus Verrucosus was one of the most illustrious political and military leaders of the generation preceding Cato and Scipio.

86.12. Market day in the Roman Republic was every ninth day.

86.13. Horace, *Satires* 1.2.27, where the name is Rufillus. Horace's full line reads, "Rufillus smells of lozenges; Gargonius of the goat." "The goat" was Roman slang for body odor.

86.14. The freedman Aegialus, according to Pliny the Elder 14.49, earned much respect for his skill in cultivating the villa at Liternum. In the same context, Pliny reports that Seneca was sufficiently interested in farming to spend a large sum on an estate in Nomentum owned by a rival, the literary scholar Palaemon; there the vineyards had been cultivated with renowned success by one Acilius Sthenelus.

86.15. Virgil, *Georgics* 2.58.

86.16. Virgil, *Georgics* 1.215–16.

86.20. Grapevines were planted at the roots of elm trees, which normally served as their lifelong supports.

90.1. Like other Stoics, Seneca emphasizes that the human capacity for reason gives us not wisdom itself but the possibility of developing wisdom. Further specification is needed, however, as to the nature of wisdom itself. Does the standard definition "knowledge of things human and divine" (e.g., at 104.22) pertain only to the virtues of individuals and the government of human communities, or does it extend to all kinds of inventions and acquired skills? Seneca will argue for the former, taking issue with a historical work by Posidonius.

90.3.   Stoic theory held that any person who possesses one of the virtues necessarily possesses them all, and further, that any action done on the basis of one virtue is simultaneously, though secondarily, done on the basis of every other virtue as well. Nonetheless, the virtues are not merely different names for a single condition, for each virtue has its own distinctive sphere of application: temperance regulates our impulses, justice makes fair distributions, and so on. Compare 113.14, and for the Stoic background, Diogenes Laertius 7.126; Stobaeus 2.7.5b5, 63W [LS 61D].

90.4.   These would be persons who had not yet become subject to moral corruption (see the note on 31.2).

90.5.   For Posidonius see the note on 83.10. The material cited in this letter must derive from his historical writings.

90.6.   A list of "seven sages" was traditional among the Greeks as early as Plato (*Protagoras* 343a); all were intellectual and/or political leaders of the sixth or fifth century BCE. Solon, who wrote a law code for Athens, was among them; Lycurgus, traditionally named as the lawgiver of Sparta, lived too early.

Zaleucus and Charondas were remembered as lawgivers for the Sicilian cities of Locri and Catania, respectively; both in fact predated Pythagoras, but by Seneca's date a lack of concern for chronology in speaking about Pythagoras was itself traditional.

90.9.   Virgil, *Georgics* 1.144.

90.11.   Virgil, *Georgics* 1.139–40.

90.13.   Seneca's word *sapiens*, for "sage" (i.e., for an inventor or teacher of long ago, as described by Posidonius) is also his word for "wise person" (the intellectual and moral exemplar; see the note on 9.1).

90.14.   Diogenes of Sinope was the best known of the Cynic philosophers of the fourth century BCE. Like other Cynics, he practiced a rigorous asceticism that included sleeping outdoors with minimal shelter. Daedalus, the legendary inventor (his name means "ingenious"), is credited by Pliny the Elder (7.80) with the invention of carpentry and of such carpenter's tools as the saw, drill, and plumb line.

90.20. Ovid, *Metamorphoses* 6.55–58, but the version Seneca gives differs significantly from our texts of Ovid.

90.29. The language used here is that of Stoic physics. The Stoics held that the universe is completely infused with rationality in the form of a "designing fire" that is identified with the creator god, or Zeus. (See also the note on 9.16.) This designing fire imparts generative principles of structure and function to everything that exists through the admixture of *pneuma* (breath), a fine-textured material in which the warmth of the designing fire is blended with the coolness of air (Alexander of Aphrodisias, *On Mixture and Increase* 224 [LS 47I]).

For the Stoics, the mind or spirit is corporeal in nature, being composed entirely of *pneuma* "disposed in a certain way" (as Seneca himself says in letter 50.6; see GL, 145–46). *Pneuma* resides especially in the heart, where it serves as the directive faculty (*hēgemonikon*) of the person as a whole and provides the capacity to form mental impressions and impulses and the special attribute of reason (Diogenes Laertius 7.85–86 [LS 57A]; Stobaeus 1.49.33, 368W [LS 53K]). But *pneuma* is also present throughout the body, where it is responsible for all our life functions and especially for the faculties of sight, hearing, smell, taste, touch, voice, and reproduction. These together with the directive faculty comprise the eights parts of the Stoic soul (Aetius 4.21.1-4 [LS 53H]). For the possibility that the mind continues to exist after the death of the body, see the note on 57.7.

This third set of investigations belongs to the realm of logic, the third major division of Stoic philosophy (Diogenes Laertius 7.39–41 [LS 26B]). Logic deals with the incorporeal because it is primarily concerned with "things said" (see the note on 58.11).

90.31. Anacharsis of Scythia (sixth century BCE) was sometimes listed as one of the Seven Sages; the potter's wheel, which is mentioned already in Homer, *Iliad* 18.600–601, is much older.

90.32. In addition to his writings on physics and ethics, Democritus of Abdera was credited with treatises on a wide range of technical subjects (Diogenes Laertius 9.48); he did not, however, invent the arch.

90.33. The Romans were familiar with techniques for producing colored enamels and for softening ivory for carving by soaking it in an acidic solution.

90.35. The philosophy criticized is Epicureanism. For Seneca's attitude toward the school, see the note on 2.5.

90.37. Virgil, *Georgics* 1.125–28.

91.1. The Roman colony of Lugdunum, modern Lyon, was the empire's most important administrative center north of the Alps. If this fire is the disaster mentioned in Tacitus, *Annals* 16.13, it must have taken place shortly after the great fire at Rome in the summer of 64 CE. Seneca's friend Aebutius Liberalis is the addressee of his treatise *On Benefits*. The present letter summarizes a letter of consolation previously sent to Liberalis himself. For this type of letter, see the note on 63.1.

Seneca assumes that Liberalis has "armed himself" by reflecting daily on all the many kinds of misfortune that can happen to a person. (Compare 76.35.) Frequently recommended in consolatory works, this technique was meant to afford an accurate assessment of what a human life is likely to include, thus mitigating the psychological impact of inevitable misfortune. Cicero, in describing the same practice in *Tusculan Disputations* 3.28–31, supplies the term "prerehearsal of future ills" (*praemeditatio futurorum malorum*).

91.12. For earthquakes caused by subterranean wind or water, see Seneca, *Natural Questions* 6.7 and 6.12–13.

91.13. Timagenes of Alexandria came to Rome as a prisoner of war in 55 BCE and later worked as a historian under Augustus and Asinius Pollio. Both the elder and younger Senecas tell of him that he had an acid wit and that after falling into disfavor with Augustus, he had his record of the princeps's achievements publicly burned (Seneca the Elder, *Controversiae* 10.5.22; Seneca, *On Anger* 3.23).

91.14. The founding of Lugdunum by L. Munatius Plancus is confirmed by his funerary inscription; *Corpus Inscriptionum Latinarum* 10.6087. As the colony was founded in 43 BCE, it was in fact somewhat more than a hundred years old.

91.16. Rome was captured and sacked by a Gallic tribe in 390 BCE; Ardea, a small hill town nearby, was devastated by the Samnites later in the same century.

91.17. On Alexander, see the note on 53.10.

91.19. On Demetrius, see the note on 20.9.

97.1. Cato the Younger was present when Publius Clodius Pulcher was put on trial in July of 61 BCE, on a charge of violating the ritual of the Bona Dea by using it as cover for adultery. Cicero prosecuted Clodius on behalf of the Senate, and it is his account of it in a letter to his friend Atticus that supplies Seneca's information here. For more on Cato, see the note on 14.12.

97.4. Cicero, *Letters to Atticus* 1.16.5.

97.6. Quintus Lutatius Catulus was a prominent member of the Senate; his witticism appears in the same words in *Letters to Atticus* 1.16.6.

97.8. Cato was said to have been so revered by the plebeians that in his presence they would not call for that part of the festival of Flora which involved ribald joking and public nudity (Valerius Maximus 2.10.8).

97.13. Compare Epicurus, *Principal Doctrines* 35.

97.15. The view attributed to Epicurus is similar to what he states in *Principal Doctrines* 33 and 34: that justice is not "something in itself" but consists in a mutual nonaggression pact, and that injustice is bad not in itself but because of one's fear of detection and punishment.

104.1. The letter is written from Seneca's villa at Nomentum, about eighteen miles northeast of Rome. Although traveling this far has enabled him to recover from a fever brought on by the dust and smoke of the city, Seneca objects to the notion that long-distance travel can improve concentration by relieving anxiety and other mental afflictions.

Following Roman custom, Seneca's father had allowed a close friend, the senator Lucius Iunius Gallio, to adopt Seneca's older brother Novatus. It is the brother, now known as Lucius Iunius Gallio Annaeanus, who is referred to here. He is Seneca's mentor (*dominus*) in that he is the head of the family, the elder Seneca having died in 39 or 40 CE. Gallio Annaeanus also served as governor of the province of Greece (Achaea) in 51–52; he is mentioned in the Bible in Acts 18:12–17 for dismissing the charges brought against the apostle Paul.

104.2. Seneca's wife Pompeia Paulina was a member of a prominent senatorial family. Her devotion to her husband figures prominently in the account of his death in Tacitus, *Annals* 15.63–64.

104.7. In letter 28, Seneca quotes Socrates as saying, "Why are you surprised that traveling does you no good, when you travel in your own company? The thing that weighs on your mind is the same as drove you from home" (28.2, in GL, 97).

104.10. Virgil, *Aeneid* 3.282–83.

104.21. The first group are typical examples of moral rectitude from the Roman Republic. Both Gaius Laelius and Quintus Aelius Tubero were associates of Scipio Aemilianus: Laelius, called "the Wise," was remembered for his political restraint and for his qualities as a friend; Tubero for frugality and self-control. For the two Catos, see the notes on 7.6 and 14.12. Zeno of Citium, Chrysippus, and Posidonius were all Stoic philosophers. For Zeno's suicide, see Diogenes Laertius 7.28, and compare 58.34–36.

104.23. The wise resemble God in perfect rationality and in blessedness; see the note on 31.8. That they consciously imitate God is a further idea which Seneca expresses also in 124.23–24. The theme is characteristic of the Platonic tradition under the influence of Plato, *Theaetetus* 176b, but it is also fully compatible with Stoic thought; see, for instance, Epictetus, *Discourses* 2.14.11–13.

104.24. Virgil, *Aeneid* 6.277.

104.27. Seneca now brings together a number of biographical details about Socrates. The tradition concerning Socrates's wife goes back to Xenophon, *Symposium* 2.10.

The word "freedom" (*libertas*) refers to the Athenian democracy, since it was after the democracy was restored that Socrates was tried and sentenced to death.

104.28. This claim about Socrates is made also by Cicero, *Tusculan Disputations* 3.31, and by Seneca in *On Anger* 2.7.

104.29. The biographical sketch that follows recapitulates points that have already been made (cf. especially 14.12–13) but also provides further details. Seneca's knowledge of Cato's life may owe something to the biography written at around this time by Thrasea Paetus (mentioned by Plutarch, *Cato the Younger* 25.1).

104.30. The prosecution Seneca has in mind is probably that of Murena in 63 BCE, described as especially stern in Cicero's speech for the defense. The province is Cyprus, which Cato administered on special commission in 58 BCE with scrupulous honesty.

104.31. Virgil, *Aeneid* 1.458.

104.33. These events are vividly described by Lucan, *Civil War* 9.371–618.

The story of Cato's playing ball after losing the election for the consulship of 51 BCE is told also by Plutarch, *Cato the Younger* 49–50.

108.1. It is only at the very end of this letter that we learn anything more about Lucilius's overly technical inquiry; namely, that it is the question treated in letter 109, "whether one wise person can help another" (109.1, in GL, 434). In the meantime, Seneca writes at length about the purpose of teaching and learning, including some of his own experiences as a young student. The plan to write a comprehensive book on ethics is mentioned also in letters 106.2 and 109.17 (in GL, 421, 437). If it was in fact written, the work was perhaps identical with the *Books on Ethics* (*libri moralis philosophiae*) quoted several times by the Christian author Lactantius. See further Leeman 1953; Vottero 1998, 204–9, 340–54.

108.3. On Attalus, see the note on 9.7.

108.7. Certain festivals of the goddess Cybele, thought to be of Near Eastern origin, involved ecstatic dancing to the music of flutes, cymbals, and tambourines, with some worshippers practicing self-castration.

108.8. Our innate tendencies to prefer certain kinds of objects serve as the starting points for our development toward perfected rationality; hence they are sometimes referred to as the "seeds" or "sparks" of the virtues. These tendencies would include our instinct for self-preservation (121.17–18) and for the companionship of others (9.17). For the Stoic background, see Stobaeus 2.7.5b3, 62W and 2.7.5b8, 65W [LS 61L]; Cicero, *On Duties* 1.11–17, and *On Ends* 3.16–21 [LS 59D]

108.9. The two lines appear consecutively in the collection attributed to Publilius Syrus (Friedrich [1880] 1964, 49); see the note on 8.9.

108.10. Cleanthes became head of the Stoic school in Athens in 262 BCE. His philosophical poetry is represented especially by a hymn to Zeus [LS 54I] and by another, shorter hymn, which Seneca quotes in his own translation in letter 107 (see GL, 425).

108.11. The source of these lines is unknown.

108.12. Faults of character, such as avarice and ambition (see the note on 53.7), are less deeply ingrained in the young than in older persons.

108.17. Seneca mentions studying with Sotion also in 49.2, indicating that this was at an age when he had not yet begun to argue cases; i.e., in his early teens. From the passage here, it appears that Sotion offered the Pythagorean rather than the Sextian justification for vegetarianism. Quintus Sextius the Elder and his son, also called Sextius, are described by Seneca as proponents of a philosophy that emphasized practical ethics, extolling frugality, self-control, and courage and recommending such practical expedients as looking in a mirror to control anger and mentally reviewing each day's conduct at bedtime (*On Anger* 2.36, 3.36; *Letters* 64.2–5, 73.12–16; *Natural Questions* 7.32).

108.18. For this sense of the word "cruelty" (*crudelitas*), see the note on 83.25.

108.24. Virgil, *Georgics* 3.284.

Virgil, *Georgics* 3.66–68.

108.29. Virgil, *Aeneid* 6.275.

108.30. Cicero's *On the Republic*, which survives only in part, combines theoretical issues in political philosophy with much anecdotal information on the historical development of the Roman government. In book 3 of that work, the skeptical philosopher Philus speaks as a devil's advocate "against justice"—i.e., against there being any natural basis for ethics.

According to both Cicero (*On the Republic* 2.33) and Livy (1.32), Ancus Marcius, the grandson of Numa Pompilius through the maternal line, was made Rome's fourth king by popular acclamation. Servius Tullius, the sixth king, is said (in *On the Republic* 2.37) to have been the child of a slave woman of the Tarquins and an unknown father.

108.31. For these historical details, compare Cicero, *On the Republic* 1.25, 63. Fenestella wrote a lengthy chronicle of Roman history through the Late Republic.

108.33. These and the following lines concern Scipio Africanus, who was Ennius's patron late in life; compare 86.1, and see also Lactantius 1.18.10. If, as seems likely, both quotations derive from the same passage in Ennius, we might venture with the aid of Vahlen 1903, 215–16, to combine these fragments from *On the Republic* with Cicero's Ennian quotations in *On Laws* 2.57 and *Tusculan Disputations* 5.49 into an epitaph similar in meter and style to the one Ennius composed for himself:

> Here lies a man whom neither citizen nor foe
> could ever repay the price of his assistance.
> "From the Maeotian sea, from furthest east
> there is no one to rival my achievements.
> If it be right for anyone to mount the skies,
> for me alone does heaven's great portal open."

108.34. Virgil, *Georgics* 3.260–61.

112.1. In letter 36, Seneca advises Lucilius about how to counsel a young friend who is embarking upon philosophical study (36.1, in GL, 114). Here, it is Seneca who is attempting to teach a friend of Lucilius, with the latter contributing his insights.

112.2. Seneca was strongly interested in viticulture; compare Seneca, *Natural Questions* 3.7.1 (where he calls himself "a meticulous digger of vines"), and see the note on 86.14.

113.1. According to one of the surviving compendia of Stoic doctrine:

> The virtues are multiple and are inseparable from one another;
> they are the same in substance as the soul's directive part. Accord-
> ingly each virtue is and is called a body, since the mind and soul
> are corporeal. For they hold that the warm breath that is innate
> in us is our soul. They also want the soul that is in us to be an ani-
> mate creature, since it is alive and has sensation. . . . Hence, every
> virtue is also a living creature, since in substance it is the same
> as the mind. In addition, they say that intelligence is intelligent.
> (Stobaeus 2.7.5b7, 65W, *SVF* 3.305–6).

While Seneca accepts the idea that the mind is corporeal in nature
(see the note on 90.29), he finds it absurd to conclude that each of
the virtues is an animate creature in its own right. It becomes even
more so when we keep in mind that the term here translated "animate
creature" also means "animal."

113.2. The Latin word *animalia* is derived from *animus*, meaning "mind".

In Stoic metaphysics, a substance—in this case, breath—is "disposed
in a certain way" when it takes on a further attribute. The mind or
spirit is already "breath disposed in a certain way"; but it may take
on a further attribute: it can be a courageous mind, a just mind, and
so on. For the Stoic background, see Alexander of Aphrodisias, *On
Soul* 118 [LS 29A]; Sextus Empiricus, *Outlines of Pyrrhonism* 2.81–82
[LS 33P].

113.5. Here and in 113.16, the argument appeals to the Stoic metaphysical
doctrine that each numerically distinct entity has its own distinctive property (*proprium* or *proprietas*; Gk. *idiōs poion*), which persists
though many kinds of change (Simplicius, *On Aristotle's Treatise On
Soul* 217–18 = LS 28I). Because the virtues are not individuated in this
way, they cannot be considered animate beings in their own right.

113.14. The Stoics held that while each virtue is a distinct disposition, anyone
who possesses one virtue necessarily possesses them all. (See the note
on 90.3.) On this basis, Seneca rejects the view of his opponent that
a person could take on the virtues successively, like different suits of
clothing.

113.18. An impression whose content is "it is fitting for me to walk" is what the parallel text in Stobaeus calls an "impulsory impression of what is appropriate in that moment" (Stobaeus 2.7.9, 86W [LS 53Q]). When Seneca speaks of the creature's having "entertained an impulse" (*impetum cepit*), he means that it must have generated such an impulsory impression before giving assent to it. (A clear example of the Latin usage may be found in 78.2).

113.22. Chrysippus held that the human soul when separated from the body assumes a spherical form (scholiast on *Iliad* 23.65 [*SVF* 2.815]); compare Jerome, *Letter* 109.23 (*SVF* 2.816). Seneca is also familiar with a Stoic claim that the gods themselves are round, for which he cites Varro (*Pumpkinification* 8); compare Cicero, *On the Nature of the Gods* 1.18, 2.46–48.

113.23. Cleanthes was the second head of the Stoic school in Athens; Chrysippus succeeded him in 232. On Chrysippus, see further the note on 9.14. On vital breath and the directive faculty, see the note on 90.29.

113.25. "Arms and the man I sing" begins the opening line of Virgil's *Aeneid*, each (complete) line of which has six metrical feet.

113.26. Caecilius Statius was a comic playwright of the second century BCE.

113.28. On Posidonius, see the note on 83.10.

113.29. On Alexander, see the note on 53.10.

116.1. Seneca here confronts directly the view of the Peripatetics, later followers of Aristotle, on the nature and management of the emotions. These philosophers held that emotions are part of human nature and are often useful to us, and that in any case they cannot be eliminated but should instead be moderated; i.e., experienced in moderate amounts. To this he responds that while the emotions do indeed stem from a natural source, they are not indispensable: we can want to have the necessities of life without experiencing desire for them, and we can have concern for ourselves without feeling anxious. The moderation approach is logically flawed: given that the emotions are inherently unhealthy (since they depend on false notions of value; see note on 9.3), it is better to have none of them than to have a moderate amount. Besides, the vehemence of emotional impulses makes them ungovernable: we cannot limit their extent, so it is better to resist them at the outset. Compare Seneca, *On Anger* 1.7–17, 2.35; and *Letters* 85.3–9; and for the Stoic background, Cicero, *Tusculan Disputations* 3.22, 3.71, 4.38–42; Galen, *Precepts of Hippocrates and Plato* 4.2.14–18 [LS 65J], with Graver 2007.

Desiring (*cupere*) differs from wanting (*velle*) in that it regards its object as a genuine good rather than as a preferred indifferent. Hence desire counts as an emotion, while wanting is an instance of "selection" (*eklogē*); i.e., an impulse directed toward a preferred or dispreferred indifferent (Stobaeus 2.7.7g, 84–85W [LS 8E]; Cicero, *On Ends* 3.20). See also the note on 31.6.

116.3. The view that pleasure is a by-product that supervenes when we obtain the necessities of life is attested for the Stoic Chrysippus (Diogenes Laertius 7.86 [LS 57A]). In *On the Happy Life* 9.1–2, stating the same doctrine, Seneca compares it to poppies that grow around the edges of a cultivated field.

116.5. Panaetius of Rhodes assumed leadership of the Stoic school in Athens about 129 BCE. His statement here is in keeping with his interest in practical ethics.

121.1. Letter 120 (in GL, 479–84) had discussed at some length the process by which human beings, in the course of their development, come to grasp a notion of the good, which for Stoics is also a notion of what behavior is honorable. The present letter treats a question that is logically prior: how it is that animate beings generally, both human beings and nonhuman animals, are aware of their own physical structure and abilities. The Stoic answer, which Seneca recapitulates here, is that this awareness is innate, although it will naturally change as the animal's constitution changes during its life. The topic is in fact highly relevant to Stoic ethics, since it is only insofar as we are aware of what accords with our constitution that we are able to develop a concept of what is good for us. See further Diogenes Laertius 7.85–86 [LS 57A]; Cicero, *On Ends* 3.16–24, 62–68.

Seneca implies that his primary sources for the discussion that follows are Posidonius (see the note on 83.10) and the second-century-BCE Stoic Archedemus. From our perspective (given that the works by

Posidonius and Archedemus do not survive), his presentation of the issue, with its many examples from the animal world, has most in common with the *Elements of Ethics* by Hierocles (text and commentary in Bastianini and Long 1992; translation in Ramelli and Konstan 2009).

121.4. For the corrupting influence of well-meant prayers, see the note on 31.2.

121.6. Pantomime dancers were highly popular entertainers who used singing and movement to enact episodes from mythology.

121.10. For the terminology, see the note on 113.2.

121.14. For this process of instinctual attachment (*oikeiōsis*), see the note on 9.17.

121.18. In letter 82, Seneca writes, "There is in us an innate love of self, an innate wish to survive and preserve ourselves, and an innate horror of disintegration, because it seems to deprive us of many goods and to remove us from the surroundings we are used to. Death is made alien to us also by the fact that we know this world already, but we do not know what the world toward which we are headed is like, and we have a horror of the unknown. Besides, we have a natural fear of darkness, and people believe that death will lead us into the dark" (82.15, in GL, 274). Other relevant passages include 14.1 and 116.3.

123.1. Seneca's villa in the Alban Hills would have been located about fifteen miles southeast of Rome. The delay in his meal occasioned by travel to that location occasions this reflection on how one can rise above things that are superfluous. An important step is to dismiss the voices of those people who encourage self-indulgence; and all the more so when their encouragement pretends to have the authority of philosophical doctrine behind it.

123.4. A state dinner given by a newly elected magistrate, normally at great expense.

123.10. The speech that follows is that of a crass hedonist who offers as a pretext the Epicurean claims that virtue is an empty name (cf. Cicero, *On Ends* 2.48) and that sensual pleasure is the goal of existence. Compare 21.9. The commonplace that life is "irretrievable" recalls Virgil in *Georgics* 3.284 and *Aeneid* 10.467–68; compare Seneca's own treatment of the theme in 108.24.

123.12. See the second note on 31.2, on the corrupting influences of the surrounding culture. As in that passage, the voices that beguile us are compared to the song of the Sirens in Homer, *Odyssey* book 12.

123.13. To make a fully rational decision, one needs not only to understand the Stoic position on naturally preferred and dispreferred indifferents (see the note on 31.6) but also to correct for the natural preference itself.

123.15. The second speaker, likewise a crass hedonist, gives a philosophical veneer to his position by referring to two Stoic doctrines: that the wise person falls in love, and that the wise person has knowledge of proper conduct at drinking parties (Stobaeus 2.5b9, 65–66W [*SVF* 3.717]; Diogenes Laertius 7.129–30).

124.1. A quotation from Virgil, *Georgics* 1.176–77, introduces the relatively technical question that Lucilius is supposed to have asked. By what faculty do we come to understand the human good? Is it by the senses, or by the intellect?

Both nonhuman animals and human infants lack the ability to use spoken language; the Latin word *infans* actually means "nonspeaker." However, it is not speech in itself that puts mature human beings into a different ethical category; rather, it is the rational capacities that are typically manifested in the use of language.

124.2. Hedonist philosophers, among whom Seneca is especially concerned with the Epicureans, maintain that our instinctive attraction to pleasure and aversion to pain are indicative of what is good or bad for us. Seneca objects that on this basis it will be difficult to refute the crass hedonist who uses Epicureanism as a pretext for an entirely unregulated manner of living. Compare 123.10, and see the second note on 21.9.

124.5. Vision is our most accurate sense; when dissimilar objects are very small, we need vision to tell them apart. If any of our senses were able to tell us whether an object is good or bad, it would have to be vision.

But in fact, we cannot *see* goodness or badness. It follows that the good is grasped only by the intellect.

124.11. As human children develop, they begin to think and act as rational creatures, and thus to have the potential for perfecting their rational nature. It is at this point that attaining the human good becomes a possibility for us. Compare 121.14–16, and for the Stoic background see the note on 121.1.

124.17. The point about memory and anticipation appears in similar terms in Cicero, *On Duties* 1.11.

124.18. Animal behavior is disordered and unsystematic in the sense that nonhuman animals, by their focus only on the immediate present, lack the capacity to subject their behavior to a rational plan. Consequently, they have no access to the good as Stoics understand it. Compare Seneca, *On Anger* 1.3.7.

124.23. On the mind's godlike potential, see the notes on 31.8 and 104.23.

124.24. The extant collection ends with a return to the theme of letter 23: the powerful sense of joy that comes from the realization that all goods come from within oneself. The final sentence exploits the Stoic paradox that only the wise person is rich; cf. 90.34.

Angle brackets indicate words that are not in the manuscripts.

1.1. *maxima . . . magna.*

11.5. *lenti.*

12.6. *includit.*

12.7. *<unus>.*

12.7. *<licet dies sit>.*

14.13. *et probris infandis.*

15.4. *usu redde facile.*

15.8. *et latus.*

15.8. *media oris vi abeat nec.*

15.9. *munus Graecum.*

20.11. *gloriosus.*

21.4. omit *<sibi>.*

21.10. *et inscriptum videris.*

33.5. omit *<continuando>*; move *et* to follow *per lineamenta sua.*

40.2. *una.*

40.2. *iuveniori oratori.*

40.7. *pondere se rapit.*

40.9. *ut P. Vinicius qui titubat.*

40.10. *numquid dicas.*

49.10. *da aequanimitatem.*

53.9. *adesse.*

54.4. *et.*

56.3. *Crispum.*

58.10. *animam.*

65.15. *potiora.*

84.1. omit *<non>.*

86.14. *quid quod vidi illud arbustum trimum et quadrimum haud fastidiendi fructus deponere.*

90.28. *perpetuae.*

90.36. *secutast.*

104.11. *ut virides frondes.*

104.27. *foris vero.*

104.29. *in pace.*

104.29. *in servis se libertati addixisse.*

108.7. *galli.*

108.21. *crudelitatis.*

108.31. *et alii quiqui.*

113.20. *exibit.*

113.20. *<cenare bene>.*

113.25. *<lis est>.*

113.31. *doce.*

123.3. *ad voluptatem prohibentes.*

123.5. *aliquod enim.*

123.10. *eo.*

123.10. *sine tibi interire.*

123.12. *in turpem vitam misera nisi turpi spe inludunt.*

124.14. *qua.*

Barnes, J. 1997. *Logic in the Imperial Stoa*. Leiden: Brill.

Bartsch, S., and A. Schiesaro, eds. 2015. *The Cambridge Companion to Seneca*. New York: Cambridge University Press, 2015.

Bartsch, S., and D. Wray, eds. 2009. *Seneca and the Self.* Cambridge: Cambridge University Press.

Bastianini, G., and A. A. Long, eds. 1992. "Ierocle: Elementi di Etica." In *Corpus dei papiri filosofici greci e latini*, vol. 1.1.2, 268–362. Florence: Olschki.

Beltrami, A., ed. 1937. *L. Annaei Senecae ad Lucilium epistulae morales*. Rome: Typis Regiae Officinae Polygraphicae.

Boys-Stones, G. 2013. "Seneca against Plato: *Letters* 58 and 65." In *Plato and the Stoics*, edited by A. G. Long, 128–46. Cambridge: Cambridge University Press.

Brennan, T. 2005. *The Stoic Life: Emotions, Duties, and Fate*. Oxford: Oxford University Press.

Cancik, H., and N. Schneider, eds. 2002–10. *Brill's New Pauly: Encyclopaedia of the Ancient World*. Leiden: Brill.

Damschen, G., and A. Heil, eds. 2014. *Brill's Companion to Seneca*. Leiden: Brill.

Dillon, J. 1996. *The Middle Platonists: 80 B.C. to A.D. 220*. 2nd ed. Ithaca, NY: Cornell University Press.

Edwards, C., ed. 2018. "Conversing with the Absent, Corresponding with the Dead: Friendship and Philosophical Community in Seneca's *Letters*." In *Letters and Communities*, edited by P. Ceccarelli, L. Doering, T. Fögen, and I. Gildenhard, 325–52. Oxford: Oxford University Press.

———. 2019. *Seneca: Selected Letters*. New York: Cambridge University Press.

Fantham, E., trans. 2010. *Seneca: Selected Letters*. Oxford: Oxford University Press.

Friedrich, O. (1880) 1964. *Publilii Syri Mimi Sententiae*. Reprint, Hildesheim: Olms.

Garani, M., A. Michalopoulos, and S. Papaioannou, eds. 2020. *Intertextuality in Seneca's Philosophical Writings*. Abingdon, UK: Oxon; New York: Routledge.

Graver, M. 2007. *Stoicism and Emotion*. Chicago: University of Chicago Press.

———. 2012. "Seneca and the *Contemplatio Veri*." In *Theoria, Praxis, and the Contemplative Life after Plato and Aristotle*, edited by T. Bénatouïl and M. Bonazzi, 73–98. Leiden: Brill.

———. 2014. "Honeybee Reading and Self-Scripting: *Epistulae Morales 84*." In *Seneca Philosophus*, edited by J. Wildberger and M. Colish, 269–93. Berlin: De Gruyter.

———. 2020. "Seneca and Epicurus." In *Oxford Handbook of Epicurus and Epicureanism*, edited by Phillip Mitsis, 487–506. Oxford: Oxford University Press.

Graver, M., and A. A. Long. 2015. *Seneca: Letters on Ethics to Lucilius*. Chicago: University of Chicago Press.

Griffin, M. 1968. "Seneca on Cato's Politics: *Epistle 14.12–13*." *Classical Quarterly* 18:373–75.

———. 1992. *Seneca: A Philosopher in Politics*. 2nd ed. Oxford: Clarendon Press.

———. 2007. "Seneca's Pedagogic Strategy: Letters and *De Beneficiis*." *Bulletin of the Institute of Classical Studies* 50:89–113.

———. 2008. "Imago vitae suae." In *Seneca*, edited by John Fitch, 23–58. Oxford Readings in Classical Studies. Oxford: Oxford University Press.

Gummere, R. M., ed. and trans. 1917–25. *Seneca: Ad Lucilium Epistulae Morales*. 3 vols. Loeb Classical Library. Cambridge, MA: Harvard University Press.

Hense, O., ed. 1914. *Seneca: Opera quae supersunt*. Leipzig: Teubner.

Inwood, B., ed. 2003. *Cambridge Companion to the Stoics*. Cambridge: Cambridge University Press.

———. 2005. *Reading Seneca: Stoic Philosophy at Rome*. Oxford: Clarendon Press.

———. 2007a. "The Importance of Form in the Letters of Seneca the Younger." In *Ancient Letters: Classical and Late Antique Epistolography*, edited by R. Morello and A. Morrison, 133–48. Oxford: Oxford University Press.

———. 2007b. "Seneca, Plato and Platonism: The Case of Letter 65." In *Platonic Stoicism, Stoic Platonism: The Dialogue between Platonism and Stoicism in Antiquity*, edited by M. Bonazzi and C. Helmig, 149–68. Leuven: Leuven University Press.

———. 2007c. *Seneca: Selected Philosophical Letters*. Oxford: Oxford University Press.

Inwood, B., and L. Gerson. 1997. *Hellenistic Philosophy: Introductory Readings*. 2nd ed. Indianapolis: Hackett.

Kidd, I. G. 1988. *Posidonius II: The Commentary*. 2 vols. Cambridge: Cambridge University Press.

Leeman, A. D. 1953. "Seneca's Plans for a Work 'Moralis Philosophia' and Their Influence on His Later Epistles." *Mnemosyne* 6 (4): 307–13.

Long, A. A. 2001. *Stoic Studies*. Reprint, Berkeley: University of California Press. First published 1996.

———. 2017. "Seneca and Epictetus on Body, Mind and Dualism." In *From Stoicism to Platonism: The Development of Philosophy, 100 BCE–100 CE*, edited by T. Engberg-Pedersen, 214–30. Cambridge: Cambridge University Press.

Long, A. A., and D. N. Sedley, eds. 1987. *The Hellenistic Philosophers*. 2 vols. Cambridge: Cambridge University Press.

Préchac, F., ed. 1945–64. *Sénèque: Lettres à Lucilius*. Translated by H. Noblot. 5 vols. Paris: Les Belles Lettres.

Ramelli, I., and D. Konstan. 2009. *Hierocles the Stoic: "Elements of Ethics," Fragments, and Excerpts*. Atlanta: Society of Biblical Literature.

Reydams-Schils, G. 2010. "Seneca's Platonism: The Soul and Its Divine Origin." In *Ancient Models of Mind: Studies in Human and Divine Rationality*, ed. A. Nightingale and D. Sedley, 196–215. Cambridge: Cambridge University Press.

Reynolds, L. D., ed. 1965a. *The Medieval Tradition of Seneca's Letters*. Oxford: Oxford University Press.

———. 1965b. *Seneca: Ad Lucilium Epistulae morales*. 2 vols. Oxford: Clarendon Press.

Romm, J. 2014. *Dying Every Day: Seneca at the Court of Nero*. New York: Knopf.

Ross, G. M. 1974. "Seneca's Philosophical Influence." In *Seneca*, edited by C. D. N. Costa, 116–42. London: Routledge and Kegan Paul.

Schafer, J. 2011. "Seneca's *Epistulae Morales* as Dramatized Education." *Classical Philology* 106 (1): 32–52.

Sedley, D. 2005. "Stoic Metaphysics at Rome." In *Metaphysics, Soul and Ethics: Themes from the Work of Richard Sorabji*, edited by R. Salles, 117–42. Oxford: Clarendon Press.

Usener, H. 1887. *Epicurea*. Leipzig: Teubner.

Vahlen, J. 1903. *Ennianae Poesis Reliquiae Iteratis Curis*. Leipzig: Teubner.

Veyne, P., ed. 1993. *Sénèque: Entretiens, Lettres à Lucilius*. Revised translation, introduction, and notes. Paris: Laffont.

Volk, K., and G. Williams, eds. 2016. *Roman Reflections: Essays on Latin Philosophy*. Oxford: Oxford University Press.

von Arnim, H., ed. 1903–24. *Stoicorum Veterum Fragmenta*. 4 vols. Leipzig: Teubner.

Vottero, D. 1998. *Lucio Anneo Seneca: I Frammenti*. Bologna: Pàtron.

Wilcox, A. 2012. *The Gift of Correspondence in Classical Rome: Friendship in Cicero's "Ad Familiares" and Seneca's "Moral Epistles."* Madison: University of Wisconsin Press.

Wildberger, J. 2006. *Seneca und die Stoa: Der Platz des Menschen in der Welt*. 2 vols. Berlin: De Gruyter.

Wildberger, J., and M. Colish, eds. 2014. *Seneca Philosophus*. Berlin: De Gruyter.

Wilson, E. 2014. *The Greatest Empire: A Life of Seneca*. Oxford: Oxford University Press.

Wilson, M. 2015. "'Quae quis fugit damnat': Outspoken Silence in Seneca's *Epistles*. In *The Art of Veiled Speech*, edited by H. Baltussen and P. Davis, 137–56. Philadelphia: University of Pennsylvania Press.

135–36, 244; rational capacities, xx–xxi, 135–36, 219, 280, 289, 291; study of, 226. *See also* instinctual attachment

Idomeneus (associate of Epicurus), 51, 257
illness, 92, 110, 115, 192–93, 259
impassivity (*apatheia*), xx, 17–18, 249, 273. *See also* emotion
impressions, 90, 219, 231, 278, 288
impulses, 136, 219, 229, 280, 288; in animals, 104, 136, 215, 243; emotional, 273, 288–89; in the world-soul, 269
incorporeals, 104, 176, 268
indifferents. *See* Stoic doctrine: values
infants, 227–28, 239, 240, 291. *See also* children
infirmities of mind. *See under* faults
instinctual attachment, 251, 285; to other people, 22, 251; to self, 229–32, 286–87

joy, xx–xxi, 54–56, 140–41, 244, 258, 292
Julius Montanus (Roman poet), xxviii
Jupiter, 21, 251. *See also* God
justice, xxiii, 211, 222–23, 285–86; in Epicurus, 191, 282; metaphysical status of, 217–20. *See also* virtue

Laelius (associate of Scipio Aemilianus), 26, 167, 247, 283

Latin language, 82, 101–2, 267; poverty of, 101, 267
letters, xv–xvi, 70–71; in moral instruction, 69–70, 129–30, 261, 273. *See also under* Cicero; Epicurus
Letters on Ethics (Seneca): date of composition, xii; genre, xvi–xviii; influence, xxxi; title, xi
Liberalis. *See* Aebutius Liberalis
Libo Drusus, Marcus Scribonius (relative of Augustus), 124, 272
lightning, 100, 266
literature, xxviii–xxx, 86, 144–45, 156–58; immortality through, 51–52, 257, 267; pedantry in studying, 102, 209–13, 267
Liternum (town in Campania), 161, 277–78
Livy (Roman author), 77, 262–63
logic puzzles, xxv, 86, 87, 150–51, 206, 220, 264, 274
love, 20, 225, 237, 250, 251, 291. *See also* friendship; sexual behavior
Lucilius (Gaius Lucilius Iunior, Seneca's addressee), xi, xiii, xvi–xviii, 85; governor of Sicily, 65, 253, 260–61; hometown, 121, 262, 272; philosophical position, 257, 260–61; pupils, 286; writings, xxix, 17, 77–78, 144–45, 248, 262, 274
Lucretius (Roman poet), xxviii, 104, 259, 265, 266; quoted, 161
Lugdunum. *See* Lyon
Lycurgus (lawgiver for Sparta), 168, 279

Ulysses, 62, 236

Varius Geminius, Quintus (Roman orator), 73, 262
Varro of Atax (Roman poet), 96, 266
Varus, Publius Quinctilius (Roman general), 81, 263
vegetarianism, 207–8
vice. *See* faults
vineyards, 165, 194, 214, 278, 286
Vinicius, Publius, 73, 260
Virgil, xxviii, 101–2, 106, 144, 210–11, 257–58, 288; quoted: *Aeneid*, 29, 45, 52, 65, 75, 86, 89, 97, 102, 122, 142, 157, 195, 199, 201, 221; quoted: *Georgics*, 101, 101, 164, 169, 178, 212, 209, 212, 238
virtue, 63–64, 135–41, 147; interentailment of virtues, 279, 287; metaphysical status, 215–22, 287; progress toward, 180–81, 204, 287. *See also* courage; justice; wisdom
void, 107, 247, 268
volcanoes, 143–44, 145, 184–85

volition, 41, 136, 274–75. *See also* assent; impulses

wealth, 35–36, 41, 50, 159, 195, 202, 260, 261. *See also* greed; poverty
will. *See* volition
wisdom, 48, 145, 174–76, 278–79. *See also* philosophy; wise person
wise person, xx, 248; and drunkenness, 153, 155–56; and God, 91, 260; and involuntary feelings, xx–xxi, 24, 99, 249; self-sufficiency of, 18–23, 248–49
women, 67, 82, 114, 124, 188–89, 193, 263, 270
writing: as nourished by reading, 156–58, 277; punctuation of, 73, 262; as service to others, 14–15, 69–70; style of, xxviii–xxx, 78, 129–30, 261, 273. *See also* books; reading

Zeno of Citium (Stoic philosopher), 10, 67, 198, 213, 247, 249; syllogisms of, 150–51, 274